D0411463

UNQUIET SPIRIT

First published in 2008 by
Liberties Press
Guinness Enterprise Centre | Taylor's Lane | Dublin 8
www.LibertiesPress.com | info@libertiespress.com
Editorial: +353 (1) 402 0805 | sean@libertiespress.com
Sales and marketing: +353 (1) 415 1224 | peter@libertiespress.com
Liberties Press is a member of Clé, the Irish Book Publishers' Association

Trade enquiries to CMD Distribution
55A Spruce Avenue | Stillorgan Industrial Park | Blackrock | County Dublin
Tel: +353 (1) 294 2560
Fax: +353 (1) 294 2564

Copyright © Yseult Thornley, 2008

The author has asserted her moral rights.

ISBN for PB: 978–1–905483–47–1

2 4 6 8 10 9 7 5 3 1

A CIP record for this title is available from the British Library

Liberties Press gratefully acknowledges the assistance of RTÉ and SIPTU
in relation to the publication of this title.

Cover design by Liam Furlong at space.ie
Set in Garamond

Printed by ScandBook | Sweden

UNQUIET SPIRIT

ESSAYS IN MEMORY OF DAVID THORNLEY

EDITED BY

YSEULT THORNLEY

ERRATUM

The reference to Edward Thornley on page 43 is incorrect. He is a registered auditor, practising accountant and tax expert. He has an honours degree from UCD and a master's degree in economics from TCD for research in the field of taxation. He has contributed to anti-evasion legislation.

Contents

ACKNOWLEDGEMENTS

I would like to express my sincere gratitude to Peter Feeney, Head of Public Affairs Policy in RTÉ, and Joe O'Flynn, General Secretary of SIPTU, for their early and continued support for the publication of this book. I would also like to thank the RTÉ Reference Library for their patient and generous assistance to me in my research. My thanks must also go to Brendan Halligan, who was an invaluable source of advice and practical help in the long process of producing this book and without whom it may never have happened. I want, also, to thank Seán O'Keefe and Peter O'Connell of Liberties Press for putting their faith in a book about someone who is, after all, dead more than thirty years. They are two people who genuinely love what they do. Finally I would like to thank my loyal friends and my family, in particular my mother, Petria, who was unstinting in her encouragement, advice and, most of all, wisdom.

*

The publishers gratefully acknowlege Blackstaff Press for granting permission to reproduce the following material: 'Postscript, 1984' and 'Freehold' from *Freehold and Other Poems* (1986); 'Bogside, Derry, 1971', 'An Ulsterman', 'The Glens', 'Conacre', 'The Coasters', and 'Memorandum for the Moderates' from *The Collected Poems of John Hewitt*, ed. Frank Ormbsy (1991).

PREFACE

YSEULT THORNLEY

In 1969, David Thornley, along with Conor Cruise O'Brien and Justin Keating, was elected to the Dáil as part of the new wave of intellectuals in the Labour Party. He was almost thirty-four. By that time, he had achieved a First in political science in Trinity College, completed a PhD on Isaac Butt and written a book on the subject. He was appointed an Associate Professor of Political Science in TCD at the age of twenty-seven and had embarked on a highly successful career as a broadcaster in RTÉ's current affairs division, giving him a profile which helped to get him elected. But nine years later, on 18 June 1978, he was dead. This book is, at least in part, the result of a desire to understand why. I also wanted the brilliance which came before the decline to be illuminated once more.

David Thornley was born on 31 July 1935 in Sutton, Surrey, in England. His Irish mother wanted her third – and last – child to be born in Ireland but did not make the boat journey home in time for that to happen. His parents, Maude Helen (née Browne) and Frederick Thornley, met in Dublin at a time when the new Irish state was being forged. They both worked in the Inland Revenue. After the Treaty, some senior British civil servants were given the choice of transferring to the Irish Revenue, but Frederick was not one of them, even though he wanted to stay. He was redeployed to Burnley, Lancashire, then spent six and a half years in Derry as Inspector of Taxes, before moving to Manchester and finally south to Surrey, after suffering a serious heart attack. They lived in a house on Cedar Road in Sutton. But the Irish connection was kept very much alive. David, his brother Edward and their sister Primrose would spend summers with their aunt Eva back in Sandymount. From a young age, he was already developing a keen sense of Irish history and the country's republican tradition. As he told the Dáil in December 1971: 'We were taught to believe all these traditions were right. I was taught to believe they were right. In 1944, on my ninth birthday, my birthday presents were: Dan Breen's *My Fight for Irish Freedom* and Desmond Ryan's *Sean Treacy and the Third Tipperary Brigade*. I was brought up on this.' David's parents were products of two very different cultures. She was a well-educated Irish nationalist and he was English, a democrat, and largely an agnostic. This extraordinary mixture would help to shape and inform David's own sense of conflict in his identity.

In Surrey, David attended Homefield Preparatory School. By the age of eight, he was at the top of the highest form. He was already showing signs of precocious intelligence. His headmaster encouraged him to study for a scholarship to St Paul's – the Greek scholarship. He was awarded the scholarship but did not take it because he did not want to board. In 1944, Maude had returned to Dublin with her three children, living in Sandymount with her sister until they bought their own house in Ballsbridge in 1950. Frederick and Maude reconciled in 1947 but they would never live together permanently again. He died in 1953, long before retirement. Instead of attending formal schooling, David took a correspondence course, read voraciously and sat the London matriculation in Belfast. He was accepted by TCD but was too young to enter the university. In 1951, at the age of sixteen, he did enter TCD, beginning a degree in Modern History and Political Science under Professor T. W. Moody. He graduated with first-class honours. He was truly a brilliant student.

Just as he was a hugely gifted student, his academic career was also enormously successful. In 1957, he was awarded the Blake National History Scholarship, and two years later his thesis on Isaac Butt and the Home Rule Movement earned him a PhD. This subsequently became a book, published in 1964. At the age of twenty-four, he was a junior lecturer on the staff of the History Department. In 1965, at the age of thirty, he was elected a fellow of the college, and in 1968 he was appointed Associate Professor of Political Science under Professor Basil Chubb. His students loved him, as can be seen from the contributions in this book from former students. In one year, three of his students achieved Firsts, and I am told that such was the brilliance of his lectures that non-history students would sneak in to hear them. David had always been planning to write a biography of Patrick Pearse, a figure with whom he empathised, partly because Pearse also had an English heritage, but also because he shared Pearse's romanticism and republicanism. Sadly, David never wrote that book.

David was also a very keen boxer and had a fine singing voice. He joined the Trinity Boxing Club, where he was coached by Freddie Tiedt. In 1964, he was the Dublin University Staff Middleweight Champion. Singing as a tenor, he took part in Feis Cheoleanna from an early age, accompanied by his brother Edward on the piano. In 1970, he was awarded the Ludwig Cup for singing by the Royal Irish Academy of Music. He sang regularly in the Westland Row Church Choir. One would think that he wanted to be Il Primo Tenore in La Scala in Milan and middleweight champion of the world!

Although he had been baptised in infancy, he was not brought up a Catholic. His later return to the Catholic Church was more a result of his being enraptured by the writings of Cardinal Newman and Graham Greene. He took his First Communion in 1954 and would remain committed to the Catholic Church whilst also supporting rights to divorce and contraception. In those years, the History Societies of UCD and Trinity would meet for discussions, walks and social functions. It was through these that David and my mother, Petria, met. They were married in 1958 and would have two children, my brother Gerry and myself. They would also, along with students and graduates of UCD and Trinity, establish the 1913 Club in 1958. This was a political discussion group named after the tumultuous events of 1913. David was also involved in Tuairim, a national organisation conceived with the purpose of involving young people more in the economic, social, political and cultural issues which were then facing Ireland. It wanted to create a forum for discussion and try to carve out solutions to the country's many problems.

From the age of sixteen, David had also been politically active. He became a supporter of Noël Browne; he wanted to work for him in the 1951 election but was unable to do so because he was sitting his London matriculation exams in Belfast. He did work in Browne's unsuccessful Fianna Fáil campaign in 1954 and ran Browne's 1957 campaign to return to the Dáil as an independent after Fianna Fáil rejected his nomination. Browne was elected a TD for Dublin South-East in 1957. The Thornley family, living in the constituency, were heavily involved in this campaign, and my grandmother, Maude, gave financial support as well as allowing her house to be used as a headquarters. In his autobiography, *Against the Tide*, Browne carefully diminishes the role David played in these political campaigns. Browne could be very spiteful. They would always have a turbulent relationship.

In 1966, David was recruited to the new weekly current affairs programme *Division* after he was spotted on the programme *The Professors*. As is clear from Muiris Mac Conghail's chapter in this book, David became a key component of RTÉ's fledgling current affairs programming. It was a new departure for David, and he was entirely successful as a broadcaster. He was an incisive, probing interviewer of politicians and ministers, who at that time were not accustomed to being held to account for their actions. When the Fianna Fáil government proposed to hold a referendum in 1968 (for the second time on this issue) to change the electoral system from PR to first-past-the-post, David, along with Basil Chubb (then head of the new Department of Political Science in TCD), did a forensic analysis for RTÉ's *7-Days* programme on what the effects of such a change would be – and demonstrated that Fianna Fáil would enjoy massive overall majorities in perpetuity!

The referendum was defeated. It was an example of how public service broadcasting can be hugely influential and can alter the course of events. There are some who feel that the tribunal established by Fianna Fáil a few years later to investigate a *7-Days* programme on moneylending (rather than moneylending itself, which was a huge social problem at the time) was an act of revenge for the Thornley/Chubb programme.

Such was David's impact on television that Brendan Halligan, then general secretary of the Labour Party, was asked to approach David by the then Labour leader, Brendan Corish, to sound him out as a potential candidate in the 1969 general election. David, always eager for new challenges and adventures, agreed. Perhaps he saw himself as a parliamentarian and educationalist. As it was, he attracted more than eight thousand first-preference votes in the constituency of Dublin North-West, drawing out a young vote with his own youthful appeal, enhanced by his profile on television. Undoubtedly, he had charisma. One person told me that he and my mother would have featured in a celebrity magazine if such a thing had been around in 1969. However, for the Labour Party, this would prove to be a disappointing election. The Electoral Act of 1969 reduced the number of five-seat constituencies and greatly increased those with three seats, thus aiding Fianna Fáil and blunting the Labour Party's advance in Dublin (as some theorists think was its crude intention). But for David personally, the move to Dáil politics would prove to be disastrous. The kind of parliamentary politics he envisaged would never be practised in this country. The back-stabbing which went on in his own constituency only deepened the disillusionment which would inevitably come to him. He would later say: 'Those first six months were terribly exciting, and I think there was a good performance by the opposition. But things have changed now. My mood is a melancholy one, and I think there are good grounds for it.' His time in politics and in the Labour Party, largely unhappy, is detailed in the chapters of both Michael D. Higgins and Barry Desmond, and need not be described here. As early as 1971, in an interview with Bruce Arnold, he spoke about the 'paralysis' of the Dáil: 'How can one not feel hopeless? It bears out what I have always had – a sense of the impossibility of achieving anything in this world.'

As mentioned earlier, there was a conflict in David's own sense of identity. He once said of his half-English, half-Irish background: 'I have an Irishman's capacity to dream dreams, an Englishman's capacity to shatter them. And there is always conflict.' He was brilliant, but also egocentric and, at times, selfish. He could be unnecessarily hurtful and was the cause of some degree of lasting pain, if only through his far too early death.

So why publish a book commemorating David Thornley's public life? Surely we shouldn't measure a man just by the manner of his ending? Brendan Behan was an alcoholic who died young, but he was also a brilliant writer. Oscar Wilde died a sad, lonely death in a dingy Parisian hotel room, but look at the writings and plays he left behind.

David is a significant figure of his time. He was an outstanding broadcaster and a superb historian and teacher. He believed passionately, perhaps informed by his Christianity, in equality and also in change. He was a radical and a thinker. If he were alive today, he might well be asking: 'Yes, but where are we going?' In truth, there have been few politicians and public figures asking that question – and seeking an answer – in the last fifty years in this country.

His tragedy was an all-too-human one. Appropriately inscribed on his gravestone is the Latin phrase: *Homo Sum: Humani Nihil a me alienum puto.* 'I am human, therefore nothing human is alien to me.'

Through my own research, through talking to the contributors, absorbing what they told me and reading these essays, my knowledge and understanding of a father I never really knew have been greatly enhanced. For that, I owe them a profound debt of gratitude.

FOREWORD

JAMES DOWNEY

David Thornley had star quality. He had it in his outstanding intellect, in his versatility, in his magnetic personality. He had it even in his numerous eccentricities.

Thirty years after his death, he is remembered more vividly, by a remarkable variety of people, than many of his contemporaries and successors who rose higher in the worlds of academia, television and politics and could lay claim to greater achievements, whether substantial or illusory.

But admiration and fondness are shadowed by the knowledge that in all those fields – and in others, in which he merely dabbled – he never reached the heights for which his dazzling talents qualified him. His star quality made him. It also destroyed him.

For David, sad though it is to say, was blessed – or cursed – with too many talents and scored too many instant successes. And for all the clarity of his thought and writing, for all his dialectical skill and his genius for coming to the point of any issue, there was another important, and contradictory, part of his character. He was a romantic.

After all these years, I still think with affection and amusement of how this romantic aspect of his character was displayed in his musical and literary tastes. He loved Mario Lanza, and sweet, sorrowful arias like 'When Other Lips' and 'Remembering You'. Together with his father-in-law John Hughes, he sang Jacobite songs with gusto. Every Christmas, he re-read all of Dickens's Christmas books. He wallowed in the sentimental passages.

More to the point, at a very early age he embraced – more or less simultaneously – the Catholic Church, Irish nationalism and socialism. All were of a piece with his romanticism. They did not sit well with a coolly academic, or pragmatically political, view of the world.

His first career set a pattern which would be repeated more than once. At Trinity College, he was a brilliant student and, what is less often remembered, a brilliant teacher. His doctoral thesis, published under the title 'Isaac Butt and Home Rule', was recognised immediately for its contribution to our knowledge of the development of constitutional nationalism. He also wrote pamphlets, including one published by the discussion group Tuairim on the confluence of the national, land and religious questions in the late-nineteenth century; a subject that would become a staple of Irish historical studies.

He planned a major work, a definitive biography of Patrick Pearse, but never wrote it. After his death, Ruth Dudley Edwards published a very fine biography of Pearse, but there is no knowing how much more David might have achieved. One can only speculate as to whether he might have, had he lived longer and stuck to his academic and literary last, outdone in volume and quality the historians of the generation that succeeded his.

One may speculate, too, on whether he might have made a name as an administrator – whether he might have become provost of Trinity, for instance. He did have a taste for administration, and sat on the college board.

He told a story against himself from this period. He proposed at a board meeting that the college should run a course in 'Catholic social teaching'. What form might that take as an academic discipline? What do the words themselves mean? At the meeting, Dr A. A. Luce, a Church of Ireland clergyman, observed mildly: 'I'm a Catholic.' That was enough to torpedo the suggestion.

This happened at a time when most journalists were too humble to parade themselves as pundits and when economists and accountants had not yet taken over the airwaves. Academics found themselves much in demand to talk on television about growth rates and other subjects which were not necessarily within their fields of competence. David was spotted by the superb RTÉ producer Muiris Mac Conghail as not just an occasional commentator but a potential star. The interviews conducted by Thornley under Mac Conghail's direction were unequalled for information and excitement. One of the most gripping was the one with John A. Costello, Taoiseach at the time of the Mother and Child Scheme fiasco in 1951. Pressed on the subservience of his government to the Church on that occasion, Costello almost leapt out of his chair as he declared that he would make no apology for obeying the Church in matters of faith and morals.

David had a particular reason for his interest in that controversy. For many years, he was a devoted follower of the central character, Dr Noël Browne. So dedicated was he to him that he followed Browne out of Clann na Poblachta, into Fianna Fáil, out of that party again, and into the National Progressive Democrats. He ran Browne's election campaigns tirelessly and ruthlessly. In 1957, when Browne, having been denied a Fianna Fáil nomination, stood for the Dáil as an independent, canvassers were forbidden by David to mention the word 'socialism' and told instead to remind middle-class and upper-middle-class voters that the candidate had stood up to the bishops. The strategy worked perfectly.

He got poor thanks for his efforts. In his memoirs, the petulant and self-centred Browne dwelt on David's physical deterioration in his last years and wrote about suspicions that David might have had political ambitions of his own. So he did, but he had every right to them.

For his own sake, however, David would have done better to put these ambitions aside. His lifestyle and his health had suffered from his encounter with the febrile world of television. They would suffer more from his venture into electoral politics.

At the 1969 general election, he stood as a Labour Party candidate for a largely working-class Dublin constituency. He approached the event in a characteristically emotional style. At an election rally in O'Connell Street, he said that he and other 'celebrity' candidates, like Dr Conor Cruise O'Brien and Justin Keating, were 'laying ourselves on the line'. Their livelihoods, to say nothing of their heads, were not at stake. Electorally speaking, those whose heads rolled in the ensuing disaster for the party were the scores of less glamorous Labour candidates who were rejected by the voters.

I was one of the rejects, and I am profoundly grateful that I polled a mere 895 first-preference votes. The experience cured me forever of the electoral bug. David was less fortunate. He was elected, and served two Dáil terms before losing his seat. In addition, he served for a while as a member of the European Parliament – in the days when MEPs were nominated by their parties rather than being directly elected. This must have been far more injurious to lifestyle and health than television or domestic politics: a deadly combination of lack of serious work, so much fatiguing travel, and so many late nights of what the widow of a Fianna

Fáil MEP, musing on her husband's experiences, called 'the fleshpots of Strasbourg'.

But the fleshpots of Strasbourg are, after all, only fleshpots. They do not compare with the misery, for someone of David Thornley's intelligence and abilities, of sitting on a Dáil back bench, impotent, hopelessly underemployed, wholly out of sympathy with his party and, in his second term, with the government in which that party served.

Seared by the debacle of 1969, the Labour leadership reversed the party's anti-coalition policy and in 1973 took office in alliance with Fine Gael. David, in common with Conor Cruise O'Brien and Justin Keating, did not share the left wing's passionate objection to that decision, or the belief that Labour could replace Fine Gael as the second party in the state. On the contrary, they considered Fianna Fáil such a danger to the well-being of the state that it had to be driven from office by whatever means were available to them. Notoriously, Thornley and O'Brien clashed on the 'national question', but before the Northern eruption of 1969 and the Arms Crisis of 1970, David had said that the activities of Neil Blaney and Kevin Boland, with their lack of care for the norms of democracy, frightened him.

Besides, all of them were sufficiently pragmatic to know that politics is about power. But power comes only with office. O'Brien and Keating were Cabinet ministers. David was not even a junior minister. His time and his talents were wasted in a public and humiliating fashion; and, in my opinion, fatally.

Another humiliation awaited him. Perhaps he should have rejoiced when he lost his seat. Instead, he wept; and not only for the failure of a political career, than which nothing is more commonplace, or the folly of his ever having chosen that path. He lamented the severing of his link with the ordinary people of his constituency. That link may have been emotional, sentimental, romantic, but to him it was real, and the rejection by them was also real.

When he died, thousands who knew him mourned, and scores of thousands who never knew him mourned with them. They recognised his star quality; and they recognized his sincerity.

Those who knew him best had, and have, another reason for lamentation. He made a mark in three separate careers, but in none of them were his mighty capabilities realised beyond a fraction of their potential. And here is an irony. Those capabilities, his character, his life, deserve some memorial. Although he is so well remembered, until now he has had none.

*

One summer evening eighteen months ago, his daughter, my cousin Yseult, sat with me in the courtyard of the United Arts Club in Dublin and discussed with me what has become the present work. I was delighted to learn of her intention to undertake the project, and honoured when she invited me to write the foreword. It is only a sketch of an unforgettable personality and an extraordinary life. The contributors will broaden the canvas and fill in the many colours, dark and light. She has chosen them well. Among them, they will build him a memorial in the best of all media and the one he loved most. Television and the blogosphere are well enough in their way, but nothing beats print. *Litera scripta manet.*

Jim Downey was formerly London editor, political correspondent and deputy editor of the Irish Times. *He now writes a weekly political column in the* Irish Independent. *He has won several journalism awards, including the Liam Hourican Award for his work on Europe-related affairs in the* Irish Independent *and* Business and Finance *magazine.*

PART ONE

ESSAYS

1

'THAT YOUNG MAN MEANS WHAT HE'S SAYING':

RECOLLECTIONS BY FRIENDS AND COLLEAGUES

OF DAVID THORNLEY

EDITED BY JOHN BOWMAN

This is a transcript of an edition of the RTÉ Radio 1 programme Opinion *which was broadcast on the night that David Thornley died. All the interviews for the programme were recorded in the immediate aftermath of the announcement of his death. The interviews were therefore recorded at short notice and the judgements expressed were 'of the moment'.*

The transcript follows the sequence of voices as heard on the original radio programme. Devices such as the introduction of a new speaker who is not identified until the end of their first sentence have been retained. Some few minor corrections and changes have been made to the original transcript, always in the interest of accuracy and comprehension. Where changes are of any consequence, they have been indicated in the footnotes.

The original recording is in RTÉ's Sound Archive, no. BB 796, first broadcast: Opinion, *RTÉ Radio 1, 23 June 1978.*

JOHN
BOWMAN: Despite his short life, David Thornley had many careers. As well as being a politician, he had been a television broadcaster, a political commentator and an academic. His failure, his very public failure, in the most recent of these careers – that of politician – has to too great an extent obscured his earlier achievements, which were considerable: as a publicist, a

catalyst, his work in Tuarim, his lectures, his pamphlets, his work as a television interviewer; and the central role which he played in the development of political broadcasting in Ireland. And also there were his achievements as an academic, a scholar, an historian.

T. W.
MOODY: He came as a student to Trinity in the session 1951–52.

JB: T. W. Moody, then Professor of Modern History and David Thornley's first tutor.

TWM: And you know that a tutor in the Trinity sense has a special relationship to a student. So I well remember David coming to see me in my rooms in Number 1 and telling me all about his expectations of college and impressing me very much as an extraordinarily eager and gifted and attractive young man.

JB: As well as being his tutor, Professor Moody was to be David Thornley's teacher and, later, supervisor of his main research work on Isaac Butt.

TWM: He really had all the qualities that one hopes for in a student: immense zest for the subject; immense intellectual energy; dedication to anything that he was working on at the time; great fluency; an incisive style; and originality.

JB: And to all of these qualities, David Thornley added meticulous scholarship. Professor Moody remembers him as a model PhD student.

TWM: He worked away for four years. He did all the right things and was a model student. He would make regular progress reports, some of which I still have and which were models of their kind. He discussed his work regularly with me. He would come bubbling over with some fresh discovery and it was a great pleasure to supervise him. He worked on all the obvious sources here and went over to London and dug out things there and elsewhere. He was very systematic; organised his work extremely well; had an impressive card index and so on. Then he presented the thesis in 1959 and it was well approved by the extern examiner and, of course, by me and had a very glowing report.[1]

22

JB: He then joined the staff of Trinity College lecturing in history and political science. He was extraordinarily popular with his students.

TWM: They found his exuberance and his enthusiasm and his vitality and his pugnacity . . . they found this all very attractive and they rallied around him. For example, when, as happened once or twice, he was ill, they used to go to the nursing home where he was and take seminars from him from his bed. Yes, they had a special sense of loyalty to him.

MICHAEL
McINERNEY: I met him as a very young lecturer in Trinity College Dublin. At the time I was what they called a mature student and I must have been about twice David Thornley's age, at least.

JB: Political journalist Michael McInerney.[2]

MMcI: And I can still see him, a handsome, slim young man, obviously really gifted, and I think every one of us in the class really liked him very much. I can still hear his voice ringing out when he was talking to us about Marx: 'We must *smash* the bourgeois state!' And I thought to myself: that young man means what he's saying.

JB: Thornley's intellectual allegiances to socialism, to Irish republicanism and to Catholicism were sometimes in conflict. His attempts to resolve these conflicts in public debate and in political pamphlets made him an important figure in the mid-1960s. A friend, Enda McDonagh, Professor of Moral Theology at St Patrick's College, Maynooth.

ENDA
McDONAGH: Well, he was perhaps the first politician or academic interested in politics – because at that stage, of course, he was lecturing in Trinity – who seemed to me to take seriously both the need and the possibility for an understanding between Catholicism and socialism. He took his Catholicism very seriously – partly perhaps because of his family background, partly perhaps because of the Trinity situation.[3] But he had this vision of a socialist Ireland, I suppose a socialist republic essentially; and he felt that these two great forces in his life should be worked out and could

provide a vision for Ireland which was badly needed in these rather pragmatic times in the 1960s. He was undoubtedly inspired to this to a certain extent by the euphoria which had been generated by Vatican II, by the encyclicals of Pope John XXIII on socialism, peace in the world, human rights. And in that context through his work in Tuarim, and through his own lecturing on politics and through his many discussions with his friends like myself, he was seriously undertaking the task of developing an understanding of this kind. At the same time in that period in Britain you had the *Slant* people developing the Christian Marxist dialogue.[4] David was never either so Marxist or so Christian in that sense; he was both most self-consciously an Irish Catholic, although in no way narrow or unecumenical, and he was also a socialist who wanted to retain, I think, part of a liberal tradition which was important to him.

JB: He also impressed as secretary of the Irish Federation of University Teachers. Garret FitzGerald.

GARRET
FITZGERALD: Well, he had this vigorous and trenchant way of speaking. He kept people amused while he pushed us through the business. He was the secretary of the organisation for its formative years and from that position he managed efficiently, energetically and with a humour which perhaps reduced the kinds of tensions which can arise between academics. He enjoyed every moment of it and we enjoyed every moment of working with him, I think.

JB: And at about this time David Thornley became a frequenter of the television and radio studios; at first, answering questions; establishing himself as one of the foremost and most forthright political commentators in the country.

DAVID
THORNLEY: [*from the election results broadcast of the 1965 general election, Radio Éireann*] Well, I agree that you can't predict this thing with any confidence; but after all, that's what we're here for; to stick our necks out . . . at least one of the things we're here for; and on the basis of expert knowledge, which we are supposed to possess, to fall flat on our faces, to the general

delectation of the listeners. And this I am prepared to do, for one.[5]

JB: Soon he was *asking* the questions, as a television interviewer, first on *Division*, later on *7-Days*. Muiris MacConghail, the producer and editor with whom he worked, considers David Thornley's recruitment highly important in the development of political broadcasting.

MUIRIS MAC CONGHAIL: It was understood at the time, I think, that the Broadcasting Act and the ethos of the period required RTÉ to be solid, quiet and manifestly with a shut mouth. And I think it was an attempt to break through that kind of era and to introduce our own expertise and, rather than interview people constantly who were experts in their own fields, [we should] attempt to integrate some of them within the broadcasting service. Thornley was one of those first picked for that role.

JB: And the qualities which David Thornley brought to his broadcasting work?

MMacC: The first thing, of course, he brought to broadcasting was his own authority as a political scientist. Secondly, and, perhaps, it's not a broadcasting trait but it's important to remember it – and it's still something which we very much lack, I think – he actually wrote English extremely well. He could express himself precisely, and he brought in addition to that the precision of a political scientist. He was an actor; he enjoyed performing; and it gave him perhaps a unique opportunity to combine all of his talents with, I think, not a whole lot of effort on his part. It didn't require great effort. He had worked for the previous ten years acquiring most of the information which he was subsequently to use in political broadcasting for us; and he then became very much an activist. What broadcasting gave to him was an opportunity, I think, to go on the floor, so to speak, among the politicians. So it gave him something in return for his contribution to us.

JB: 'An instrument of public policy' was how Sean Lemass as Taoiseach had described RTÉ.[6] It was not a definition easily accepted by the broadcasters. In MacConghail's view, Thornley's work played an influential role in redressing the balance between politicians and broadcasters. His authority and independence helped to change the relationship between Donnybrook and Leinster House.

MMacC: I think this was recognised by the public, who accepted him in turn as 'their man', putting the questions – which, of course, is the ideal position for any broadcaster to be in. And he behaved, in a way, on behalf of his constituents, who were the wider public, and I think they trusted him. And the politicians, I think, accepted that triangular relationship: they versus him; and he on behalf of the general public. Now he made it possible, I think, in the broadcasting sense to do the hard interview. It was he more than any other person who actually did the hard, face-to-face, frontal interview in which the answer, if not given in accordance with the information available, [would prompt Thornley to] come back and say: 'Well, minister, really that isn't true, is it?', and ministers and leaders of the opposition of the day accepted that from him and, perhaps, qualified their answer. I'm not saying they were misleading, but I think they were used to, perhaps, giving a general answer and not expecting the kind of cross-examination which became a feature of television in the late 1960s.[7]

DAVID
THORNLEY: [*archive recording of an aside taken from a live television broadcast*] There's a great danger I feel that many people will think that watching Manchester United next Wednesday is more important than voting in the referendum. I'm here on behalf of those people asking in effect what are you gentlemen at? Why is this important?

JACK LYNCH: Having come face to face with him, I think the very first time was shortly after I was elected Taoiseach . . . it was at a Fianna Fáil Ard Fheis and it was he – I think it was with Brian Farrell – conducted with me a most incisive interview; a lot of people thought it was too incisive. Personally, I didn't regard it as such.

JB: As an interviewer, Jack Lynch found him informed, incisive and fair. Frank Cluskey also faced his questions.

FRANK
CLUSKEY: I could only use the word 'brilliant' as an interviewer. He was gentle but yet very incisive,[8] very probing in his questions. He had this marvellous facility, which I think is essential to a good interviewer, where he did not intrude into the interview and just led you along gently; but [he] wasn't interviewing himself, which some interviewers have a tendency to do.

JB: *7-Days* was a controversial programme. Thornley relished the controversy. And contributed to it, notably in the PR referendum campaign of 1968, when his and Basil Chubb's forecast of how the abolition of proportional representation would favour Fianna Fáil – the publication of that forecast after careful research on the *7-Days* programme – changed the very nature of the referendum campaign. Muiris MacConghail.

MMacC: And it was the enthusiasm not only of David Thornley but of those associated with him, including his academic colleagues, who were only too willing . . . I mean there were statisticians of all kinds associated with the figures as well, and the work of Basil Chubb, who was regarded as a kind of god figure who guided us through the mists of these difficulties. And it was that kind of cooperative effort that put that [programme] on. The impact of that forecast was very great and it has been said subsequently that it, perhaps more than anything else, brought about the proposal's defeat. I have no doubt that that is correct.

JB: A verdict corroborated by the Taoiseach, Jack Lynch, who recalled that the Fianna Fáil Party's own survey conducted during the campaign looked promising until the publication of the Chubb–Thornley forecast.

JL: But I believe myself that even if that [Fianna Fáil's optimistic opinion poll during the initial campaign] were the case, that the survey done by Basil Chubb and David Thornley would have beaten us anyway, because nobody was going to give a party ninety-odd seats, ninety-five seats[9] – I forget the exact number – a huge majority which they estimated. I think if anything killed our aspirations about the change in the system, that certainly did.

JB: Nor was David Thornley's contribution as a broadcaster confined to his appearances on screen. At programme conferences – as Muiris MacConghail remembers him – he was full of ideas, critical of last week's programme, critical of his colleagues, and self-critical.

MMacC: Very critical, I think, perhaps of what he regarded at times as being our rather isolated position in relation to the general public; and [he] frequently brought us right down to earth. He had – notwithstanding the suavity of his accent and his general debonair appearance – he had a common touch: he was a showman; he knew precisely what 'would go'; and he certainly, I think, helped us very much to formulate a public affairs policy on television. And I don't think it would have been anything like as effective as it was if he hadn't been with us. In fact, I doubt if it would have existed really had he not been a member of the team at the time.

JB: Having established himself on television, David Thornley turned to politics. In 1969, he was recruited to the Labour Party and elected to the Dáil for Dublin North-West.[10]

RETURNING
OFFICER: [*from RTÉ election results broadcast, 1969*] 'Accordingly I declare Mr Thornley deemed to be elected. [*Cheers and applause*]

JB: Much was expected of David Thornley's career as a politician, not least by David himself: he was Labour Party spokesman on education; he was highly popular in his constituency; and he had topped the poll with over eight thousand votes at the election. He was an advocate of coalition with Fine Gael. It was perhaps typical of his sense of mischief that in 1972, in Cork, he mingled with the delegates at the Fine Gael Ard Fheis before joining an RTÉ broadcast from that Ard Fheis on the prospects of coalition. Despite, as he said, the sharpening knives of the Left within his own party, he was an advocate of a coalition with Fine Gael.

DT: [*RTÉ archive recording*] One of my first rules in politics is you count first and you talk afterwards. And I am not prepared to indulge in a political exercise which maintains Fianna Fáil in power for my lifetime and my children's lifetime.

JB: But he added a postscript to that interview.

DT: If we're talking about coalitions or anything like that, let me make one thing absolutely clear: no government that interns or uses special tribunals to put Irishmen like Cathal Goulding behind bars will ever get a vote of any kind from me.[11]

JB: Later he disagreed with his party's Northern Ireland policy as enunciated by Conor Cruise O'Brien. At the Wexford conference of the party in 1972, an O'Brien-versus-Thornley showdown was expected. It didn't materialise. Dr O'Brien's views prevailed.[12]

DT: [*addressing Labour conference in Wexford*] There may be people who will come to this rostrum or raise their hands with bitterness or personal malice against Dr Conor Cruise O'Brien. It is not true in my case. I have the utmost admiration for Conor. I think his attitude to the North is unfortunately incorrect; but I think he is one of the finest intellects in western Europe; and on every other liberal issue, of contraception, divorce, community schools and everything else, I will be found standing with Cruise O'Brien and against his enemies, and I want to make that clear. [*Applause*] I sometimes think you must be sick of all the doctors collectively and that you wish that both Cruise O'Brien and Thornley – and even Browne[13] – would be manacled together and tossed into the Liffey and solve a lot of problems. [*Laughter, some heckles indecipherable; then heckler shouts:* 'What about Stevie?';[14] *further laughter*]

DT: Now, now, now, you're[15] . . . The leader spoke of discipline this morning; I will accept discipline in this party without the slightest question, provided every other deputy in the party does the same. I am no advocate of violence. The most I have said was that the IRA, both wings, are a fact of life and must be brought into any talks that take place in the North. If that makes me an advocate of violence, well then the following are also advocates of violence: Ivan Cooper, Paddy Devlin, Peter Hain and the Young Liberals in England, Dr John O'Connell, and the novelist Graham Greene.[16]

JB: When coalition government came after the 1973 election, no office, no Mercedes[17] came David Thornley's way. That was no surprise, presumably even to himself. He was Labour deputy at the European Parliament. He was generally uncomfortable as a backbencher in coalition. He expressed himself as sick and tired of the erosion of civil liberties. In defence of free speech, he said that he had found it necessary to attend Provisional Sinn Féin's Easter Rising celebrations in 1976. He was expelled from the parliamentary party. [18]

DT: *[RTÉ archive recording]* As for pragmatism, I'm getting a bit sick and tired of pragmatism in politics. And my soul is not for sale for the price of a seat or a Mercedes car or anything else. And if I lose my seat over this, if I lose my membership of the Labour Party, well then I will just depart quietly with regret into the background.

JB: And at the 1977 general election, he lost his seat; indeed he lost his election deposit.[19] Michael McInerney.

MMcI: But I believe his death at forty-two years of age is the saddest thing I have known among politicians in something like forty-five years' experience of journalism, mainly dealing with politics, with *The Irish Times* and with other papers. And I think he really was another victim of the Northern troubles. Here was a man who had a commitment, an obvious commitment, to Catholicism, to socialism and to Irish republicanism, which is different to any other form of republicanism. His emotions, his impulses, seemed to dominate his intellectual mind; and some of his actions were very irrational.[20]

JB: It's early and difficult to assess David Thornley's contribution to Irish life. His failure as a politician is of such recent memory that it makes more difficult what is never an easy task. But some attempt must be made. Labour Party leader Frank Cluskey.

FC: If you take together all his various activities, I think he made a very major contribution to Irish political life; you had his teaching; his writings; you had his major work on *7-Days* television, which brought to the ordinary public an awareness of political matters that I believe that otherwise they would not have had. So I think that – taken all together – it was a very major contribution.

JB: Garret FitzGerald.

GF: I think it's going to be difficult in the short run to evaluate what he achieved. But he played a role at a point of transition in Irish life which involved challenging many preconceptions; but doing so always constructively, always with an eye to how things might be done better. And the fact that he came on the scene and was active on the scene during a crucial period meant that he played, I think, a very important role. There were others with him at the same time, but because of his extraordinary skill in broadcasting, he made [a] particular impact, and that carried through into the early years in politics. And I think that his contribution to making us rethink many aspects of our society should not be undervalued. And anybody who ever came in contact with him was stimulated – stimulated to think, and to think twice about one's preconceptions.

JB: Enda McDonagh believes that David Thornley made an important contribution in the mid-1960s. He sees him as a political theoretician, challenged by the pragmatism of the Lemass years.

EMcD: So he was at that time active, involved as it were in [the] educational process of the wider public, and a learning process for himself which involved this development of his thinking both as a Catholic and as a socialist.

JB: And his contribution there?

EMcD: His contribution there, I think, is still, as it were, undeveloped. In my view, after that period, politics, and the theoretical grounding of politics, had changed somewhat again. This was partly due, undoubtedly, to the development of the Northern Troubles; partly due to the losing out at the time of the Just Society concept promoted by Declan Costello, which interested and even excited David at the time.[21] And I think partly due then to, in a sense, his own shift of interest in the later stages of his life. So that he has left some unfinished business there, I think, for the rest of us, that Irish thinkers and Catholics and politicians will still have to face. Can you explore the relationship between Catholicism and socialism? Can you develop a proper understanding between them and generate a political ideal and a political theory and a political movement that will capture the mass of the Irish people for a genuine socialism? He has provided some of the groundwork, some of the inspiration, but it's obviously unfinished.

JB: And David Thornley also made a considerable contribution as an historian. Professor T. W. Moody.

TWM: And what David Thornley undertook to do and what he succeeded in doing was examining the years from 1870 to Butt's death in 1879, when the Home Rule movement was effectively started. That had never been critically examined before, and Thornley's work on it was of a kind that I am quite confident will last. I have had occasion – many times since it was published – to use it in the context of work of my own; and the more I use it, the more respect I have for it.

JB: David Thornley will also be remembered as a friend to generations of his students and to his colleagues in the universities, in politics and in broadcasting. Muiris MacConghail remembers his sense of fun, of mischief, and his great generosity.

MMacC: Warm, generous, a lot of difficulties, the sort of difficulties which all great men who are ebullient and involved with life have – he was full of life. He was very demanding of his friends; he insisted on their full and total attention; and it's a trait of many broadcasters, and it was especially so in David's case. But he was extremely loyal, kind, and very attentive to all his friends.

JB: Garret FitzGerald remembers him . . .

GF: . . . with very deep affection indeed; somebody I was very fond of from the time I first met him. In later years, I would like to have been able to help him more than I was able to; and I suppose, like many others, we feel we should have tried more to help him. But certainly, he is somebody whom I will never forget.

JB: Professor Moody remembers the undergraduate, the young historian.

TWM: David changed a great deal in the course of his short life, from the time when he was a young ardent student. We all know that. But I would like to recall the memory that I retain, and will continue to retain, of that ardent spirit: refined and perceptive, sympathetic, tactful and warm-hearted. I recall these qualities very vividly, and I would like to continue to think of these in my memories of David, because I wasn't so closely associated with him, of course, in later years. But I did retain some connection with him, and always an affection for him, and I believe that there was in him a single-mindedness and a purity of heart that never vanished.

Dr John Bowman is a broadcaster, political scientist and historian. As an undergraduate in the history and politics department in Trinity, he was among David Thornley's students. His PhD thesis, De Valera and the Ulster Question: 1917–1973, *was later published by the Oxford University Press and won the Ewart-Biggs literary prize for its contribution to North–South understanding. He presents current-affairs and historical programmes for RTÉ radio and television. He is a past president of the Irish Association for Economic, Cultural and Social Relations.*

NOTES

1 David Thornley, *Isaac Butt and Home Rule* (London, 1964). Moody describes this as 'a learned and perceptive study' in his *Davitt and Irish Revolution: 1846–82* (Oxford, 1982), p.120, n.1.

2 Michael McInerney, formerly a member of both the Communist Party of Ireland and the Labour Party, was political correspondent of *The Irish Times*.

3 A reference to the ban by the Roman Catholic hierarchy on Catholics attending Trinity College. In April 1967, Thornley, with two Roman Catholic colleagues on the Trinity staff, Dr Louis Cullen and Dr James Lydon, met the Archbishop of Dublin, Dr John Charles McQuaid, to invite him to appoint a Roman Catholic chaplain to the university for the many Catholics who – despite the ban – were enrolled in the university. Lydon recalled McQuaid addressing them 'in full canonicals' from his throne in his library. Lydon admitted: 'We got nothing.' Interviewed by author on *John Charles McQuaid: What the Papers Say*, Esras Films for RTÉ, 1998. *The Irish Times*, 15 April 1967.

4 *Slant* was edited by Father Herbert McCabe (1926–2001); sometimes considered a Marxist, his real belief was that 'Christianity, not Marxism' was the 'really revolutionary creed'. Obituary, *The Independent* (London), 25 July 2001.

5 This was Thornley's riposte to his fellow panellist, Brian Farrell, who had said that engaging in the prediction of a constituency result would be 'a waste of time' since the result would be known within twenty-four hours. For the context of these exchanges, see John Bowman, 'Reminiscences of an on-the-run psephologist', in Tom McGuire (ed.), *The Election Book* (Dublin, 2007), pp.15–29.

6 In 1966 the then Taoiseach Sean Lemass – betraying how politicians initially viewed the new service – said that RTÉ had been 'set up by legislation as an instrument of public policy'. Dáil Debates, vol. 224, cols. 1045–46, 12 October 1966.

7 Instances would be Thornley's interview with Jack Lynch as incoming Taoiseach, *Division*, RTÉ television, 18 November 1966, and his robust and incisive interview with the former Taoiseach, John A. Costello, *7-Days*, RTÉ television, 24 June 1969. See also report of Thornley's address to the Dublin Rotary Club on 'Television and Politics', *The Irish Times*, 21 November 1967.

8 Cluskey says 'decisive' but clearly 'incisive' was intended.

9 On the broadcast, Lynch mistakenly said 'votes' instead of 'seats'. Given Fianna Fáil's traditional support base – from 1932 to 1965, they had always exceeded 42 percent of first-preference votes – most commentators reckoned that under the proposed first-past-the-post system, Fianna Fáil would retain power indefinitely by winning at least ninety seats. Basil Chubb and David Thornley, 'In pursuit of a majority: some possible results of changing the electoral system', *The Irish Times*, 15 January 1968; Basil Chubb, *The Government and Politics of Ireland* (London, 1992, third edition), pp.148–9; Michael Gallagher, *The Irish Labour Party in transition: 1957–82* (Manchester, 1982), pp.74–5 [hereafter, Gallagher, *Irish Labour Party*]; Garret FitzGerald, *All in a Life: An Autobiography* (Dublin, 1991), p.79; Cornelius O'Leary, *Irish Elections: 1918–1977* (Dublin, 1979), pp.68–70; *The Times*, 6 March 1968. Labour TD Eileen Desmond – quoting the Chubb–Thornley forecast – argued that the proposed change would yield Fianna Fáil 65 percent of the seats from 40 percent of the vote, *The Irish Times*, 1 October 1968.

10 'Thornley explains choice of party', *The Irish Times*, 24 May 1969. He was one of three new recruits who won seats for Labour in Dublin, Dr Conor Cruise O'Brien

and Dr Justin Keating being the others. For accounts of Labour's expectations and the outcome of the 1969 election, see Gallagher, *Irish Labour Party*, pp.83–103; for an entertaining account of Drs Thornley, Keating, Cruise O'Brien and Noël Browne sharing the same room in Leinster House, see Conor Cruise O'Brien, *Memoir: My Life and Times* (Dublin, 1998), pp.321–4. See also 'Labour welcomes the intellectuals', The *Irish Times,* 12 June 1969.

11 Cathal Goulding (1923–98) had been 'behind bars' on four occasions: interned in 1940 and three times convicted and jailed for IRA offences in Ireland and Britain. IRA chief-of-staff throughout the 1960s, he stayed with what was known as the Official Republican Movement when the Provisionals broke away in 1970.

12 For the background to Labour's internal disagreements on Northern Ireland policy, see Niamh Puirseal, *The Irish Labour Party:1922–73* (Dublin, 2007), pp.288–95 [hereafter, Puirseal, *Irish Labour Party*]; and Gallagher, *Irish Labour Party,* pp.135–53; for an account sympathetic to Cruise O'Brien, see D. H. Akenson, *Conor: A Biography of Conor Cruise O'Brien* (Montreal, 1994), pp.361–74.

13 Noël Browne (1915–1997), maverick loner during his thirty-four-year political career, represented four political parties but was probably most comfortable – as were they – when he contested elections as an independent. Thornley was not alone in finding him a difficult Labour Party colleague. No doubt Browne had some reason to think the same of Thornley, but readers would not need to rely on Browne's self-serving memoir for an understanding of their complex relationship, Noël Browne, *Against the Tide* (Dublin, 1986), pp.250–3, 262–7. These pages provide a 'deeply wounding' portrait of Thornley according to Browne's biographer, John Horgan, who characterises Thornley's initial regard for Browne as 'only just this side of idolatry'. Horgan suggests that their subsequent relationship underwent 'many vicissitudes, ruptures and reconciliations' before ending in tears as Thornley's 'expansive but vulnerable personality clashed fatally with Browne's unforgiving temperament'; *Noël Browne: Passionate Outsider* (Dublin, 2000), p.182.

14 This was a reference to Stephen Coughlan (1910–1994), Labour TD for Limerick East (1961–77) and a deeply divisive figure who had already risked expulsion from the party for what were considered anti-Semitic and illiberal views. His continued membership was again in question at this Wexford conference for his refusal to accept Labour's proposed reforms of family-planning legislation. Thornley, in the interests of party unity, had not supported Coughlan's expulsion. Puirseal, *Irish Labour Party*, pp.242, 245, 278–81, 287, 294.

15 Thornley wisely decides not to rise to the bait of the heckler who invites him to comment on Coughlan's suitability to be manacled to the Doctors.

16 Cooper and Devlin had been civil rights leaders in Northern Ireland and founder members of the SDLP; Hain – a future Secretary of State for Northern Ireland – was then a Young Liberal and had expressed support for the Troops Out movement; O'Connell was a Labour TD who had incurred the wrath of his party's leadership by secretly attempting to broker a ceasefire between the Provisional IRA and the British government in 1972; Greene had recently written to The *Times* [26 November 1971] that the British government would in time learn the folly of vowing that they would never sit down 'with murderers'. See Thornley's citing of Greene's letter in Dáil Debates, vol. 257, col. 2500, 16 December 1971.

17 From the 1960s, when it became customary for Irish ministers to be driven in Mercedes cars, the term became a shorthand for becoming a minister.

18 Gallagher, *Irish Labour Party*, pp.211–12.
19 Thornley polled only 1,615 votes in Dublin Cabra in the 1977 election. Justin Keating and Conor Cruise O'Brien – both outgoing Labour ministers – also lost their seats.
20 McInerney was referring to Thornley's joining the Provisional rally at the Mater Hospital in Dublin where IRA chief of staff Seán Mac Stíofáin was on hunger strike; and his sharing a platform at the Provisionals' commemoration of the 1916 Rising in 1976. Puirseal, *Irish Labour Party*, p.303; *The Irish Times*, 26 April 1976. For a spirited defence of Thornley's line, see his contribution – some eight thousand words – to a charged Dáil debate on 16 December 1971; Dáil Debates, vol. 257, cols. 2486–2509. For an account of Thornley's expulsion from the party, see John Horgan, *Labour: The Price of Power* (Dublin, 1986), p.118.
21 For the Just Society initiative in Fine Gael, see Dermot Keogh, *Twentieth Century Ireland: Revolution and State Building* (Dublin, 2005), pp.291–4; Diarmaid Ferriter, *The Transformation of Ireland: 1900–2000* (London, 2004), pp.558–9.

2

The Thornley Family and Noël Browne

Edward Thornley

Noël Browne's claim to fame arises from the Mother and Child Scheme, a scheme for free pre-natal and post-natal services. This was bizarre, since he was not even the author of the scheme, having inherited it from the previous Fianna Fáil government when he became Minister for Health in the 1948 coalition government – the so-called inter-party government. Behind the scenes, the Catholic hierarchy, bitterly, and part of the medical profession, to a lesser extent, lobbied against the scheme. The arguments produced by the former were rather unconvincing; the real objection was believed to be the fear that non-Catholic doctors operating the scheme would make contraception available to Catholic mothers. This antediluvian attitude to birth control persists, and, through the banning of condoms, does untold damage in the Third World by facilitating the spread of AIDS. In better-educated countries like Ireland, most Catholics vote with their feet in their frequent visits to the chemist while nodding politely in the direction of dogma. It is exactly like the educated Romans of two thousand years ago who burnt a pinch of incense at Caesar's statue while not believing for one moment that he was 'the unconquerable God'.

Browne's constitutional obduracy, which meant that he was incapable of negotiating on an equal footing with anybody in any matter whatsoever, brought down the government and blew the whole affair, which otherwise would have been dealt with behind closed doors, into the public domain. The publication of the correspondence, of which act of exposure de Valera later expressed disapproval, was a particularly valuable contribution to democracy, letting daylight into hitherto secret areas. In a word, on this occasion at least, a politician's inflexibility served the Irish nation well.

My mother, David and I were delighted at what appeared to be a wind of change in Irish politics. During the ensuing election, David, who had already met Noël Browne, intended to canvass strenuously on his behalf. But he also was resolved to sit his London matriculation, a tradition in our father's family, at the nearest centre in Belfast, and this unfortunately coincided with the election. David was fifteen at the time. While my mother was driving him north, I hired a car and canvassed in his place. Browne was swept back into the Dáil as an independent.

After the election, I was summoned with others to a meeting. Browne arrived late and sat for a few moments at a table. One hand shading his eyes, he mumbled his gratitude. Then, without a word to any of his followers, he got up and left. His followers dispersed. I was unfavourably impressed, and conveyed the fact to David and our mother when they returned from the North. This was only the first of a number of occasions when I had personal experience of his bad manners.

In September 1953, Browne told his followers that he was joining Fianna Fáil; David, reluctantly, followed him. Many of Browne's supporters defected. These were people who did not equate contempt for the most priest-ridden government in the history of the state with support for Fianna Fáil. Initially, things went well for Browne. In May 1954, however, he lost his seat in the general election, but this did not appear to alter his standing in Fianna Fáil. The real crisis was to come in 1956.

It may not have been entirely coincidence that two events took place at virtually the same time: the Anglo-French-Israeli adventure at Suez, and the Soviet invasion of Hungary to put down Dubcek's very mild reformist 'Socialism with a human face' government. For some time, all of us had been worried at Browne's tendency in conversation to refer with admiration to what he called 'the socialist democracies of Eastern Europe': that is to say, the murderous puppet police states that ultimately, when Gorbachev refused to send in tanks to put down local dissent, were consigned to the dustbin of history.

Both invasions were at their height when a letter signed by Browne appeared in the press. It argued that far too much attention was being devoted to 'the reported aggression in Hungary'; our minds should be concentrated on Suez. It was precisely the sort of letter that a communist fellow-traveller would write. I asked David if he had had anything to do with this letter. 'God, no!' was the reply. One should remember that this was a situation where people were photographed lying down in the streets in an effort to stop the Russian tanks. A few days later, the lawyer Noel Hartnett, a faithful acolyte of Browne, came round at lunchtime. I always came home for lunch. Hartnett never mentioned the letter. When he was leaving, I challenged him. 'Were you responsible for that disgraceful letter about the *reported* aggression in Hungary?' To my surprise, his face twisted with rage. 'Edward, my boy, you have no idea what I have had to put up with from that man.' Browne, he said, could go round for a fortnight with a letter in his pocket – a damaging, self-defeating letter which he would then post off without a word to him, Hartnett, supposedly his closest friend.

The immediate effect of this letter was not apparent, but the long-term effect was serious. It was probably the main reason Browne was refused a nomination by Fianna Fáil in the general election of the following year. This refusal was well planned: it was timed to inflict the maximum political damage, being announced just before nomination day, so that Browne would have very little time to mount a campaign as an independent. He had no inkling of what was to come. He arrived at our house in a state of collapse. He was retiring from politics; he 'could not face the lorry again'. By this, he meant that he could not face addressing the crowds once more on a lorry through an amplifier. 'You won't have to,' said my mother coolly. 'We'll do it all. We'll hire the lorry; we'll draft the speeches; we'll print the election literature; we'll make a martyr of you; you won't even have to appear.' A look of dawning hope appeared on his face.

And so it was. The sympathetic vote was marshalled, and he was swept back into the Dáil. After the election, he wrote a letter to my mother. It concludes:

> . . . yet this letter I have found to be quite beyond adequate expression. I must only then say simply thank you and thank you and thank you again.
> Yours
> Noël C. Browne

But it was not an election without its setbacks. It is difficult to convey the energy and enthusiasm with which David hurled himself into the campaign. It was like Blücher, the Prussian general, driving his troops into action at the climax of the Battle of Waterloo. He drafted speeches; he delivered them himself; he issued press releases, the content of which was 20 percent Hartnett and 80 percent David. Like the Scarlet Pimpernel, he was here, there and everywhere. Then, following ten days of striving for Browne night and day, David collapsed. He had contracted pleurisy. When Browne saw the first X-ray, he exclaimed: 'Jesus! I'm a murderer.' This was Browne at his best. For a full week, no effort or attention was spared. When the third X-ray showed that David was out of danger (but only barely), he lost interest. He did not call any more; he did not even telephone.

For most of the election campaign, the main burden of directing the campaign fell upon my shoulders. Our mother provided endless meals for the canvassers coming and going.

I also prepared the electoral accounts. Topping the list of contributors were our humble selves.

Since the Browne vote had been by definition anti-Fianna Fáil, most of his followers assumed that he would vote as a matter of course against de Valera as Taoiseach. Instead, he decided to abstain – for which he received a hearty handshake from Lemass.

The subsequent meeting of Browne's followers in a hotel was stormy. Noël Browne sat silent, while Hartnett, on the dais beside him, produced marvels of forensic justification. Whatever tensions there may have been in the past had now, at least for the moment, been buried. There were a number of walkouts, one of them by a prominent trade unionist.

Despite warnings from all sides, Browne, when he formed the National Progressive Democratic Party in 1958, put up Hartnett as a candidate for the Dáil. He actually went through the motions of consulting my mother. 'I'm lonely in the Dáil without Noël,' he told her. 'I need him beside me.' 'Yes,' said my mother, 'but do the voters?' Hartnett forfeited his deposit.

This was not the only time when Browne's obduracy was maddening. He approached me on two occasions for assistance. On the second occasion, he asked me if I could draft some parliamentary questions that would elicit figures of a damaging nature about Aer Rianta, since he was convinced that there was gross mismanagement at the airline. I did what he wanted. To my disgust, I found that he had boiled down my queries into a single question, of the form: 'Is it true that . . . ?' The answer was the shortest on parliamentary record: the one word 'No'. The whole exercise had been fruitless. In recent years, I had better luck in drafting several questions on taxation which were put to the then Minister for Finance, Charles McCreevy, by Joan Burton, the Labour Party spokeswoman on Finance. She, at least, knows when to leave well enough alone.

I have indicated the stages of increasing disillusionment in our relationship with Browne. The climax came when I walked into our dining room one day to find David deep in conversation on the telephone. 'Shssh,' he said. 'N.B.' David had the list of supporters in front of him. I could see that lines had already been drawn through many of them. David was reading out the names that had not yet been struck out; every so often, I could hear Browne at the other end of the line say: 'Out! Out!' David would then draw a line through the name. He put his hand over the mouthpiece for a moment to explain: 'This is the phenomenon of the Purge.' In my article of 15 November 1986 in the *Sunday Independent*, I described the process, and continued:

> The number of supporters dwindled as a result at successive meetings. I had asked David what was the fault of these unfortunate non-persons in the Dr Browne microcosm of a Socialist state: were they IRA, communist or fascist? David explained to me that they were nothing of the sort; they were merely people for whom Dr Browne had an aversion . . . Noël Browne never engaged in political discussion at these meetings, and the more fluent and intelligent contributions seemed to elicit an expression of tight-lipped hostility from him.

One of the names crossed out that day was that of a woman doctor. I was appalled. She had spoken brilliantly and at length at the previous meeting. Her idea was that policy should be expanded beyond the scope of health to issues such as redistributive taxation, without which there cannot be a healthy society. There was no hint of criticism of Browne, or of anybody else for that matter, in what she had to say. I said all this to David. 'That's the problem,' he remarked drily. 'She spoke too long for N.B.'

David rushed off to deal with other business. I discussed the matter with my mother. We resolved to raise the whole thing with David, which we did the next day. I put the case for having nothing further to do with Browne; my mother said that she agreed with me completely. If he or Hartnett called on her again, she would remain polite, because she hated public rows, but her involvement with him would cease. David said that he fully agreed with our appraisal of Browne – that he was a raging neurotic – but he said that Browne was the only figure in Irish politics with the courage to say what most other people were thinking but did not dare to say.

The impossibility of Browne as a colleague in almost any context was vividly illustrated by the case of the barrister Ernest Wood. Hartnett phoned us one day in a state of jubilation. A new Browne party had at last been officially formed: the National Progressive Democrats. (Later, Des O'Malley *et al.* borrowed the name, but scrapped the word 'National'.) I had already received my membership card: the only membership card of any party I have ever held. Hartnett's elation appeared to be fully justified: Ernest Wood had joined the new party. This was a coup indeed. A few days later, there was an important announcement: he had left the party on some point of principle. My mother was vastly amused; not so David. It reminded us of Brendan Behan's famous witticism: 'The first item on the agenda of every new Irish political party is a split.'

The rest of Browne's career in relation to David's was punctuated by successive public spats. These arose ostensibly over different issues, but in fact the essential problem was that they were tugging in different directions. David envisaged a great new movement of the Left of which Browne would be the *fons et origo*; Browne's only desire was to tuck his feet under the Fianna Fáil executive table, be on first-name terms with their top people, and have the donkey work at election time taken over by others. All the indications are that he suffered a controlled nervous breakdown when he was ditched by Fianna Fáil, a breakdown from which he never completely recovered.

In September 1970, he decided at last to nail his colours to the mast: he openly espoused what he called 'the Marxist-based revolutionary socialism of James Connolly'. During the Cuban missile crisis of 1962, he had already been photographed picketing the United States embassy and being savaged by police dogs (an event captured in a famous photograph). Even a communist fellow-traveller deserves better than this. To what depths can our so-called democracy descend?

The relationship between David and Noël Browne was uneasy from the start. First, David laboured under the illusion that Browne was a democrat, but the illusion was short-lived. Second, Browne, whose own speaking voice underwent a rapid metamorphosis from breezy RAF style to mumbling monotone, deeply resented David's fine delivery, which he jeers at in *Against the Tide*. Third, Browne, who is normally included with David, Conor Cruise O'Brien and Justin Keating among the 'intellectuals' who all arrived on the Irish political scene at about the same time, was not really an intellectual at all. On his first day as a minister, he was asked what distinctions he had acquired in the field of medicine. 'I passed my exams,' he replied coldly. This explains the intense intellectual jealousy which he could not conceal even in his venomous autobiography. Thus he writes that David, 'to judge by his reading', was fascinated 'to an unusual degree' by the development of Nazism. Nothing could be further from the truth. David, as a historian and political scientist, was obliged to lecture on Nazism, communism and all the other isms, and had an extensive private library on these areas in consequence.

And the impact of Browne upon David's career? This, I submit, was entirely harmful. David was a democrat, a socialist and a constitutional republican, 'in that order of importance', as he used to say. It was his misfortune that he ran full tilt, first into a crypto-communist, Browne, and later into a crypto-unionist, Conor Cruise O'Brien. The latter, ultimately, like Browne, nailed his colours to the mast when he joined, for a time, one of the northern unionist parties. This was not much use to David, who, by then, had gone to his reward.

Edward Thornley is David Thornley's older brother. He is a retired tax consultant and lives in Sandymount.

3

'AN ELEMENT OF ELECTORAL POLITICS

INTRUDED INTO HIS LIFE'

W. E. VAUGHAN

About a quarter of those who graduated in history and political science in 1967 gathered for a weekend in September 2008 at St Etienne-du-Bois. Although they did not meet to mull over the past – certainly not the remote past – the setting was a good one to collect memories of David Thornley for Yseult's book. The fact that such a large proportion of the class met after nearly fifty years said something about the School of History in the 1960s. The fact that the main argument of the weekend was not about Ireland in the 1960s, or about David Thornley, but about the conduct of the French government and people in 1940 also said something about the History School.

A remarkable amount about David was remembered, and there was remarkable agreement about his strengths and weaknesses. It was agreed that he had brought a sense of contemporary involvement to the course in political science by his own involvement in politics, especially his involvement in 'non-party' politics. For one of those present, it had been a revelation that there was politics with a lower-case 'p' as well as politics with an upper-case 'P'. This distinction, for example, was exemplified by his lecture to Tuairim, one Sunday afternoon in the Shelbourne Hotel, when he talked about Catholic social teaching and its relevance to Ireland. That talk complemented his course on Catholic political thought, which was in itself a notable achievement. Such a course, taught by a layman in a university from which Catholics were excluded by the archbishop of the diocese, and in a university where more than a few probably regarded

Catholic political thought as propaganda concocted during the Modernist controversy, must have been rare in Europe. That course was not the only ecumenical factor operating on undergraduate opinion (as well as David, the influence of John XXIII was acknowledged, as was the fortuitous confessional composition of the undergraduates at that time), but the course led one graduate to take a postgraduate course in a French university on the social teaching of the papal encyclicals. At another level, it probably accounted for the fact that three members of the class (two Northern Protestants and one Northern Catholic) attended Opus Dei weekend courses at a country house near Navan.

The thing that was most vividly remembered was the way David organised his special subject on Irish political movements, which covered the period from before the First World War to the 1930s. The highlight of the course was the interviews he arranged with men such as Seán MacEntee, who turned up with the gist of his information written on a cigarette packet; George Gilmore, with his earnestness and disfigured face; Ernest Blythe, with his unblushing memories of the civil war and of even more bitter engagements in the Abbey Theatre; and Peadar O'Donnell, who was mischievous, misleading – and apparently younger than most of his interlocutors. Sean Lemass took part in the interviews in later years, although not during the first year. These interviews were a startling innovation for undergraduates who were bred on documents and books. The enthusiasm with which these remarkable men talked to students in their early twenties was in itself a breath of fresh air. David carefully prepared the class for each session, warning us of what subjects to avoid and which to pursue. Blythe talked with zest on all of the forbidden topics, and fascinated the class like a snake-charmer with a gentle Northern accent and a compelling eye.

For students who were spending their undergraduate years within the walls of a self-confident but detached university, it would have been possible to ignore the 1920s and 1930s and to think that it was enough to have heard and seen Pádraig Colum, Patrick Kavanagh, Brendan Behan and Father Cremin (whose memorable prophecy on the effects of the Vatican Council turned out to be only slightly true). The students who came in contact with David were lucky in that he guided them into what was then, in historiographical terms, a remote and bitter period of Irish history. In a way, David was lucky with his students, with his colleagues in History and Political Science, and with the times in which he was most active as a teacher. The students were a remarkably diverse bunch – some were Protestants, some were Catholics; one third of them came from the North, one third from England, and one third from the South. It was also a good time to be in Dublin: hopes were high in the wake of the Programme for Economic Expansion and after the meeting between Lemass and Terence O'Neill.

David was also lucky in his niche in the School of History. His approach to political science and history slightly contradicted, but nicely complemented, the predominant ethos of the School, which was based on the strict examination of documents, cautious generalisation, a modicum of speculation, and no moralising. Where T. W. Moody was exactingly precise, David was attractively speculative; where Moody was balanced in his judgements, David was exuberantly personal, and where Moody expected thought to precede speech, David encouraged speculation. David's preoccupation with Irish politics was also complemented by Moody's serious commitment to public affairs, which was exemplified by his membership of the Commission on Higher Education and of the RTÉ Authority. David's interviews with prominent figures of the 1920s were also complemented by Moody's austere study weeks at Townley Hall, which dealt with topics such as Parnell's involvement with the Fenians and, in a rare gesture to near-contemporary history, with partition.

One aspect of David that was not generally remembered at St Etienne-du-Bois was his one monograph, *Isaac Butt and Home Rule*, which was published in 1964. The book was an original contribution to the political history of nineteenth-century Ireland, describing the rise of Home Rule under Butt and basing itself on detailed analyses of the general elections of 1868 and 1874. It fitted into a pattern that had been established by Conor Cruise O'Brien and John Whyte. *Isaac Butt and Home Rule* would have been a better book if it had simply been a study of the early stages of Home Rule or of Irish electoral politics in the 1860s and 1870s, but it uncomfortably combined a study of electoral politics with a biography of Butt, with whom David felt a strong sympathy. It was easy to understand David's feelings for Butt: both were remarkable public speakers; both were men for the large questions (a speech by Butt might save a prisoner on trial for his life; his sketchy grasp of the details of the case might deliver him into the hands of the hangman); both were from backgrounds which did not predict their eventual political milieu (Butt was a Northerner, an Orangeman, and a Tory, who ended up leading a party whose electoral success was largely dependent on clerical support in

Southern constituencies); both were closely identified with Trinity (Butt held the Whately Chair of Political Economy from 1846 to 1851). Yet the biography does not work: little of Butt's charm comes across, there is not much about his legal career, and above all there is no sustained study of his Toryism, which might have given his biographer an entrée into a vein of Irish patriotism as rich as anything to be found among the Fenians or the Home Rulers of the 1870s. There was a strange correspondence between *Issac Butt* and David's life: the scholar might say a large biographical element intruded into a detailed study in electoral politics; those who enjoyed his teaching in the 1960s might say that an element of electoral politics intruded into his life.

W. E. Vaughan is a member of staff in the Department of History in TCD. He is also a Fellow of Trinity College and has written on Irish landlords and tenants in the nineteenth century, and was an editor of A New History of Ireland. *He has just completed a book on murder trials in Ireland in the nineteenth century.*

4

'More passionate, more modern, and definitely more irreverent'

Willie H. Maxwell

The 1960s were a time of great change in Ireland, Europe and the world as a whole. I arrived in Trinity to study history in 1963. I hailed from south Tipperary but had gone to boarding school in Dublin. Trinity was an exciting and exotic place at that time. The group of forty who made up our year in history were an eclectic set. The mix then would be hugely different from the make-up of today's class. There was a strong representation of Northerners, English, and people from overseas, and it was difficult to place exactly the Irish students who had gone to school in England or elsewhere. There were locals, but we represented a small element in the overall class. It took some of us locals additional time to feel comfortable and assertive in this mix.

The School of History had a fine academic staff made up of established legends whose reputations had gone before them – F. S. L. Lyons, Theo Moody, Jocelyn Otway Ruthven and R. B. McDowell were all impressive characters. Then there was Dr David Thornley. David made a huge impression on most of us immediately. He was so different from most of the others: younger, more passionate, more modern, and definitely more irreverent. David was so modern and informal that he made the gap between teacher and student more bridgeable.

Trinity was slower to participate fully in the Irish state and mainstream Irish society than other institutions and elements within the state. The church ban on Catholics attending Trinity increased the university's isolation from mainstream Irish life. The fault for this state of affairs rested with both parties. There may have been a logic and acceptance of this position by Trinity in the early years of the state. This situation became intolerable to many of us in the sixties, and we were increasingly impatient to be allowed to play a full and active part in all aspects of Irish life.

Thornley became a natural focal point for this position and provided a leadership role among his students throughout the college and beyond. He exhorted his students to become activists in our political and civic lives rather than mere observers. He himself adopted that activism, first by becoming a respected commentator on *7-Days* on RTÉ television and then by being elected as a TD for Dublin North-West in a resurgent Labour Party.

David seemed to know every important historical figure and every other mover and shaker in the Ireland of his day. This connection was invaluable in securing access for his students to interesting and important figures of the day who appeared glad to accept David's invitation to come and share their experiences with his pupils. Earnan De Blyth, George Gilmore, Peadar O'Donnell and Sean McEntee all enhanced our studies of 'Ireland, 1913–39' with personal live experiences. Michael O'Leary, Declan Costello, Donough O'Malley and Brian Lenihan were among the political activists of the day whom we got to meet.

David's example and leadership influenced many of us deeply and shaped our thinking and beliefs on Ireland and life in general. He also influenced the debate about the future of Trinity. His position irritated and angered many people who were content with the status quo. These criticisms would have reassured him that he was being effective and would not have caused him to lose much sleep.

David was eccentric and had a well-developed ego, and yet he displayed great insecurity as well. He overstated his credentials: his Catholicism, his Irishness and his radicalism. He appeared to want to be admired for what he was rather than to be content with his beliefs.

These characteristics, coupled with his flirtation with alcohol, served him poorly later in life. He had the potential to achieve greater things. He succeeded in getting elected, along with a bunch of talented Labour Party TDs, and for a short time in the seventies Ireland did indeed seem to be heading towards a socialist golden era. Justin Keating, Michael O'Leary, John O'Donoghue and others survived this era better than David and settled more easily into parliamentary politics. The emergence of the civil-rights movement in the North and the beginnings of the Troubles threw up new uncertainties and dilemmas for everyone in both parts of Ireland. David was always strong on the need to have a base ideological position, both in life and politics. Many of us wept as he seemed to fail his own test this time by flirting with Provisional Sinn Féin and other elements – with little conviction, and to little effect.

David was a powerful and attractive teacher to many of us who were lucky enough to be taught by him. He provoked and influenced us greatly. It is a pity that the potential we experienced in the classroom and saw on the hustings did not develop further, to a happier and more effective conclusion.

Willie H. Maxwell was born in Dundrum, County Tipperary. He studied History and Political Science at Trinity College Dublin where he graduated in 1967. He then went into business joining Northern Foods plc in Hull in 1967 where he became a director in 1977. He worked in Saudi Arabia for two years and later established his own business consultancy in 1990. He went on to become the first Programme Director of the all-island Inter-Trade Ireland Acumen Programme and is currently President of the Institute of Management Consultants and Advisers (IMCA). He lives in County Dublin.

5

Taking on the Three Biggest Men in the Room

Rodney Rice

Universities were different then. At least so it seems to me. Trinity College Front Square: the sweep of the billowing robes of professors and dons, down to the more insouciant wave from the sleeveless gowns of undergraduates. Each overgarment a clear statement of the hierarchical position of its wearer.

Students walked past the seeming great names of their chosen course of study. In my case, from the History Department, Professor T. W. Moody, its head; Professor F. S. L. Lyons; Professor Annette Jocelyn Otway-Ruthven; the eccentric Junior Dean – the man charged with maintaining College discipline – Professor R. B. McDowell. From the newer Department of Political Science, Professor Basil Chubb, seeming a little less remote, but nonetheless with the full mantle of authority.

And then there was Dr Thornley. David Thornley: don, teacher, intellectual. To those of us interested in politics, an inspirational figure, a man whose aura of excitement outshone his academic gown, a man with an altogether more contemporary 1960s rapport with his students.

It was not alone the callow youths straight from school who felt this. Professor Moody, who oversaw David's doctorate studies in the 1950s, had immediately recognised him while an undergraduate as an 'extraordinarily eager, gifted and attractive young man'. When Thornley joined the staff on completion of his doctorate in 1959, Moody could immediately see that 'students found his enthusiasm, exuberance, vitality and pugnacity very attractive'. The older man recognised that his protégé enjoyed 'a special sense of loyalty'.

And to this writer at least, that loyalty has survived not just the many years since his premature death but also the decline of that great mind that the disappointments of life caused in his last years. Before that sad occasion, though, our paths had intertwined under several headings.

II

We begin at Trinity. In 1950s Dublin, it was still something of a place apart, still seen as part of a Protestant, even English environment. In 1951, David entered at the age of sixteen, young even by today's standards, where the mad rote-taught rush that is the Irish education system pushes children into university mostly not long after their seventeenth birthday. Back then, the university, which had perhaps just a couple of thousand undergraduates, received many of them from the public schools of England, those who, by choice or from failure, had chosen Trinity, Dublin, over an Oxbridge college or St Andrews in Scotland.

Perhaps significantly to the teenage Thornley, some of his contemporaries may have been young men returned from the world war that had ended just six years previously. Many others would have arrived having completed their two years' national military service, which was compulsory in Britain until the late 1950s.

What effect did this mix have on a youngster brought up in England, country of his birth? (Family legend has it that his mother fervently wished him to be born in Ireland but that the taxi to take her to the boat arrived only after she had gone into labour.) He was a Catholic returning to his spiritual home yet still surrounded by those Protestants among whom he had grown up. Our relationship was never such as would have led us to discuss this, but I do recall a contemporary of his judging that the age discrepancy had driven him through a period of shy immaturity into a competitiveness that was more typical of his later persona.

It may also have contributed to what Professor Moody is quoted as calling 'his pugnacity', for later, as a lecturer, he accepted an offer from the college boxing club to become its president. I'm not sure if David had ever actually boxed up to that time, and his appointment perhaps came only because it was a university rule that a club president must be a member of staff. In any case, David took his position seriously and put on the gloves and got into the ring.

Unfortunately for him, emerging from the other corner was not an eighteen-year-old ingénue but the man who trained the Trinity team –

Freddie Tiedt, silver medallist in the welterweight division at the 1956 Melbourne Olympics. For the first – but not the last – time, he broke David's nose. Nothing personal, you understand. Just boxing.

III

He wore the newly shaped nose as a mark of pride, and boasted of it each time he told the story of what was really a non-existent boxing career. Facing superior physical forces, as will be mentioned later, was something apparently almost demanded by David Thornley's character.

Intellectual forces he could confront on a more equal footing. Not that many of his students could have matched him on that front. But his easy and open relationship with those he taught allowed them to challenge him, either in class or in social settings, and to be let give of their best.

The university cohort was changing as David's teaching career began. Free secondary schooling, the state funding of university fees and the introduction of student grants through 'Rab' Butler's 1944 Act revolutionised education in the UK. By the 1960s, this brought the first generation of British government-funded Northern Ireland Protestants to Trinity. (Catholics, if they came to Dublin at all, chose UCD, the Earlsfort Terrace establishment much disparaged by those at our end of Grafton Street, though the majority seemed still to opt for Queen's Belfast, where, by the start of the civil-rights campaign in 1968, they outnumbered the traditional student majority of middle-class Protestants.)

So the college was now very representative of three, and perhaps four, groups – an apparently (and sometimes ostentatiously) wealthy English cohort, a Northern Irish grammar school selection, and a middle-class group from the Republic, at first with a clear Protestant majority, which narrowed significantly as more parents either ignored or found a way round the ban the Catholic Church had placed on attending Queen Elizabeth I's 'College of the Most Holy Trinity near Dublin'.

It was now the 1960s, the rock'n'roll generation's first public appearance, long hair and jeans replacing a more conservative dress code. Women, whose presence in college had not been allowed past the 6 PM watershed, were now permitted to remain for the meetings and debates from which they had for so long been excluded. And to socialise too in ways perhaps less common in that quite recent past. Though midnight was still the official cut-off time for their visits!

53

IV

This atmosphere was conducive to the relationship David Thornley chose to encourage with the students in his classes. His tutorials were more interactive than those of many of his colleagues. Of course, that may have been assisted by the fact that the subjects under discussion were of more obvious interest to this new generation than many of the alternatives within history and politics: Marx and Engels seemed more immediate to an early sixties student than the nonetheless necessary understanding of Plato and Aristotle, or even the relationship between the Irish earls and the Queen in whose name the august college stood.

At that time, the history courses ended with the outbreak of the First World War in 1914, a time so distant to most of us that it might have been centuries ago. Though David's tutorial course on 'Working-class movements, 1864–1914' suffered the same official cut-off date, the mid-century currency of Marxism in its Soviet guise was such a reality in the immediate aftermath of the Cuban missile crisis as to bring a form of immediacy to our tutorial debates.

For one of my own contributions to that course I presented a paper on anarchism. David congratulated me, saying that students of previous years who had looked at the subject had centred on issues such as the tossing of a bomb into one of the recently installed phone boxes by a French anarchist as a blow for his cause, while I had focused on the early-twentieth-century development of anarcho-syndicalism, which had been for a while influential in some parts of the trade-union movement as a weapon in the class war. I recall feeling quite flattered by the attention! Very much an undergraduate response, I'm sure.

An undergraduate response of a different kind came when Ernest Blythe accepted an invitation from David to address another of his seminar classes. Mr Blythe (Earnan de Blaghd) had been Minister for Finance in the first Free State government.

V

Blythe may be best remembered as the minister who cut a shilling off the old-age pension, but his talk to us that day was on the seizure of the Four Courts at the start of the Civil War and the subsequent execution of four of the anti-Treaty leaders concerned: Rory O'Connor, Liam Mellows, Joseph McKelvey and Richard Barrett.

The years had not mellowed the old IRB veteran of the Easter Rising, the War of Independence, the Civil War and the early days of the establishment of the new state. This time the undergraduates were gape-mouthed as he coldly explained what he described as the absolute necessity of killing these and the others of the seventy-seven anti-Treaty rebels executed during the Civil War. Some of us who had what seemed like sufficient courage to challenge him were easily batted off by a man who had himself experienced imprisonment and hunger strike, and who had known one of his fellow ministers to be shot dead as he went about his private business.

This was living history, an in-your-face personal reminiscence of a time still barely confronted by the Ireland of the 1960s. And in inviting Mr Blythe to speak to us, David again seemed to us like an instigator of a new mood, where students were encouraged to confront their own immediate concepts and perceptions. This view may be truer of a cohort more used to the study of distant history rather than of more obviously current and immediate subjects such as economics, modern English or Irish literature or the sciences. But even so, it left some of us viewing Dr Thornley as an innovator in how he taught his subject.

In part, this reflects a perception of how professors related to students. In fact, that may not have changed very much in the intervening period. Students were (and are) very young people just emerged from the discipline of secondary school, thirsting for the freedoms on offer, and still perhaps wary of how they were expected to relate to the older men and women who stood before them in the lecture hall.

VI

There may now be a suggestion that at least some modern students regard a university education as a right rather than a privilege, and indeed some of Trinity's students back then came from financial and educational backgrounds that made them also of this mind. But for most of us, university was an unknown. And in the case of the History and Political Science classes of the 1960s at least, David Thornley was one of the guides to the gates of the wider world.

This we saw not just through his informal style of interaction with us, but also in his lectures, the plenary sessions of our course. Professor Chubb lectured us in the broad course of political science from the Ancient Greeks till the nineteenth century. Then, in the post-Industrial

Revolution period, he took responsibility for giving us an understanding of capitalism.

Youthful arrogance may have been responsible for some of us believing that since that was, and is, the system within which we lived, there was a more exciting prospect to hand in David's course on Marxism. Besides, it was the sixties, the high point of investigation into Marxism-Leninism, Stalinism, Trotskyism and Maoism. With the Cuban missile crisis, the cold war was at its apex, and with the Swinging Sixties and the growing mood of student revolt, any of the varieties of Marxism, properly understood or not, attracted the enthusiasm of students.

It was cool to be Left. And David Thornley was openly Left. Yet never a tub-thumping Marxist – if he really was one at all. Was this perhaps because he was also a believing Catholic? He indeed had a vision of a socialist Ireland, one which eventually led him into national politics. But he also sang in the choir at Westland Row Church. Whether this was an expression of a deep devotion or of a traditional belief system allied to an opportunity to put himself (in however small a way) in front of an audience as a performer, I do not know. But certainly it is my understanding that he was well able to discuss, define and, if necessary, debate his faith with Catholic Church thinkers of the time. Father Enda McDonagh of Maynooth College is on record as believing he was a Catholic and a socialist but that in neither case did he take a doctrinaire view.

VII

That in itself may have been most fitting to the time. The mid-1960s were indeed a time of much personal liberation, but in the Ireland of the period, and with the structure of the student cohort at Trinity just then, it was not a revolutionary era. At that time, David Vipond seemed a lonely Maoist propagandist in Front Square, and Marxism was less preached than simply discussed in O'Neill's of Suffolk Street, the most 'political' of the student bars around Trinity.

Indeed, when students did first take to the metaphorical barricades, it was not in Trinity but in UCD, an establishment much derided by those of us at the older university. It was not, I think, until the later Joe Duffy generation that Trinity became a short-lived centre of revolt.

David was an inspiration for many of us who at least debated the revolution, but my recollection of my association with him outside the college walls was not in O'Neill's but rather on Saturday evenings in 'The

Lincoln', Lincoln's Inn, outside the back gate, when a sporting crowd would gather for copious pints after the on-field exertions of the day. Then he would always be in the company of his wife, Petria, and both of them enjoyed the social company of students, whether political scientists or 'rugger buggers'.

So that's where the first phase of my relationship with David Thornley ended – physically, possibly in the bar of the Lincoln, intellectually as I sealed my final paper in the Examination Hall. Two subsequent periods of contact were to follow.

I suppose most people recall their university days through the most rose-tinted of glasses: a period of growing dogmatic certainty that the holy grail of knowledge has been opened by the particular student personally; and he or she is now ready to face a wider world without a trace of self-doubt.

One is certainly very quickly disabused of that notion in the broader world, but it may be no harm to start the journey of adulthood with a fair degree of self-belief. Trinity College was a good place to gain that confidence.

VIII

In my case, that was assisted not just by relationships with fellow students but, in what seems to me to have been that new informality that was changing the university, with hours spent socially with lecturers Terence McCaughey from the Irish department and Jim McGilvray and Charlie Mulvey from Economics. But where the social and the formal academic mixed, the deepest influence was that of David Thornley.

As I returned to Belfast to enter journalism, I suppose I thought that that was the end of that relationship. But just a little more than a year later, he was again to influence my life and its direction in a very lasting way.

The *Belfast Telegraph* was Northern Ireland's leading newspaper. Any time I see it these days, it seems to be an organ of much less substance, but at that time, just before the civil-rights campaign and the destructive violence that superseded it, it was a forum not just for good reporting but also for interrogating the society in which it thrived, moving under the editorship of Jack Sayers more objectively to a questioning of the unionism from which it had grown. For a young trainee journalist, it could have been a springboard to a larger platform or a respectable home in which to devote a career.

In my case, it was to be the former. A phone call from a man called Muiris MacConghail informed me that he was editor of *7-Days*, the bi-weekly current-affairs programme of RTÉ television. He wished to recruit a new reporter, and David Thornley had told him that I had entered a career in journalism.

Muiris sounded surprised to learn that I had never heard of *7-Days*, and had never watched it while a student in Dublin. But what student had a television in college rooms? What lunchtime discussions related to last night's TV debates? In fact, at this remove I'm not sure I even knew that one of my lecturers, David, was a star interviewer on the programme.

However, whatever the shock to the show's ego, MacConghail maintained his interest and suggested I apply for the job.

IX

Subsequently, he interviewed and assessed many applicants over two evenings, and my sceptical analysis of a Stormont speech by Northern Ireland's Home Affairs Minister, Bill Craig, owed more to the influence of my nationalist Dublin experience than to my unionist *Belfast Telegraph* employer. If my 'test' interview with Labour TD Michael O'Leary as guinea pig sounded incoherent to me, the slight familiarity of having been a peripheral canvass-team member for him during his 1965 election may have helped me sound less nervous than I otherwise would have. Whatever, a couple of months later, another phone call offered me the job. So my former professor and I were reunited, this time as colleagues.

Radio Éireann was still broadcasting from where it had first begun in 1926 – the top floor of the GPO in O'Connell Street. But the new, exciting Radio Telefís Éireann was headquartered on its now well-known Donnybrook site. It was an exciting time for television, which, when it began in 1961, was described by Taoiseach Sean Lemass as 'an instrument of government'. That was not how the fresh young programme-makers saw it, and of course it was in current affairs that the battlefields between establishment and modernity lay.

7-Days had developed from earlier programmes and had already fallen foul of the external and internal authorities. The result was that some of its team had resigned, but not editor MacConghail, who had already recruited Bill O'Herlihy as a reporter and now added me to a front-of-camera unit that was completed by presenter John O'Donoghue, Dáil specialist Ted Nealon and, as new-style interviewers, a political scientist from each of Dublin's two universities, UCD and TCD, Brian Farrell and David Thornley.

X

Farrell to an extent modelled himself on the style of the BBC's Robin Day – direct, sharply worded, and with, for the age, an aggressive approach to politicians. For more than thirty years, he was to remain a model for many RTÉ interviewers. But he and David Thornley were rivals, each vying to conduct the main political interview of the night. Thornley's style was in some ways more discursive, less threatening, but nonetheless sharp at its point. As Jack Lynch was later to say: 'He was incisive. Some thought *too* incisive.' Labour TD and later party leader Frank Cluskey had a different way of describing how the interrogator extracted information: 'He was gentle yet probing. He did not intrude, but led you on.'

Both men were models for any young interviewer to study. Naturally my preference was for David, though it is for others to decide which style came closer to my own approach in my earlier days as a studio interviewer on television and then in radio.

An element of the build-up of David's reputation as a political guru had already taken place by the time I joined. The Fianna Fáil government had proposed a constitutional referendum to change our voting system from proportional representation to the British first-past-the-post method.

The old Trinity political science team of Basil Chubb and David Thornley put on their statistics hats and demonstrated that such an election method would see Fianna Fáil returned pretty much in perpetuity. Jack Lynch didn't try to finesse the point. 'Chubb and Thornley beat us,' he said later, 'by saying that Fianna Fáil would have a huge majority.'

In a strange way, I had perhaps less, and certainly not more, contact with David as a colleague than I had had with him as a student. For a start, he was still a full-time member of the staff of TCD and came to the TV office only for meetings and when he was going to be on air. At the same time, the Northern civil-rights protests had escalated into violence and the threat of bloodshed was in the air. As a result, though I had thought I had finally left Northern Ireland, I began spending nearly as much time there as I had done while with the *Belfast Telegraph*.

XI

We did, however, have the occasional social foray still; one in particular stands out in my mind. David and Petria always held a New Year's party in their Sandymount home. On this occasion, I was chatting in one room when a crash was heard from next door.

We all rushed in, and there was David on the floor wrestling with the burly Sean Bourke, the Limerick man who had recently helped the Soviet spy George Blake make his escape from Wormwood Scrubs Prison in England. Bourke had met us all when telling his story on *7-Days*. And here he found himself in an unequal fight with tonight's host. Bourke soon subdued David and the party continued, many of us still confused and a little unsure of what had occurred.

Some time later, another body crashed to the floor and the crowd parted. This time it was Brother Eamon – a Marist educationalist who was a programme regular when relevant matters were under discussion – who had been sent sprawling. Another large man, he too pacified his assailant. And the rest of us more or less pretended it hadn't happened.

Next time, however, I was no longer able politely to ignore the brouhaha. For this time it was me who unexpectedly hit the ground. 'What the f—! Stop it, David!' I yelled, as I struggled from underneath him and pinioned his arms to the ground. I relaxed. Prematurely. And found myself again facing the ceiling as his fists pounded my chest. Again I spun him over and this time didn't release him until I was sure he was calmed. I moved off, still not seeking an explanation for this extraordinary behaviour.

Later, with most of the guests gone, I sat with Petria and a glowing David as he proudly boasted that he had taken on the three biggest men at the party. And that Sean Bourke was the dirtiest fighter of the three of us.

This time I saw it. It was back to those days at College and the liaison with the boxing club, and the rounds in the ring with Freddie Tiedt. David could easily match any of us intellectually; he dreamed of matching bigger and stronger men physically. For him, continued effort was its own reward.

XII

That anecdote, I feel, is worth including because it points again to the complex personality we are considering. But it has no more significance than that. What is really important at this stage of David's life is the contribution he made to current affairs broadcasting.

This will be analysed in greater depth elsewhere in this book, but it cannot be overstressed that without David's work, the transition of RTÉ from state servant to modern broadcaster may have been slower than it was. Those who led protest meetings in the canteen – who, in their own words, felt they must 'stand up and be counted' – were the up-front expression of the discontent of a new generation with the establishment and were important catalysts for the change that came. But under the editorship of Muiris MacConghail, *7-Days* was surely the strongest on-air expression of this mood, and a great deal of its success was built around the new-style interviewing of David and Brian Farrell, as well as on the approach the programme took in its film reporting of public issues.

But by this time, David's restless intellect was looking for a new challenge. That was to come in June 1969, when he ran for the Labour Party in Dublin North-West, succeeding Michael Mullen, the general secretary of the Irish Transport and General Workers' Union (the ITGWU, the predecessor of SIPTU).

Labour in this election successfully introduced as candidates four heavy-hitting intellectuals: David Thornley, Conor Cruise O'Brien, Justin Keating and Noël Browne, who previously had been a TD and minister. The slogan was 'The Seventies will be Socialist', but though the four newcomers took seats, Labour suffered an overall loss and the wags soon had it that by the time Fianna Fáil lost an election, 'the Socialists will be Seventy'.

So it was life on the backbenches for some who had expected to be destined for greater things. For Cruise O'Brien and Keating, elevation to the cabinet was to come in 1973, when a pre-election pact on a specific programme between Fine Gael and Labour ended Fianna Fail's sixteen years of uninterrupted power.

XIII

In 1971, David had joined the Liaison of the Left, a Labour Party group led by Noël Browne that was opposed to coalition with the more conservative Fine Gael. Perhaps it was this, plus the fact that his re-election had been with fewer votes, that resulted in his view from the Leinster House benches being still from the rear, even if now from the government side of the House.

Morally, he may have been correct to team up with a group more aligned to his personal socialist beliefs; pragmatically, he was wrong if he hoped, as he did, for promotion to the ministerial ranks. And this, I believe, was his downfall. Governments at that time had the support of six parliamentary secretaries. Today, that auxiliary group incredibly totals twenty Ministers of State, five more than the constitution provides for the number of full ministers.

What do all these people do? I was about to suggest that under current arrangements even David would have been sure to have been offered a place among those junior ranks. That's probably true, but would such thinly spread work have been sufficient to engage that brain, and would it have been enough to save him from the personal downfall that was to come?

So the penance of life in Opposition was followed by the purgatory of being government lobby fodder. He was dispatched in consolation to the European Parliament in Strasbourg in the first Irish delegation to the then nominated, not elected, democratic fulfilment of the young Community long before it became a Union.

And in Strasbourg, David may have been among the first – though he was certainly not the last – to find solace for unrequited political love in the bottle so easily available to doubly paid deputies. It was a weakness that was as much in his nature as in that of so many others among us. And equally, like so many, he was able to seek and find a reason to indulge. In 1976, he reluctantly supported a government measure arising from the Northern Troubles. 'When I get very depressed, I drink too much,' he said. 'When I voted for the Criminal Justice Bill, I went on the batter for a fortnight.'

XIV

Participation in coalition he accepted, however reluctantly. What proved much more difficult for him was to acquiesce in his government's response to the Northern Ireland situation. Conor Cruise O'Brien was Minister for Posts and Telegraphs – hardly the most exalted of leadership jobs. But he was also the Labour Party's spokesman on Northern Ireland, and his steadfast opposition to the policies and methods of the perpetrators of the violence there brought his party well into tune with their colleagues in Fine Gael, who were equally strongly influenced by Garret FitzGerald, the Minister for Foreign Affairs.

David informed his party's annual conference that O'Brien's 'attitude to the North was unfortunately incorrect'. Again, to me this was another illustration of his personality, with his conventional background diced with an instinct for a life closer to the edge – a bigger-picture example of his pleasure at taking on the three biggest men in the room.

And that courting of danger became practical reality in Easter 1976, when he appeared on an O'Connell Street platform with Provisional IRA leaders who were holding a banned commemoration of the sixtieth anniversary of the Easter Rising in protest at the government's failure to mark the occasion in a significant way. This embarrassed the government and further distanced David from his own party.

The late Michael McInerney, then political correspondent of the *Irish Times*, had earlier been a mature student at Trinity College and was greatly impressed by David. Speaking about this event, he later commented: 'He really was another victim of the Troubles. Here was a man who had an obvious conviction to Catholicism, to socialism and to Irish republicanism, which is different from any other form of republicanism. Indeed, his emotions, his impulses, seemed to dominate his intellectual mind, and some of his actions were very irrational.'

XV

It was at that time that I had my last meaningful engagement with David – no longer a teacher or a colleague, but now a politician. I was the presenter of *Here and Now*, at the time the mid-morning show on Radio 1. David sat across the table to defend his appearance on that platform against the wishes of his party.

But this was more than a standard political interview on radio, the daily joust between programme host and guest. It became personal. It compressed those past years as teacher and colleague; the political nuances that had in a normal fashion been debated between us over those years crystallised into a studio cauldron. Again, it was that battle over who was the bigger, the stronger. Back again to the New Year's party.

Who won? Who knows? Reports reached me of listeners held captive in different parts of the country. It was for each of them to decide.

The following year, David's former electors decided that they no longer wanted him to represent them. He lost his Dáil seat. His health was deteriorating. Within a year, he had left the Labour Party to join another disillusioned former colleague, Noël Browne, in the newly formed Socialist Labour Party. 'There is no man in politics that I respect more than Noël Browne, despite our occasional differences,' he said. 'If the SLP is good enough for him, it's good enough for me.'

I think it was a fitting arena for him to end his political career. Noël Browne was an iconic politician, the man attributed with eliminating tuberculosis in Ireland, but not at the time receiving the thanks that were his due. He fell foul of the Catholic bishops and the medical establishment with his Mother and Child Scheme when he was Minister for Health in the inter-party government of the late 1940s. Indeed, he fell foul too of his Clann na Poblachta party leader Seán MacBride, who sacrificed him at the altar of his own conservative religious convictions.

XVI

It was this Ireland that David Thornley was never able to accept, despite his strong belief in the state and his church. He played a perhaps modest but nonetheless important role in helping to promote change, first through his moulding of a couple of generations of Trinity College students, and subsequently by impressing the audience of the new television service, who were excited to hear their political leaders questioned without undue deference.

Thirdly, whatever his failings, he was a challenging presence to his fellow politicians, for whom he was perhaps far too radical a voice – a discomforting colleague too unbending in his demand for an Ireland consistent with the vision he had developed as a leftist political scientist and caustic observer.

He died that year, 1978, only forty-two years of age. He had in fact self-destructed in his frustration at his lack of achievement at the point that should have been the pinnacle of opportunity for such a dynamic mind.

The republicanism at least of his later years was never my republicanism; his socialism may perhaps never have been my socialism. But whatever I am politically or intellectually, he helped to shape, and there is a deep satisfaction, even thirty years after his death, in putting my gratitude on the record.

Rodney Rice is one of RTÉ*'s longest-serving presenters. Currently chairing Radio 1's weekly political review,* Saturday View, *he also presents and produces* Worlds Apart, *an annual series on issues in the developing world. Rodney graduated from Trinity College Dublin in the 1960s and began his broadcasting career as a reporter on the* 7-Days *current-affairs programme on television. Subsequently he presented the Radio 1 mid-morning programme* Here and Now *for six years before moving directly into political coverage and his current positions.*

6

The Tuairim Phenomenon –
A Forum for Challenge in 1950s Ireland

Miriam Hederman

The generation that reached adulthood in Ireland in the 1950s and 60s faced a dilemma. Change was needed, as it almost always is, but revolution had taken place, civil war had come and gone and the Irish State was a reality, albeit a contested one. The veterans of the state's creation were in no mood to cede either their positions of power or the certitudes that had brought them so far against such odds. Any challenge to the social, economic and political realities was regarded at best as uninformed and, at worst, as a step towards treason. The reality called out for and received criticism but alternative policies were not pursued – or invited.

The turmoil in continental Europe had thrown up new and powerful political and social movements to respond to the crises of the forties and early fifties. The political caste of many European countries was discredited after the war; people looked for new ideas, new solutions and new faces. Ireland appeared to be in a different position. It had been saved by its neutrality and saw no reason to experiment with alternatives to familiar political mantras and well-known faces. The emergence of Clann na Poblachta[1] as a new political party in the 1948 General Election indicated a stirring in the traditional political scene, but in 1954 the party gained only one seat and it dissolved in 1964.

The backwash from political changes in the United Kingdom offered little to a country whose problems differed fundamentally from those of her close neighbour.

Yet change occurred and one of the most interesting agencies was the organisation *Tuairim*. Founded in 1954, with an upper age limit of forty years (the subject being tactfully avoided for a few members) and a culture of vigorous enquiry, the organisation offered an opportunity to young Irish people who wished to challenge prevailing orthodoxies that they saw as inadequate.

Another unusual feature of the organisation was the absence of a specific dedication to any particular political, social or economic policy. It was to provide a forum 'to encourage the younger generation to study Irish social, political economic and cultural affairs; to discover and advocate new policies where these are needed; and, in particular, to create a climate of opinion in which wiser approaches to our problems will be possible.'[2] It encouraged a membership of diverse political and personal opinions and ensured a genuine testing ground for any advocate of a particular solution to a current problem. Many bodies existed in Ireland for the pursuit of rural, social and economic activity on the basis of agreed principles, as did traditional political and sectoral movements, such as political parties and trade unions. Tuairim enabled its members to pursue rational discussion as a means of promoting solutions to serious and stubborn problems, irrespective of their background and viewpoints.

Tuairim was involved in five main subject areas. These were:

- Northern Ireland
- Economic development
- European prospects
- Social and educational policy
- The practice and development of government.

Each theme had implications for the others. Emphases changed with time and according to the individuals concerned with the research, lectures and publications but the interaction was a bracing challenge to the formulations or acceptance of any simple formula.

THE METHODS

The founders of Tuairim in 1954 were conscious of the problems facing Ireland and frustrated by the atrophy in the systems available to deal with them. The first step towards reform was to analyse those problems, the second was to identify solutions and the third to persuade those with the relevant capacity to support these solutions.

The members used openings that were available, such as meetings, lectures, study-groups and articles, and published wherever an opportunity arose. Every member was encouraged, and subtly expected, to reach out to the wider public. Tuairim, however, was neither a debating society nor a club.

No one particular process was devoted to any theme, so the general objectives can be discerned through each method or process. The issues were addressed through every available type of activity.

The Tuairim Extern Lecture scheme offered to provide lecturers on a wide choice of subjects which covered, in alphabetical order, 'Agricultural Credit' to 'Yeats as an Irishman'. There are forty-one titles and thirty-one lecturers listed on the back page of *Partition Today*, the second Tuairim pamphlet, published in 1959.

Study-groups were formed to work on aspects of potential economic and social reform before the members involved decided on the options they wanted to advance. They called on others with specific experience in the areas under discussion to help.

A seminal weekend study group was held in 1959 to respond to the Report on Economic Development by T. K. Whitaker, recently published by the government. There were two papers, one by Patrick Lynch, Chairman of Aer Lingus and lecturer in University College, Dublin on 'The Economics of Independence – Some Unsettled Questions of Irish Economics' and the other, 'A Problem of Economic Development' by Professor C. F. Carter, Professor of Political Economy in the University of Manchester. These were published as a pamphlet, which helped to extend their audience and influence.

In the pamphlet, Patrick Lynch refers to the two conclusions he drew from the Whitaker Report: that past policies, though given a fair trial, have failed and the other, 'implicit but no less important – that the true character of the Irish economic problem has often been wrongly diagnosed, and even when rightly diagnosed, the solutions have been stultified because policy has aimed at contradictory objectives'. He then considers independence and economic co-operation, the myth and the reality. The second half of the paper is devoted to the important issue of the role of public enterprise.

Professor Carter concentrated on aspects of economic development which were not commonly discussed and which represented some of the most glaring weaknesses of the Irish economy. He argues, for example, that for the whole of Ireland, 'we are fairly good on principles, that information-gathering is deficient, that assessment is weak and that in the preparation and execution of specific plans we are very weak'. A bracing analysis of the weakness of the Irish political and civil service scene, North and South, follows, despite his praise for Whitaker's report.

A study weekend held in 1957 on the subject of the appropriate utilisation of sea fishing for the benefit of the Irish economy identified another and less frequently discussed factor in the Irish economy. John K. Clear, of the National Fish Industry Development Association, was also a member of Tuairim and persuaded it to explore the potential of the vast natural resources represented by the virtually untapped seas around the country. A research group was founded and identified various mistakes in the then current policy. When it was about to produce its findings, Erskine Childers became Minister for Fisheries and introduced immediate reforms, so 'the group decided that the day for pointing out obvious mistakes was over and that what was now needed was a positive constructive proposal for the development of the industry'[3]. A further study weekend was held in 1958 and 'Outlines of an Irish Fish Industry' by John K. Clear resulted in 1959. The conclusion of the detailed analysis shows an interesting attitude:

> In general the new policy of fisheries development must be considered not only sound but enterprising and courageous. Its great strength is the provisions of grants for the expansion of the fleet; its weakness an inadequate approach to the difficult fundamental problems of recruitment and to the questions of education for the commercial sector. . .
>
> Once he [Mr. Childers] turns his mind logically to deduce from the export desired, the production required, and from that in turn the size of the fleet and the numbers of fishermen, he will inevitably reach figures which, while they may not coincide with those in my paper, will be in the same order of magnitude.

THE PAMPHLETS

The pamphlet, as a vehicle for public debate and controversy, has had a distinguished history and been used effectively by many remarkable figures. Its heyday was long over by the second half of the twentieth century but it was very useful in the pre-electronic age. Its brilliant and devastating use by Jonathan Swift is enshrined in history and literature but not equalled in more modestly endowed modern times.

The sixteen pamphlets published by Tuairim between 1958 and 1970 can be classified into the main subject areas identified above: Northern Ireland; economic development; European prospects; issues of social and educational importance and the practice and development of politics and government.

THE BRANCH NETWORK

Tuairim was founded in Dublin and the study-groups and meetings led naturally to a branch network, first in Cork and London and by 1962 extended to other places including Limerick, Waterford, Clonmel, Kerry, Galway and Nenagh.

The themes explored reflected the interests of the branches. When Tuairim existed only in Dublin its first two pamphlets were produced as a result of the work of Donal Barrington, in particular, who was involved with others in its study groups to address the seemingly intractable problem of Northern Ireland. After the advent of other branches, the Dublin Branch was primarily responsible for three other pamphlets: 'Ireland and the United Nations' written by Brian O'Connor, 'Educating Towards a United Europe', researched and produced in conjunction with the European Teachers Association, and 'University College, Dublin, and the Future', written in the context of the proposed move of UCD from Earlsfort Terrace to Belfield.

David Thornley became Chairman of the Dublin Branch in 1965 and President of Tuairim the following year and added to the political engagement of the organisation.

The Cork Branch was the first to be formed outside Dublin and was responsible for supplying fresh voices to Tuairim discussions and research. In 1957-59 its secretary, Lean Scully, took on the task of extending Tuairim to other locations. This had been considered as possibly distracting from the main objectives by the founders. Largely due to her efforts, Cork was followed by Limerick, Galway, Nenagh, Clonmel, Athlone, Waterford, Kerry, Sligo, and London. Belfast was kept in touch and subsequently formed its own organisation Not all branches were equally vigorous, but Limerick was one of the most active and a vivid account is contained in 'Priest, poetry and politics; Tuairim in Limerick 1959-1975'.[4]

The London Branch brought together involuntary emigrants and those who, whether or not they wished to return, were critical of the same failures in economic, social and political policy that had been identified by those still living in Ireland. A paper published in 1961 entitled *Century of Endeavour – Independence, Partition and the Emigrants* by Roy Johnston, described as 'an occasional bulletin', challenged the accepted wisdom on the correct approach to agriculture, economic progress, industrialisation and attitudes to Northern Ireland. Johnston, particularly in relation to Northern Ireland, was a controversial figure. A London research group published *Some of Our Children: A Report on the Residential Care of Deprived Children in Ireland* in 1966, and a pamphlet on education.

THE THEMES

NORTHERN IRELAND

The first pamphlet, 'Uniting Ireland', by Donal Barrington, published in 1958, began life as a paper read to the Printers' Cooperative Society which was published in *Studies*.

Donal Barrington, one of the founding members of Tuairim, used 'Uniting Ireland' to point out the 'weakness that has bedevilled all nationalist thinking on the Partition problem for the past forty years: a complete refusal to face unpleasant facts'. 'Uniting Ireland' was rapidly followed by 'Partition Today – A Northern Viewpoint' by Norman Gibson, published in 1959, which argued for a policy for both Northern Ireland and the Republic which would address the grievances of the nationalist community and allay the more reasonable fears of the unionists. His plea for 'integration and co-operation' comes as part of 'an attempt to see the problem more clearly'.

ECONOMIC DEVELOPMENT

Economic development was a *leit motif* that rang through the discussions on Northern Ireland, political progress, improvement in social affairs, education, engagement with Europe, politics, government, emigration, the Irish language, the arts and sciences, and virtually every aspect of Irish life. It is therefore not surprising that the pamphlets and other activities reflected the prevailing concern of the members that, without economic growth, Northern Ireland would never seriously consider closer ties, social and educational policy would not advance, European and international relationships would be unattainable and the renewal of public and private sector institutions would not take place.

71

Emigration was a live issue in Ireland during that period. Virtually every family had members working throughout the English-speaking world. The remittances sent home kept the elderly in modest comfort and the children clothed but the absence of sons, daughters and husbands eroded not only families but communities, business and enterprise of every kind. As GAA clubs sprang up in England and the U.S they died away in Connemara and Munster. The economy and emigration were tied together.

THE FUNCTION OF POLITICS

In 1959 a Fianna Fáil-led government proposed a referendum to change the system of proportional representation, which had been operating in Ireland since 1918, for a direct vote system: i.e. a single-member con-stituency with a non-transferable vote.

Tuairim set up a research group of twelve members:[5]

> . . . not to attempt to tell the reader how he should vote in the coming referendum. We present the evidence and arguments on what we regard as the more important issues, so that the intelligent reader may be bet-ter equipped to decide the matter for himself.

The research group acknowledges the help of an impressive and diverse group of political practitioners and observers[6] and makes the customary warning against attributing the views expressed to anyone other than the twelve members of the research group.

On re-reading the pamphlet so many years later, it appears remark-ably even-handed on the merits and disadvantages of the two choices before the electorate. Only on the final page do the obvious alternatives which might have been on offer emerge: 'Should a Commission have been appointed?' After underlining the obvious difficulties, the authors declare 'we think it a pity that the people were not given the benefit of the advice of a commission before being asked to make a choice.'

Regret is expressed that the issue is being debated as a party political issue and a hope advanced that the Tuairim group has succeeded in pre-senting the issues as objectively and clearly as possible. The referendum was not carried, nor was a similar one in 1968.

A much later pamphlet, 'Dail Deputies, Their Work, Its Difficulties, Possible Remedies' by J. H. Whyte, was published in 1966. It was based on the results of a questionnaire sent to all sitting TD's (except the Ceann Comhairle) asking about practical aspects of their work such as how time was spent and expenses met. The response rate was 52 per-cent (good when compared with a similar questionnaire circulated among British MPs in 1963)[7]. The problem of multi-seat constituencies figured largely in the replies.

The format of the pamphlet remains much the same but the practice of charging an explicit amount is now adopted and the price is a half-crown – 2/6.[8]

IRELAND: THE END OF AN ERA?

This examination of political and sociological change was described by its author, David Thornley, as 'an essay . . . [whose] most useful function is perhaps less to provide answers than to point to the really big question.'

Published in 1965, it acknowledges the changes that had occurred in Ireland over the previous twenty years. Four new political factors are identified:

- the retirement from political life of the leaders of the civil war;
- the acceptance of the principle that the maintenance of economic growth is the first charge upon the administration;
- acceptance of social responsibility in spheres that would have provoked bitter disagreement fifteen years earlier;
- the impact of the pontificate of Pope John XXIII.

There is a warning against a 'too-simplified assumption of change in Ireland' and a declaration that 'it is not enough for leaders to know what to do and have the courage to do it. They must be able to persuade the electorate . . . this, if anywhere, is where leadership that is otherwise good has failed in Ireland'.

The challenge identified for the new era was 'to overhaul the politics and sociology of this republic, with as much objectivity as we are pre-pared to allow in relation to economic problems'. Ideas, arguments and pleas for change flow from every page of this pamphlet.

The last pamphlet published by Tuairim was, perhaps significantly, 'Government and People Creative Dialogue: A Report of the 1969/70 Communications Conference'.

IRELAND AND EUROPE

The changing form of Europe and the way in which it was to impact on Ireland was a theme to which Tuairim returned on several occasions. In

1963, two years after Ireland had applied for full membership of the European Communities and immediately after negotiations on British accession had broken down, the Dublin Branch set up a study group to consider 'the social, legal and political implications in Ireland of membership of the Community'. It was pointed out that the chief emphasis of the debate on the subject of Irish accession had been on economic issues and that the 'consequences to Ireland's people in their social organisation have, by comparison, gone relatively undiscussed'. The study group held a weekend session to debate the findings of their work and the results were published in a pamphlet in which several authors contributed individual chapters.[10]

What Did Tuairim Achieve and Why Did It End?

Tuairim has been credited with being a catalyst for those who wanted change and a forum for those to whom the existing platforms were closed. Because it espoused no single view it allowed various voices to be heard. Indeed, a careful reading of the pamphlets and various articles show many views and opinions, some complementary, some conflicting.[11]

Tuairim was a stepping stone to national politics for some members; others preferred to avoid the constraint of membership of a political party. However, the vigorous atmosphere in which every assumption had to be proved encouraged members to engage in other fora. It is difficult to realise today how evolutionary was the approach of Donal Barrington to 'Uniting Ireland' and Patrick Lynch to economic development.

Tuairim was founded to bring about change. Many of the reforms called for were gradually espoused by other organisations, the political scene shifted and a younger leadership, some of them former members of Tuairim, began to play their part in political, economic and social organisations.

Perhaps those who were involved[12] paint too glowing a picture. Tuairim now belongs in the past; it was lively, it was high-minded and it was often fun!

In a way, its peaceful disappearance is a sign that it believed in its mission. When policies changed and better strategies were implemented there was no longer a need for an organisation of young people to research, examine, promote and publicise a better way to do things. A well-disposed Martian visiting Ireland might wonder if there is a place for a similar organisation today.

Miriam Hederman has a BA from UCD and is a graduate of the Kings Inns. She holds a PhD in Political and Economic Science from Trinity College Dublin. She became a member of Tuairim in 1954 and later served as Honorary General Secretary from 1956 to 1960. She is a prolific writer and broadcaster and has been chairman of many public bodies, including the Commission on Taxation from 1980–1985 and the Commission on Funding of Irish Health Services in 1989. She was chairperson of the Music Network between 1995 and is currently President of the Irish Committee of the European Cultural Foundation.

NOTES

1   Clann na Poblachta founded in 1946 by Republicans, Sean MacBride, Noel Hartnett, Michael Kelly. Contested 1948 General Electrion, secured 13.2 percent of the votes, and formed the first 'Inter-party Government' with Fine Gael and Labour. Support steadily decreased until the Party disbanded in 1965.

2   Foreword to the first pamphlet, 'Uniting Ireland' by Frank Winder, Chairman.

3   'Outlines of an Irish Fish Industry' by John K. Clear. Foreword by Donal Barrington, President. May 1965

4   An article published in History Studies (Vol 7) 2006.

5   The members of this research group were; Frank Winder (Chairman), Donal Barrington, Ronan Keane (Recorders), Patrick FitzGerald (Vice-Chairman) Deirdre O'Donovan (Hon. Secretary), Ronan Brocklesby, Richard Dennis, Patrick Daly, Garret FtizGerald, Maurice Gaffney, George Hare., Dermot Moloney..

6   Those to whom the authors expressed appreciation for their help were; Senator Brian Lenihan, Senator P. F. Quinlan, Mr Lionel Booth TD, Mr Michael O'Higgins TD, Mr Sean Casey TD, Miss Enit Lakeman, Dr Basil Chubb, Mr Owen Dudley-Edwards, Dr Seamus Fitzgerald, Professor Denis Gwynne, Mr Noel Hartnett, Mr Sean McBride, Mr Cornelius O'Leary, Dr Kennedy Roche, and the Cork Executive of the Labour Party

7   A survey of all British MPs conducted by the *Observer* newspaper in 1963 is referred to on page 3 of the pamphlet.

8   The cover reveals a change in the structure or the organisation, presumably to cope with the increase in activity and numbers: The officers are: President; Dr. David Thornley, Vice-President; Michael Collins-Powell, Treasurer; David Butler, Honorary General Secretary; Miss Jane Carty; Pamphlet Officer; Miss Doreen McNamara; followed by the Honorary Secretaries of the six branches.

9   Foreword by Arthur E. Carter, President, to the Tuairim pamphlet 'The European Challenge – Its Social, Legal and Political Aspects', Dublin, March 1963.

10   These were: 'Social Policy in the Common Market' by Adrianus Vermeulen.; 'The Common Market and the Common Law in Ireland' by Paul Jackson; 'The Irish Constitution and the Treaty of Rome' by C. Gavan Duffy and 'Political Prospects' by David Thornley.

11   An extensive study of Tuairim has been undertaken by Tomás Finn of NUIG as a doctoral thesis – not yet published.

12   The author of this article was fortunate to be involved in the early years and has refrained from trying to pay tribute to those who did so much. Space does not allow and the study of Tomás Finn should be a more comprehensive guide to the successes and failures of Tuairim during its existence.

7

Northern Unionist Identity

Garret FitzGerald

David Thornley was a political philosopher, who became a political commentator. Then he became a political practitioner – for he was too personally engaged with key issues to remain comfortably on the sidelines. His views on Northern Ireland and mine diverged, but his deep interest in the crisis that developed there from 1968 onwards has suggested to me that I might contribute to his memory by writing about the issues of political identity that it has thrown up, which I recall addressing some years ago at an annual John Hewitt commemoration at Garron Towers in Antrim.

Individual Identity

Each of us has his or her own deeply entrenched sense of personal identity. I know who I am. I know I am me: unique. In the most profound way, I am separate from everyone else. No one else can know the real me – however much they may imagine they can.

My memory unites me today with the 'me' of past decades, right back to earliest childhood. I am secure and comfortable in my continuous me-ness. Outside of me, of course, there is the mystery of others – each with their own sense of who they are, of their own separateness from everyone else. All unknowable to me – however close I may be to them.

This self-conscious sense of personal identity is the ultimate mystery of creation. Science has not unlocked this enigma. Some scientists believe that eventually they will be able to do so – that the mystery of consciousness will ultimately be conquered. I like to think they will be proved wrong.

An important part of our sense of security derives from the knowledge that we are safe in our identity – safe from the intrusion of others, safe from being fully knowable by anyone else.

That's one half of the human equation. The other half is our sense of belonging with others: of sharing with others many feelings and emotions, of being part of society at very many levels – most intimately with whatever person may have chosen to share our personal lives; with our children; with our siblings; with other relations; with friends; with colleagues at work or play. Without that sharing, our lives would be arid, unlivable.

COLLECTIVE IDENTITY

With all our sense of personal uniqueness, we are at the same time social beings: we belong with others. And not just with relatives and friends, for we are all also part of a community – or rather of a series of levels of community. Part of a family; of a work community; of a local community; of a town or city, perhaps, or even a suburb; or of a county; a region; a state; and for at least some of us, of Europe, and ultimately of the wider world.

Different people identify most fully with different levels of community, and very many people do not feel comfortable above a certain geographical level – be it beyond a locality, a region or a state. Moreover, it is notable that in our modern world very many people find it difficult to identify simultaneously with more than one level of collective identity.

MULTIPLE LEVELS OF COLLECTIVE IDENTITY

But this was not always the case. In Europe in the medieval period, the feudal system accustomed people to the idea of different levels of communal identity. For most people in the medieval era, physically fixed in one spot by the nature of the prevailing form of landholding, there was, of course, a primary sense of a very local identity, or loyalty. They knew that they owed duties to their immediate lord. But they and their lords knew also that beyond that they owed duties to a superior lord; beyond him to a king; and in much of Europe beyond that to an emperor and, in spiritual terms at least, to the pope – who at a certain period claimed and exercised, with the consent of many rulers, including some kings of England, a form of political sovereignty over them.

Thus at some level, Europeans of that period were familiar with, and in many cases largely comfortable with, multiple levels of loyalty. Their sense of belonging, their loyalty and communal identity, was often in fact much more complex and sophisticated than ours today – although in a modern world in which only a minority have any real sense of history, this past reality is unfamiliar, and for some would be uncomfortable. We like to think that we in our time are much more sophisticated than our ancestors – which, of course, is true generally, but not, I believe, in respect of this identity/loyalty issue.

One has to think only of the multiple loyalties of England's Norman aristocracy, and indeed the English monarchy itself (both of them French-speaking until at least the end of the fourteenth century), who from the eleventh to the sixteenth centuries ruled parts of France as well as England, owing – and often paying – allegiance to the French king for their French territories.

In this connection, let me also point out something else that the English have totally obliterated from their memory, viz. the fact that in the early thirteenth century the heir to the French monarchy successfully invaded England and, with the support of much of its aristocracy, deposed King John and briefly ruled half of England from London, where he was warmly welcomed by the citizens. It was only because of the sentimentality of the English – or at any rate of their ruling class – that when 'bad' King John died and was succeeded by a nine-year-old boy, these nobles chose to throw out their French king in favour of this child, who ruled for many decades thereafter as Henry III.

How Did These Multiple Levels of Collective Identity Disappear?

How was it that this easy acceptance of multiple levels of loyalty disappeared? It seems to me that this was the work of monarchs who, towards the end of the medieval period, set about establishing absolute monarchies, cutting their aristocracies down to size. Formerly powerful lords, who had exercised full jurisdiction over their territories, eventually became mere rent-collecting landlords. The monarch became the sole centre of loyalty and the state the supreme focus of identity.

Absolute monarchy disappeared in Britain in the seventeenth century – well before this happened in other parts of Europe – an event consolidated by the Glorious Revolution. (Incidentally, when in 1982 the BBC asked me, then leader of the Irish parliamentary opposition, to deliver the annual Dimbleby Lecture, a reference that I proposed to make in my talk to the 'Glorious Revolution' evoked from the editor of the programme a request that I interpolate an explanation of that phrase, for he believed that most people in Britain would not know what this phrase meant!)

ABSOLUTE SOVEREIGNTY OF THE BRITISH PARLIAMENT

What replaced absolute monarchy in Britain was the equally absolutist sovereignty of Parliament, and because Britain alone in Europe avoided the upheavals of the late eighteenth and nineteenth centuries, this antique system of government, free from any constitutional constraints to protect human rights from abuse by the executive through the legislature, survived into the twenty-first century – subject only to such influence as, since 1997, may have been exercised on this by the European Convention on Human Rights.

Just how deeply engrained in the British system of government is the concept of the sovereignty of Parliament was brought home to me forcibly when, on my first day as Minister for Foreign Affairs, I met Ted Heath to discuss Northern Ireland. When I suggested to him that, despite the fact that the protection of minority rights by the Northern Ireland courts under the provisions of the Government of Ireland Act 1920 had proved ineffective, an improved system of judicial supervision would be preferable to the then-current proposal to delegate this task to a Committee of Westminster MPs, he almost blew up. 'What!' he exclaimed. 'Her Majesty's judges overruling Her Majesty in parliament? Constitutionally impossible!'

It should be said that the two biggest threats ever posed to the somewhat anachronistic absolute sovereignty of the UK parliament were made by Ulster unionism, first in 1914 – undertaken with the connivance of the British Conservative Party of the day, which sought to deny parliament's right to give Home Rule to Ireland – and second in 1974, through the Ulster workers strike.

LOYALTY CONFLICTS

A. REGIONALISM

The modern concept of a single level of loyalty to the state has in recent centuries been challenged by two different kinds of conflicts of loyalty: regionalism and colonial settlements. In Europe, the former of these threats has been the most frequent.

Regionalism in the Iberian peninsula derives from cultural differences which reflect the piecemeal way in which over the centuries monarchies in Spain came gradually to unite peoples of somewhat different cultural and linguistic backgrounds. An attempt to incorporate Portugal into the Spanish state failed in the seventeenth century. Moreover, the totally distinct pre-Indo-European culture of the Basques has persistently inhibited the development of Basque loyalty to the Spanish state and monarchy, whilst the geographical inter-penetration of Spaniards and Basques in the area in question has made it difficult to resolve this issue in a way acceptable to all concerned. For its part, Catalonia has sought and secured autonomy within Spain, under the generally acceptable umbrella of Spain's restored monarchy.

In Italy, despite the late date at which unity of the peninsula was achieved, regional conflicts today seem to be based more on economic than on cultural differences. In Germany, the twentieth century saw the completion of the process of unification in the aftermaths of two world wars, and while regionalism is reflected in the federal structure of the German state, the sense of a single German identity and loyalty to the German state is now well-established.

Elsewhere in Europe, the twentieth century saw a succession of fissiparous developments, which have resulted in a proliferation of new states in northern and later in eastern Europe – states that generally command the loyalty of their citizens, despite the existence of many culturally distinct minorities. It looks as if the patchwork of new states in the Balkans, the formation of which was completed in the last decade of the twentieth century – with only Kosovo still challenged, through incomplete international recognition of its independence – is now fairly stable, reflecting as well as may be possible the identities and loyalties of most European citizens.

B. Colonial Identity Conflicts

The other source of identity conflicts – the one that derives from colonial settlements – is less common, and generally such problems arose overseas – most notably in North America in the late eighteenth century, where local and imperial loyalties were eventually resolved by the division of most of that continent into two states, the more northerly of which accommodated, partly by means of a population transfer, those North Americans who at that time still retained a strong sense of their Britishness.

In all this, an odd man out has, of course, been Northern Ireland. In North America, the mainly religiously dissenting settlers from Britain proved capable of displacing the great bulk of the indigenous population – through a combination of technical military superiority and the diseases they had brought with them from Europe, which proved fatal to very many of the natives. In Ireland, by contrast, settlers from Britain (most of them sharing the same religious motivation as those who went at around the same time to North America) were less successful because their military superiority over the indigenous Irish was less marked, and also because, in contrast to North America, these settlers had shared historically a similar epidemiological experience with that of the native population.

Settlers and Indigenous Population in Ulster

The settlers were not that numerous: in 1635, their numbers were estimated at not more than 35,000, and an examination of the Down Survey of 1659 – a date by which I assume much of that settlement had been completed – shows that at this stage the proportion of English and Scots in the counties forming the present area of Northern Ireland stood at less than 40 percent.

Of course, some further settlers arrived in the late seventeenth and early eighteenth centuries, including, I have reason to believe, some at least of my own maternal ancestors, and the Catholic death rate may have been higher during much of the subsequent period. But even when allowance is also made for the substantial pre-famine emigration of Presbyterians from these Northern counties, and for the probability of a higher Catholic birth rate throughout the centuries, the Protestant proportion of this area's population could not have risen to as much as 60 percent by the time of the first census that provides religious data (that of 1861), without some combination of Catholics converting to Protestantism and of inter-marriage involving children being raised mainly in the faith of what had become the dominant community in this part of the island.

Thus a fair proportion of Protestant genes today must derive from the pre-settlement population of Ulster. So, given on the one hand the likely strong pre-Celtic element in the Northern indigenous population, and on the other hand the likelihood that many unionist genes are derived from that pre-settlement population, it seems clear to me that the dichotomy between Gael and Planter reflects a cultural myth rather than a genetic reality!

IDENTITY MYTHS

Of course, that does not in any way take away from the polarising power of this cultural concept or myth, supported as it has been by persistent religious differentiation over four centuries. Far from it – for, in truth, myths are often, perhaps even usually, more powerful than any reality in determining how people feel, and thus how they act. For, unlike reality, myths are not subtle and complex – they have a grand simplicity and force that leaves no room for compromise; they rule out empathy between those who do and do not share them – and where this gives rise to fear by one side of the other, the situation can develop to the point even of excluding a sense of enlightened self-interest. John Hewitt recognised this. Did he not speak in *Postscript, 1984* of

> our unforgiving hearts
> by myth and old antipathies betrayed.

Yet the fact that he saw the mythic character of the Planter/Gael division, and the danger of this myth, gave him no immunity from the power of that myth. On the contrary, his whole work is suffused with and dominated by it:

> Mine is historic Ulster, battlefield
> Of Gael and Planter, certified and sealed
> by blood, and what is stronger than the blood,
> by images and folkways understood
> but dimly by the wits, yet valid still
> in word and gesture, name of house or hill . .

> *(Freehold)*

83

The truth is that none of us in this island are immune from the power of our genetically inaccurate origin myths, which have been hugely reinforced by religious differences.

THE CELTIC MYTH

For the majority nationalist population of this island – broadly speaking, those with a Roman Catholic background – have their own myth: the belief that they are Celts. But as I have just suggested, the genetic reality is that only a small minority of our genes are actually derived from whatever Celtic settlers may have come here between two and three thousand years ago – and there is in fact remarkably little evidence of any significant Celtic arrivals. This reality should always have been evident to any thinking person, for how could Celts, arriving in small boats to an island the population of which, even three thousand years before the Celts arrived, had been large enough to release a labour force capable of building huge megaliths, ever have come to outnumber that indigenous population of the island?

Recent genetic research enables us to put a rough figure on our genetic inheritance: something like 80 percent of our genes come from those who lived in Ireland for thousands of years before the Celts arrived. All the immigrants of three thousand years – Celts, Vikings, Normans, English, Scots and Huguenots – appear to account for only about one fifth of our genetic inheritance. We have, I think, allowed ourselves to be misled on the scale of Celtic immigration by the way in which a Celtic language totally replaced whatever pre-Indo-European tongue may have been spoken by the earlier inhabitants of this island.

How then did such a small group of immigrants, the Celts, come to dominate so totally the cultural life of this island – extinguishing every trace of the language and culture of what was at that time the great majority of the island's people? We do not know, and we find it hard to imagine how this could have come about. So far as I am aware, archaeologists, geneticists and historians have little to offer us as a resolution of this mystery.

Let me, nevertheless, hazard a guess by drawing an analogy with another situation at the other side of Europe. One of the great puzzles of eastern European history is how the Slav language, which seems to have originated about fifteen hundred years ago in a small area of the western Ukraine, manage to spread, within a couple of centuries, to the whole of the eastern half of Europe. There simply weren't enough Slavs to conquer and replace the populations of such a vast area in that timescale. So it seems that the peoples of eastern Europe may have simply found Slavonic to be an attractive language with which to replace whatever they had previously been speaking.

Perhaps, then, the indigenous Irish population may have found the Gaelic form of Celtic – which after all was the first Indo-European language they encountered – so much more attractive than their, perhaps complex, native tongue (which some think may have been close to Basque) that they adopted it relatively easily when a comparatively small number of Gaelic-speaking Celts arrived, bringing with them their impressive iron swords, horses and chariots. Just as some two millennia later, within a brief period of two centuries between 1700 and 1900, their descendants chose to discard that Gaelic tongue in favour of English?

My point is simply that, whilst the genetic composition of a population changes little with immigration – especially in the case of an island – its culture can alter radically and quickly. And, of course, our sense of collective identity – our myth about ourselves and our origins – is cultural, not genetic.

THE ANGLO-IRISH

The identity conflict that is inherent in a colonisation and land-settlement process is always potentially destabilising for those torn between their roots in the land whence they came and the roots they have put down in the land where they have settled.

Long before Ulster was settled in the seventeenth century, this had become a problem for English colonists in Ireland. Thus in 1380, legislation was passed in England to expel Anglo-Irish living there, and this was to happen again in 1440. Irritated by English interference, in 1460 the Irish parliament – all the members of which were of course Anglo-Irish – declared that Ireland was a separate entity bound only by those laws that were accepted by its parliament. In 1488, Garret More, Lord Deputy, threatened that he would 'become Irish' rather than accept terms offered to him by the English government. He was, it is true, a FitzGerald!

Thus there is nothing new about a split sense of identity amongst those descended from settlers in a colony such as Ireland – as our island, or parts of it at least, had been since the twelfth century.

As the centuries passed, and especially after England and Scotland merged into a new entity, Britain, the Anglo-Irish ascendancy came to develop a sense of double identity: both Irish and British. For the 'Old English' in Ireland – the pre-Cromwellian land-owners – the sense of being English as well as Irish may have faded somewhat in the turbulent seventeenth century, but they and the Cromwellian landowners, who kept their new properties after the Restoration, could feel themselves to be both Irish and British – just as many Scots came to feel themselves Scottish and British.

THE ULSTER SETTLEMENT IDENTITY ISSUE

For the settlers in Ulster, the problem was more difficult. Less self-assured than the Anglo-Irish landlords, and feeling more threatened by the surviving indigenous Irish in the hills and bogs contiguous to the good land they had secured for themselves, they felt much more acutely the dichotomy between their British identity and their physical location in Ireland. Their sense of being British and not Irish was often strong, and it was less easy for them to think of their identity in dual terms: Irish as well as British.

Nevertheless, Richard Rose's 1968 survey showed that before the violence started in 1968, when asked to describe themselves as 'Irish', 'British', 'Sometimes British', 'Sometimes Irish', 'Ulster' or 'Anglo-Irish', no less than 20 percent of Protestants described themselves as 'Irish', 6 percent as 'Sometimes British'/'Sometimes Irish', 2 percent as 'Anglo-Irish', 32 percent as 'Ulster' – and only 39 percent as 'British'.

But ten years later, in 1978, the IRA had wreaked a transformation in Northern Protestant self-identification. The proportion of Protestants describing themselves as Irish was by then reduced from 20 percent to 8 percent, with 3 percent replying 'Sometimes Irish'/'Sometimes British'. The 'Ulster' category was down from 32 percent to 20 percent, and the 'British' category had leapt from 39 percent to 67 percent.

But Northern Protestants emphatically reject the label 'English'. Given a choice between 'Irish' and 'English', in 1973–74 only 21 percent of Protestant men responded that they were English, as against 50 percent who *in that context* declared themselves to be Irish – with 29 percent refusing to accept either category!

Clearly, self-identification by Northern Protestants may be greatly influenced by current conditions, and there has in fact been evidence both of much confusion and of instability in the sense of identity of Northern Protestants.

86

The Belfast Agreement sought to meet some of these problems by deciding that those who live in Northern Ireland may choose, if they wish, to be both Irish and British; they are, of course, like all citizens of EU states, also citizens of Europe. We live in a world where the rigid distinctions of the past are happily blurred.

My Own Background

In this connection, I have to say that I have found John Hewitt's poetry intensely moving. For although I am a child of the revolution that founded the Irish state, my roots are in many ways deeper in the soil of the Ulster of the settlers than in that of the South, where I was born, have lived, and legislated.

My father was London-born, the child of Munster emigrants of the 1860s. But for most of my life, all that I knew of his relations in Ireland was the existence of a single great-aunt in Kerry, whom I never met and who died around the time of the outbreak of the last war.

By contrast, because a fair minority of my Northern Presbyterian mother's relations (she claimed fifty-one first cousins, although I have been able to trace only forty-nine!) remained in the North when the rest emigrated, and lived in such places as Belfast, Crumlin and Bangor – in the latter of which I spent the unremembered first two months of my life in the care of an aunt – were an intimate and cherished part of the lives of my elder brothers and myself: Belfast and its surroundings was the area where we visited our surviving grandparent, stayed with an aunt and played with cousins. And these cousins in turn spent Easters and summers with us: I recall still that when, as an early-to-bed child of six, I was to be brought to see the lights of a Dublin decorated for the Eucharistic Congress, it was a Protestant cousin from the North who woke me from my sleep for that purpose!

Understanding Unionist Fears

Just as John Hewitt could write of nationalist Derry's

> gestures which might purge in rage
> the slights, the wrongs, the long indignities

(Bogside, Derry, 1971)

momentarily at least empathising with the people of the Bogside, so also, and especially through Hewitt's work, I can understand, and make my own, the attachment to place, the sense of insecurity, and the rage against the violence that has threatened the very existence of the community into which he – and my mother – were born: all of which, with tragic intensity, permeates so much of Hewitt's work:

> This is my country. If my people came
> from England here four centuries ago,
> the only trace that's left is in my name
> . . .
> this is my country, never disavowed.
> When it is fouled, shall I not remonstrate?
> My heritage is not their violence.

> *(An Ulsterman)*

The sense of being under threat, besieged, in a land in which one's roots are centuries-deep, but still under challenge and threat, is palpable – indeed palpitating – through the verses of *Freehold*:

> Three hundred years
> are long enough for these last wayfarers,
> our fathers, now to be compacted here
> of this live soil, these peoples, this bright air.

And in the coda of *The Glens*:

> And yet no other corner in this land
> offers in shape and colour all I need
> for sight to torch the mind with living light.

In that poem, one can see also how fear is combined with a sense of cultural and religious alienation – an alienation which, however, is infused with a desire to bridge the gulf between Planter and Gael:

> I fear their creed as we have always feared
> the lifted hand against unfettered thought.
> I know their savage history of wrong
> and would at moments lend an eager voice,
> if voice avail, to set that tally straight.

> *(The Glens)*

88

Yet there is also an uncertainty about really belonging to a

> mad island crammed with bloody ghosts
> and moaning memories of forgotten coasts
> our fathers steered from . . .

However, he goes on to insist that

> This is my home and country . . .

Feeling, wistfully, however, the need to add:

> Later on
> Perhaps I'll find this nation is my own;

> *(Conacre)*

All this finds deep echoes within my own being.

But I am of course looking in from the outside. At every other level than that of the myth of origins, and the sentiment that this myth generates, I am a Southern, Roman Catholic post-nationalist: proud of my parents' roles in helping to secure independence for an Irish state, which without that independence could not have become today a prosperous country – one with the most dynamic economic growth in the industrialised world, and a full and equal participant in the creation of a united Europe.

Thus, while emotionally I empathise with Hewitt's view of things, I do so from afar. And with the detachment of distance, what I find most tragic of all is the failure of the community of my maternal origins, whose fears and insecurity Hewitt expressed so movingly, to understand how the world has changed around them – and to address these changes with self-assurance and self-confidence, rather than with fear and trepidation.

It seems to me that too many among the Northern majority perceive their world only negatively, viewing these changes simply as a threat to a way of life to which they are deeply attached. There is a failure to perceive the obverse of this coin: the prospect which these changes now offer of attaining the security which they and their ancestors throughout four centuries have never been able to enjoy.

The Prospect of Security for Unionists

What kind of security might that be? I believe: a security with two key dimensions. First, the security that has been offered by the way in which the rest of the Irish people have finally accepted the Unionist community as full and equal partners within the island – not subordinated to the majority in the island nor, of course, dominating the local minority within Northern Ireland. Throughout my political life – indeed since long before I entered politics – I have consistently fought for that kind of security for unionists – which alone, I felt, could assure Northern nationalists in turn of the security that they so badly need.

The second dimension of this security is that coming from acceptance by the nationalists of both South and North of the fact that Northern Ireland will remain within the United Kingdom for so long as a majority here may wish this to be the case. And as this is currently the case with over two-thirds of the people of Northern Ireland – some 93 percent of Protestants and 20 to 25 percent of Catholics regularly record in polls their desire to remain in the UK – that will certainly be the situation for a long time to come.

This double security is now available to the Northern unionist community, and their leaders have finally had the self-confidence to accept it. At long last, Hewitt's concern lest the unionist 'in his dullness' would 'not see the future gay with possibility' is in the process of being dispelled.

The Double Paradox of Northern Unionism and Southern Nationalism

How has this come about? I think part at least of the answer to this question may lie in what has always seemed to me to be a profound paradox about Northern unionists and Southern nationalists. First of all, the fears of Northern unionists have not just been fears of a people facing a turbulent minority within their own polity; they have quite clearly also been the fears of a people who, despite the political division of the island almost a century ago, nevertheless at a very deep level have continued to feel themselves to be a threatened minority in the island of Ireland.

By contrast, within the Irish State for many decades, the rhetoric of anti-partitionism obscured a very different, and never admitted, reality. From the 1920s onwards, the nationalist population of the South rapidly came to identify emotionally far more with their own state than with the island as a whole. Indeed, I think it is fair to say that many decades ago rhetorical anti-partitionism became a means by which a high proportion of Southern nationalists managed to hide from themselves the fact of, and sought to purge the guilt they felt about, not really treating the North in their own minds as part of their Ireland – except perhaps for GAA purposes!

Perhaps because of my own Northern background, I have always been conscious – and, I have to add, often intensely irritated – by what has seemed to me to be a deep partitionism hidden within much of Southern opinion. Moreover, I have to add, I have since childhood been deeply repelled by the hypocrisy of the kind of rhetoric about 'Partition' that was often used by many Southern politicians in the past to obscure the reality of these deeper attitudes.

If from the 1930s through to the 1960s politicians in the South had been serious in their claimed concern for the North, they would have rejected the irredentist rhetoric that alleged that it had no right to exist and claimed that the British had a duty to 'hand it back' to the Irish state – for that rhetoric served only to intensify unionist fears and to encourage the perpetuation of discrimination against the Northern minority.

If our politicians had been serious about their concern for the fate of Northern nationalists, they would instead have concentrated on mobilising opinion in Britain, and further afield, against the festering sore of the discrimination from which this minority suffered – so unjust in itself, and so potentially dangerous to the eventual stability of the North; indeed, to that of our whole island.

I feel that this double paradox, of unionists continuing to think in all-Ireland terms – seeing themselves not as a secure majority in their own polity but rather as an embattled minority in the island of Ireland – whilst Southerners thought of themselves instinctively as citizens of a twenty-six-county Irish state rather than as part of an all-island community – contributed far more than most people have ever realised to the lethal tensions that eventually developed in Northern Ireland.

This curious inversion of publicly stated attitudes in the private thoughts of both groups explains both the depth of unionist fears and the scale of Southern incomprehension of these fears. And, of course, it also explains the intense and eventually explosive frustration of the Northern nationalist minority, who, I have always thought, felt abandoned by their Southern fellow-countrymen – and with very good reason.

Of course, nothing in what I have been saying about the shared responsibility of Southern political and public opinion can mitigate the failure of the sovereign power in Northern Ireland, the British state, over a period of half a century to accept and exercise its primary responsibility for the maladministration of the North by its local majority party and government.

The truth is that both sovereign governments – that of Britain certainly, but also to a lesser degree that of the Irish state – failed the nationalist people of Northern Ireland, and thus put at risk all the people of the North.

One element in this curious inversion of stated attitudes has changed radically: Southern attitudes to Northern Ireland have evolved substantially since the 1960s. Irredentism has largely disappeared from the South; the assertion of a right to reunification against the wishes of a Northern majority is now repudiated by all political parties: by Fine Gael and Labour since 1969, and by Fianna Fáil unequivocally since 1993. And even, at least by implication, by Sinn Féin. The constitutional provisions that have been read as asserting such a right have now been deleted from the constitution of the Irish state.

THE CIVIL RIGHTS MOVEMENT – IN REALITY A UNIONIST VICTORY?

The paradox of the inversion at a deeper level of the stated attitudes of Northern unionists and Southern nationalists towards the division of the island is, however, not the only unrecognised paradox underlying the Northern tragedy. For I am certain, however incredible this may seem to many unionists even thirty years later, that history will in time record that the seeds of hope for the Northern unionist community were sown almost thirty years ago by the civil-rights marchers.

Let me justify that statement. If you look clear-sightedly at what those marchers were doing, you will see, as the historians of the future will record, that they were in fact abandoning the sterile forty-year long repudiation of the Northern state by their political, and often also spiritual, leaders.

Instead of rejecting that state, the civil-rights marchers were in fact demanding admission to it on terms of equality – an equality long denied to them by the fearful majority that had been arbitrarily created in the Narrow Ground delineated by the Government of Ireland Act of 1920.

The demands of the civil-rights movement were in fact pitifully modest. They could not even raise their sights to seek a minority role in the government of Northern Ireland: they sought merely to be admitted as a fairly treated opposition. Power-sharing in government was then a concept that nationalists in the North were some years away from even imagining as a possibility – although I have to say that from the summer of 1969 onwards, it seemed to me that some form of joint government, at any rate for a period, would be necessary in order to ensure the full and unequivocal acceptance of the Northern state by the nationalist community. That is why I incorporated this idea into a policy document accepted by my party, Fine Gael, on 18 September 1969 – two years before it was adopted in the North by the newly formed SDLP.

Unhappily, the deep-seated insecurity, indeed paranoia, of the unionist leadership of that period, together with an inherited reluctance to give up unjust privileges that had quite unnecessarily bolstered the impregnable democratic majority within Northern Ireland in favour of the Union, led these leaders – 'in their dullness', to use Hewitt's phrase – to view this unique opportunity rather as a threat. Blindly – and literally, in the streets of Northern Ireland's second city in October 1968 – they beat into the ground those who were seeking the equal treatment that was then the simple key to belated nationalist acceptance of the reality of the Northern state.

From that tragic error of short-sighted unionist politicians sprang almost forty years ago the events that led inexorably in 1972 to the collapse of the Northern polity, as it had been created in 1920. And, with that, there also collapsed unionist self-confidence and, it seems to me, the capacity of the political leaders of unionism to identify clear-sightedly, and then to pursue with skill and subtlety, the long-term interests of those whom they represent.

POLITICAL PARTIES – THE DICHOTOMY BETWEEN ACTIVISTS AND VOTERS

Although they will never admit it, political parties tend to be self-sufficient and sealed off from the rest of society – responding all too often to the emotions and prejudices of their activists rather than to the needs and aspirations of their supporters, or potential supporters, in the wider community. And political unionism has suffered more than most from this besetting sin of party politics.

Of course, one-party government, with which history in 1920 endowed the Northern polity, tends especially to cut off such a party even from the community whence it derives its support. For such a system tends to draw its active participants from an even narrower band of supporters than does a system in which parties alternate in government.

I have the impression that in Northern Ireland important elements in society, such as the professions and some significant parts of the business community, always kept their distance from unionist politics – in some cases, perhaps because of distaste for the discrimination factor (from which, nevertheless, many of them were content to benefit), and which few chose to challenge, or perhaps even to admit existed.

The 'Coasters' of Unionism

I do not think I am wrong in this. Did not John Hewitt describe such unionists as *The Coasters*?:

> You coasted along
> to larger houses, gadgets, more machines,
> to golf and weekend bungalows,
> caravans when the children were small,
> the Mediterranean, later, with the wife
>
> . . .
> You coasted along.
> And all the time, though you never noticed,
> the old lies festered;
> the ignorant became more thoroughly infected;
>
> . . .
> The government permanent, sustained
> by the regular plebiscites of loyalty.
> You always voted but never
> put a sticker on the car;
>
> . . .
> Faces changed on the posters, names too, often,
> but the same families, the same class of people.
> A minister once called you by your first name.
> You coasted along
> And the sores suppurated and spread.
>
> Now the fever is high and raging;
> who would have guessed it, coasting along?

. . .
You coasted too long.

Too long? To the point where:

> the malice and the hate are palpable,
> the flames authentic,
> the wounds weep real blood
> and the future is not to be foretold.

(Parallels Never Meet)

REBUILDING NORTHERN IRELAND

The key task of the years ahead is for the two communities, through their politicians, to turn their backs on a disastrous past, instead setting out together to rebuild the shattered economy of Northern Ireland, seeking as far as may be possible to replace its level of dependence upon UK subsidies by a dynamic and self-sustaining industrial and service economy, similar to that which has been built up in the Republic over the decades.

That will not be easy, especially as, for whatever reason, the much better-endowed Northern educational system so far seems to have failed to produce and retain within the boundaries of this area a young, educated workforce on the same scale as has happened south of the border. Much now depends on the capacity of the unionist community to end its enervating brain drain, the reasons for which, with the belated restoration of peace, no longer exist.

It is, of course, true that

> there is much to do before our pride
> can move with mercy in its equal stride;
> . . .
> lost acres to resume, and skills restore,
> and towns to trim to decency – and more,
> bright halls for art and music, rambling parks
> not fenced or gravelled by some board of works,
> and simple trades to nurture, till again . . .

And Hewitt, in this 'Glittering Sod' section of *Freehold*, goes on, you will recall, to declaim:

> let there be no wall
> to shut the warm winds out that bring us word

how over Europe liberty has fared,
how in that valley or by that low shore
poor men make kindly laws to help the poor,
and quality is possible again
to meet the leaping hopes of earnest men.

Meanwhile, Hewitt's message in 'Memorandum for the Moderates' could not be more appropriate to the present moment of possibility:

Speak peace and toleration. Moderate
your tone of voice, and everywhere avoid
what might provoke. Good will must be deployed
in efforts to restore our balanced state.
To long-held views sincere give proper weight;
one brief rash word and all might be destroyed.
. . .
This is your duty as a citizen:
hold firmly to it, deaf to cynic sneers.

Dr Garret FitzGerald was Foreign Affairs Minister from 1973 to 1977, was twice Taoiseach, from June 1981 to March 1982 and again from December 1982 to March 1987, and was a driving force behind the Anglo-Irish Agreement of 1985. Dr FitzGerald taught in the Political Economy Department of UCD for fourteen years, and is now Chancellor of the National University of Ireland. In addition to being a prolific public speaker, he is a long-time columnist for The Irish Times *and a regular contributor to various journals and political magazines*

8

THE CHRISTIAN AND CATHOLIC INTELLECTUAL
AND THE PROMISE OF DAVID THORNLEY

ENDA MCDONAGH

There is scarcely a more politically incorrect term in current media or even in the academic vocabulary than 'Catholic intellectual'. Not that 'intellectual' was ever a term favoured in Ireland, any more than it was in Britain. Such pretentious vocabulary was in British terms best left to 'frogs' and 'wogs' of continental hue. That Anglo-Saxon bias has not operated to the same extent in the United States of America, despite that country having to face for long periods a certain European, including British and Irish, educational snobbery. Indeed, one of the great contemporary breeding and stamping grounds of intellectuals from all over the world, but particularly from the English-speaking world, is the *New York Review of Books*. Who is properly described as an intellectual and what he or she does is naturally the subject of disagreement among intellectuals themselves and will be the subject of later discussion.

Whatever the current difficulties about using the term 'intellectual' – and the *NYRB* seldom if ever uses it itself – its qualification by the term 'Catholic' or even 'Christian' would be unthinkable for most intellectually serious commentators, even Catholic ones. In their world, the term 'Catholic' has lost any of the visionary breadth and intellectual depth which might be associated with the great names of the tradition, from Augustine, Aquinas and Dante to Newman, Unamuno and Schumann. If it is not dismissed as pious superstition, 'Catholic' refers at best to a particular, narrow and authoritarian Christian denomination, and at worst to a sectarian and divisive religious grouping. In Ireland, the sectarian

Troubles in Northern Ireland, combined with the scandal of clerical sex abuse, accelerated an already developing decline in engagement with the Catholic Church. Large or small 'c' as the case may be, in the self-important media, as in the university – the natural environment of so many would-be intellectual and cultural leaders – Catholicism in its intellectual character enjoys little respect and carries less clout, however much members of theology faculties and institutes or church leaders may deceive themselves and others.

It is only fair to add, both in the present Irish context and more broadly, that politicians earn no more intellectual respect than people in other walks of life and that intellectuals, wherever they come from, are equally disregarded in political circles. But all that presumes an agreed account of what an intellectual is, and not just a set of agreed prejudices about who they are and what their roles are. So it is necessary to attempt some more detailed description of the intellectual, his attributes and activities. While this desciption is drawn as fairly as possible from both scholarly study and personal experience, it cannot claim universal validity.

Intellectual Hospitality

Assuming for the moment the intellectual capacity and industry which seem essential to such an avocation, the aspiring intellectual must offer hospitality to ideas and knowledge beyond his immediate ken. Intellectual hospitality, more widely and generously embracing of the strange and difficult than simple curiosity (a necessary component), defines the intellectual life in its vitality and graciousness.

Intellectual hospitality connotes more than the conventional open mind, ready to entertain any and every view, however ill-founded or ridiculous it may appear, and without any attempt to evaluate such views. One person may be, and indeed is, the equal of any other, and is as entitled to his view as any other, but that does make the views equal as factual truth or value judgment. What is at stake here is intellectual rigour and integrity, not simple prejudice or feeling. Of course, intellectuals may, despite their rigour and integrity, finally differ in their assessment of the facts and judgment of the values involved. They can do so honourably only if they begin by welcoming the differing other and his or her positions and proceed carefully and critically in examining both positions, of self and other, to some considered and well-based conclusion.

Integral to intellectual hospitality, then, is a welcome for the other and his ideas, accompanied by a critical examination of both positions in search of the fuller truth. The critical reaction without the welcome for the different and the differer, so frequent at the level of public debate, may readily yield to distraction and personal abuse without any advance in understanding of the issues involved.

As I write this in the US (Easter, 2008) in the midst of a close-fought campaign to be the Democratic nominee for the coming presidential election, Senator Barack Obama has delivered what even his opponents, Democratic and Republican, have called a 'profound speech' and a substantially 'new analysis of the current state of the race question in the United States'. Yet despite such widespread plaudits, the debate for which he called is not taking place. Most critical commentators, from journalists to professors, remain satisfied, after their general praise of the speech's content, to ignore that content and instead raise questions about why he did not deliver it sooner, or did not distance himself personally from Reverend Jeremiah Wright, author of certain objectionable remarks, and roundly repudiate those remarks. Even friendly commentators mostly simply muse on how much damage this will do to his campaign. Of course, it will damage his campaign, but more importantly, if the commentariat refuses to debate the substantial issues as deeply and fairly as Senator Obama tried to do, it will damage the political, social and racial life of the United States itself. One is left with the depressing feeling that intellectual political debate in the United States, despite its boasted freedom of speech and its major universities and publications, is as rare as it is in other western democracies. And the initial welcome for the different is no more than headline-deep.

THE CREATIVE PHASE

The failure to deal seriously and critically, in both positive and negative senses, with Obama's analysis prevented that further phase in intellectual exchange, the creative phase. Obviously, Obama had not said the last good word on the tangled question of race relations in the United States. At best, he had said a new, good word and would claim no more himself. He had – uncynically, I believe, and within the context of the controversy generated by Wright's offensive comments and of his own sensitively worded response – attempted to open a genuine debate in which fresh understanding and creative action might follow in bringing all Americans closer together in resolving their common difficulties. It is in such hospitable and critical intellectual interchange that what Senator Hillary Clinton has called creative 'solutions' may emerge and the 'change' advocated by Senator Obama may come about. And should Senator John McCain prove the eventual winner in the presidential race, his preoccupation with security could only benefit from the creative debate which such a significant speech should prompt.

The creative side of intellectual life and debate is seldom directly associated with political life and debate. Yet the major political challenges such as bio-experimentation, health-care from HIV and AIDS to bird-flu, the environment, peace and war, world poverty and economics in the context of globalisation, transcend individual countries and disciplines. There are ethical, scientific and other intellectual issues which require serious and extended discussion across the globe. All of these areas require their specialist and sub-specialist scholars in a range of disciplines, scientific and humanistic, sociological, ethical and religious, as I learned over many years of engagement with the HIV and AIDS phenomenon in sub-Saharan Africa.

Complete intellectual hospitality to the many facts and facets of this epidemic lies beyond the capacity of any one person. So does their adequate critical evaluation and creative resolution. Collaboration and teamwork are essential, where the hospitality is not just intellectual but includes co-workers in allied and quite different disciplines. Epidemiologists, virologists and other bio-scientists have to collaborate with cultural, ethical and religious specialists in many areas in efforts to contain the effects and spread of this particular virus. Such containment with its need for public and political awareness and action requires intellectual leaders who can combine with insight and integrity a number of the results of the relevant diverse disciplines. Senior officials from WHO and UNAIDS like Jonathan Mann and Peter Piot have often provided such leadership in recent years, while visionary politicians like Nelson Mandela have on this as on other crucial public issues like human rights exercised enormous positive and creative influence.

As polymaths in such a scholarly diverse world as our own are necessarily extremely rare and because the few there are may not wish to join the hurly-burly of public debate, the intellectuals of interest here are likely to be established scholars in a couple of adjoining disciplines with a competence in some quite different areas of immediate public impact. Their reputations as scholars and their known interest and competence in other (public) areas enables them to take part in relevant public debates. To be deemed intellectuals within our description they must move beyond their original scholarly concerns to the concerns of the public forum while maintaining their scholarly and intellectual integrity and impartiality, their unyielding respect for truth, for fairness of debate and for the persons of their opponents.

This will be all the more difficult to do given the passion for truth and right which draws them into the public forum in the first place. How far such frequently named and influential intellectuals as Edward Said, Susan Sontag, Martha Nussbaum and Noam Chomsky or George Orwell, Simone Weil, Jurgen Habermas or Paul Ricoeur from this side of the Atlantic, managed to combine their passion and their impartiality is too difficult for this author to judge. Yet that combination, however skewed or unequal, is essential to the true intellectual. These few sample names are not meant to exclude or diminish the hundreds, even thousands of equally famous and effective intellectual contributors to the public square over the past centuries in which the term and so the role became accepted sometimes at the risk of death or imprisonment.

More relevantly to most of us there are numerous lesser known but effective intellectuals, as defined above, operating in the universities, in politics often with a small 'p', in the media and other institutions or quite simply as individuals, who have by their intelligence and insight, commitment and integrity helped to transform local or national communities. Some of these have, on the basis of their intellectual convictions, promoted or even inspired and initiated local movements for peace and reconciliation, for environmental protection, for just economic development at home and abroad and above all for the educational advancement of the many in all our countries, developed and underdeveloped, who remain intellectually and educationally deprived. Although they would be the last to describe themselves as intellectuals, it is their intellectual capacity and its accompanying attributes that enable them directly or indirectly to promote the true well-being of their societies.

In the discussion so far intellectuals have been described dominantly as people of serious intellectual capacity and scholarly attainment who have entered effectively and with integrity into issues of public concern. And this is certainly true as far as it goes. However as with the lesser known and perhaps less scholarly 'intellectuals' mentioned in the previous paragraph, some important and related actors in the public forum may have been overlooked. I refer in particular to the artists of all 'denominations', painters, sculptors, architects and of course writers from poets and novelists to playwrights and literary critics. In his recent book, *Absent Minds: Intellectuals in Britain*, Stefan Collini lists poet, playwright and critic T. S. Eliot among the elite, as well he might. Eliot did not shirk public controversy in defence of what he saw as right and for the good of society. Artists are by avocation, explicitly or implicitly, shapers of the public mind and mood. The most notable Irish example may be W. B. Yeats, poet, playwright, critic and controversialist, like Eliot but in such different styles. In a quite different artistic genre, that of painting rather than writing, his brother Jack B. Yeats shaped the public's vision of Irish light and colour, of Irish landscape, face and figure for generations.

The Irish intellectual influence of artists is for later discussion. The point to be emphasised here is that many artists have played and still play roles analogous to the roles of more conventionally recognised intellectuals with a background in the academic worlds of the sciences and technology, of the humanities such as philosophy, sociology, psychology and economics. Literary criticism belongs in that school of the humanities and has produced many significant and influential intellectuals as mentioned above. Architecture as crossing the boundaries between the (fine) arts and the sciences and with its monuments persisting in the public sphere across cultures, continents and centuries, has had its intellectual impact in forming minds and hearts, people and politics from long before the term or category of intellectual was invented. The buildings for the new Republic on Capitol Hill, Washington DC, provide one powerful illustration of this; medieval and later European Cathedrals very different ones; contemporary shopping malls different still.

Musical artists, both composers and performers, may be more difficult to classify in their intellectual roles. Yet from local ballads through national anthems to the towering 'Ode to Joy' by Beethoven, adopted as the anthem of the European Union, music's public and political influence has been immense. The same public influence could be attributed to religious music from Gregorian chant and the Verdi *Requiem* to Wesleyan hymns and guitar-strumming religious pop. A more recent and relevant example of public musical impact may be the efforts of conductor Daniel Barenboim to promote reconciliation between Israelis and Palestinians through his orchestral and personal performances on both sides of that great divide and his illustrated accounts of this work in the *Reith Lectures* on the BBC. Not all of the music that has been influential has had much musical or intellectual substance but the great classical composers and performers could hardly be left out of the court of intellectuals, given their intellectual endowment and positive cultural influence.

In this rather summary attempt at defining intellectuals and their roles I have of course exceeded the time-span within which intellectuals have been recognised as such. More controversially perhaps I have extended the categories of actors and activities which might be properly described as intellectual. This may be a personal failing (or virtue) as I find it increasingly difficult to separate in my own life and work the sciences (my original university studies) with their unceasing impact on the world, the study of the humanities through philosophy and theology, literature and the fine arts to social and political studies. In so many of these I remain a rank but committed and persisting amateur (lover) and revel in discovering their connections and their personal and public influence.

THE INTELLECTUAL IN IRELAND

The Irish reputation for imagination and for works of the imagination has always overshadowed any claims to scholarly and intellectual achievement. There is substance in such a claim and some good historical reasons for it but at best it is only a half-truth, ignoring the pre-Christian and early Christian tradition completely, including the works of the Irish monks at home and more spectacularly in Britain and Europe. Joannes Scotus Eriugena (*c.* 810-877) was one of the greatest philosopher-theologians of his day and the Irish reputation for scholarship was well established in Carolingian times. In the post-Reformation period Gaelic and Catholic Ireland lacked access to local centres of higher learning although a number did find their way to centres in Europe through a range of Irish colleges. Members of the established Church of Ireland (Anglican) had their own University of Dublin from 1592 and produced an impressive number of reputable scholars and thinkers, such as the philosopher Bishop Berkeley and the philosopher-politician Edmund Burke. As this theme of the Irish intellectual and scholarly tradition has been the subject of a fine collection of essays edited by Richard Kearney and entitled *The Irish Mind* and as this essay seeks to ally rather than oppose intellect and imagination, further debate on the topic may be left aside. As some at least of the intellectual exchanges dealt with religion and Catholicism in particular, their discussion may be deferred to the following section on 'The Christian-Catholic Intellectual'.

103

The close intellectual connection between, for example, politics and literature may be illustrated by the work of eminent historian Roy Foster in his highly regarded but controversial *History of Ireland* and his role as the official biographer of W. B. Yeats, two volumes of which have already appeared. Seamus Deane, poet and novelist, has played a similar major intellectual role in his production of the also contentious three volume *Field Day Anthology of Irish Writing*. While recognising both authors (and their works) as major contributors and contributions to Irish Intellectual life, the controversies they generated provoked fresh developments in Irish self-understanding, developments as yet incomplete.

Foster's critique of the standard nationalist account of Irish history was sharply criticised by some of his historian colleagues as one-sided and dubbed by many critics as 'revisionist' in a denigratory sense. In a controversy which still goes on and which played out for example in attempts to end the 'Troubles' in Northern Ireland, the 'nationalist' and 'revisionist' versions may be finding a new modus vivendi, although history in Ireland as elsewhere is always likely to be a critical intellectual battlefield.

The Field Day Anthology revealed another sharp dividing line in Irish intellectual and cultural life by its almost complete neglect of women writers in the tradition. This alleged machismo among contemporary Irish writers had already been sharply criticised by poet and critic, Eavan Boland, in her collection of critical essays, *Object Lessons*. But the reaction of the outraged women writers on the publication of the anthology went far beyond that. So much farther that they organised fourth and fifth volumes devoted exclusively to women writers and in volumes much thicker than any of the three previous volumes. This controversy and its issue in two further volumes marked in many and more significant ways the culmination of one of the great Irish political and intellectual controversies which really began in the 1960's in Ireland and had embraced en route many of the feminist and indeed liberal issues disputed throughout the western world from contraception to a whole range of women's rights. It was entirely fitting that the women's *Field Day* volumes should be launched by Ireland's first woman President and a notable defender of women's and other human rights in her years as a lawyer, Mary Robinson.

Of course there were many other public issues debated in Ireland in the last century and many other notable debaters. Among politicians might be counted former Taoiseach Garret FitzGerald, former ministers Conor Cruise O'Brien, John Wilson, Michael D. Higgins and John M.

Kelly, Senators Alexis FitzGerald, Mary Robinson, John A. Murphy and David Norris, as providing intellectual political debate on occasion. However more pragmatic and partisan attitudes and actions usually dominated.

At a further remove from the hot-plates of politics, history and even feminism, the comparatively cool arena of the arts offered the Irish public fresh insights into their own lives and culture. One of the more notable of these was playwright Frank McGuinness's *Observe the Sons of Ulster Marching to the Somme*, a brilliant reconstruction of Ulster Protestants in their heady sacrifices in the Great War by somebody of nationalist and Catholic background. A parallel dramatic achievement was that of Sebastian Barry in his *Steward of Christendom*, about a retired officer of the Royal Irish Constabulary, which had been disbanded at the time of Irish independence because of its British provenance and presumed loyalty. As Fintan O' Toole, intellectual columnist and journalist with the *Irish Times*, said on the occasion of the death of that remarkable novelist John McGahern, (I quote from memory): 'He changed Irish society not by prescribing for it but by describing it'. He would be joined by many other Irish novelists and short-story writers, both men and women who made such an impact on the Irish public imagination and public life. It is hardly necessary to go through the list from Joyce and Kate O'Brien at the beginning of the twentieth century to William Trevor (still at it!) and Ann Enright at the beginning of the twenty-first.

This could be said of many other Irish artists in the twentieth and early twenty-first centuries. Two of our foremost playwrights, Brian Friel and Tom Murphy, had their initial success with independent plays dealing with the great Irish curse of the twentieth century, emigration. Friel dealt magically with pre-emigration agonising in *Philadelphia, Here I Come!* and Murphy dealt powerfully with post-emigration trauma and violence in *Whistle in the Dark*. From the plays of Sean O'Casey through those of Samuel Beckett to the latest by Conor McPherson and Marina Carr, and including directors like Gary Hynes and performance colleagues, Irish theatre has exposed some of the most powerful strengths and weaknesses of the Irish and human psyche and society, one of the true tasks of the intellectual.

Poets have been no less influential if usually in a more indirect way. Much of the best and most influential poetry of the twentieth century has emanated from poets born in Northern Ireland. That 'tight-assed trio of Heaney, Longley and Mahon', to borrow a phrase which Michael

Longley had already borrowed for his inaugural lecture as Ireland Professor of Poetry at University College, Dublin, earlier this year, have continued to open us up to dimensions of Irish life and that of the broader world otherwise too easily ignored. Heaney's 'Republic of Conscience', Longley's 'Ceasefire' and Mahon's 'A Disused Shed in County Wexford' stand out among their lyrical and other poetry as powerful social commentaries as well as fine poems. Women poets like Eavan Boland, Nuala Ní Dhómhnaill, Eiléan Ní Chuilleanáin and Medbh McGuckian provide penetrating insights into public and cultural life as well as writing marvellous poems. More conventionally, Irish literary critics of the calibre of Denis Donohue, Edna Longley and Declan Kiberd and a range of others have been engaged directly in Irish intellectual life.

The tasks of the Irish Intellectual are not sharply different from those in other similar countries. One might however criticise the limited role played by the university communities, especially the scientists, while recognising the expanded role of the artistic community.

One last note on the role of intellectual journals as distinct from professional or news journals. Ireland has never been rich in them and they have seldom lasted very long. Perhaps the potential readership is too small or those interested get what they want in other publications. However it would be unfair to overlook *The Bell* in its heyday in the forties and fifties and the people like Sean O'Faolain, Frank O'Connor, Peadar O'Donnell and others who founded and fostered it.

The Christian/Catholic Intellectual

It may have been Ronald Knox who said that the adjective can be the enemy of the noun. No doubt as indicated earlier many critics would regard the phrase 'Christian Intellectual' as oxymoronic. Even Christians and their sympathisers might wonder what Christian adds to intellectual at least in terms of the qualities required. The qualities or attributes already ascribed to the Intellectual, intellectual hospitality etc, are also proper to the Christian/Catholic species. So are many of the tasks to be undertaken in society. One might however point to resources available to the Christian and unlikely to be used by others, the resources of the biblical and later Christian traditions, in theology, liturgy, prayer and way of life. These may also underline attributes that are not so intimately associated with intellectuals in general and the public tasks they undertake.

Before examining these further attributes and engaging with some of the personalities it is necessary to consider the possible distinction between apologists and intellectuals. Apologists occur in many domains of human living outside the religious. Amid the present campaigns of nomination of candidates for the American presidential election apologists abound for all the remaining potential candidates. As their apologetic endeavours usually do not have much intellectual content and even where they have, given their uncritical or non-dialogical defence of their favoured candidate, they could not be regarded as the work of intellectuals. Yet some might. Defence of causes rather than personalities might more easily attract genuine intellectuals. Indeed it is difficult to see how they could engage long-term with their society without supporting the truth and justice of significant causes or movements. In this line Said, Arendt and many unnamed here became apologists for the historical truth about totalitarian, colonial, ethnic or economic oppression for example and the parallel contemporary cause of freedom.

Christian apologists as a class originated in the Christianity's second century in response to criticisms by Roman critics. While their work was intelligently and often quite fairly presented it would not be appropriate to describe it by what, as we saw, is really a modern term, intellectual. Given his intellectual capacity, his range of interests, his sheer erudition and the volume of his work, St Augustine must be included in any list of the world's great intellectuals, even modern style. But his work as a bishop inevitably had an apologetic flavour in its defence of Christianity. His famous *Confessions* would be read as an apology for his own life but the bulk of his writings were directed to the public square of his time in criticism of its short-comings and its need of the saving truth of the Christian faith. His legacy to later generations of Christians was by no means all positive but his genius and commitment to truth cannot be denied. The same might be said of Thomas Aquinas, although his temperament allowed for a a just integration of such different thinkers as Augustine and Aristotle, a more balanced address to the 'gentiles' and a critical integration of natural and revealed truth. His close contemporary Dante transposed this well of truth into the splendid poetry and prose which marked the imaginative high-point of Christian intellectual life.

However for our purposes and our times one point needs to be clarified. The Christian intellectual as distinct from the intellectual in the Church is engaged primarily in dialogue with the world about him. He is focused *ad extra*. This will have repercussions *ad intra*, within the Church but that is not his main concern as he seeks to use the intellectual resources of Christianity in dialogue with outsiders. In using these he will sometimes at least be acting defensively or in an apologetic way. So long however as he is faithful to the truth and fair to the outside partners he can be a true intellectual.

The thrust of his tradition emphasises qualities that may be ignored outside it. The first of these is humility. All great intellectuals are humble before the truth and behave with humility towards their critics and opponents but it is to be particularly expected of Christians. The arrogance of some Christian and other commentators of the 'left' or 'right' is bound to have a blinding effect on themselves in their pursuit of truth and make it impossible for others to enter into dialogue with them. Many Christian fundamentalists whatever their intelligence and pretensions to scholarship fall into this category. So do other fundamentalists, both religious and non-religious. It is very difficult for example for a believer to initiate any real dialogue with someone so arrogantly and often ignorantly dismissive of religious belief as atheistic biologist Richard Dawkins.

The Christian engagement with society should always be characterised by compassion. So should that of the Christian intellectual. He will use his intellectual gifts and Christian insights to analyse the lot of the marginalised or poor and its causes as a contribution to a more just and free society. This may appear to make him partisan but he will be seeking the underlying truth of the structures of society in order to promote its common good.

One last attribute ought to be required of the Christian intellectual that might be neglected by others. Aware of human limitations, enshrined in the theology of sin, the Christian recognises that no one person is absolutely right about everything in his own specialty, still less as that specialty impacts on a complex and ambiguous world. So he will be open to compromise or at least tolerance of difference while seeking personal reconciliation with opponents. Such personal reconciliation within society without surrendering commitment to the truth is essential to a peaceful and humane society. This for the Christian is the only limited realisation possible in history of the Reign of God which Jesus preached and inaugurated.

In early student days *The Intellectual Life* by French Dominican, A. D. Sertillange, was a significant read. The much later book, *The Christian Intellectual* by American Lutheran theologian and historian, Jaroslav Pelikan, was only the second study dealing directly with some of these issues which came my way. They have long been forgotten and, as far as I can tell, have had little enough influence on this essay or on my intellectual life generally.

John Henry Newman, in his lectures on *The Idea of a University*, his *Grammar of Assent* and his *Apologia pro Vita Sua* among other writings, offers classical exemplars of the work of the Christian intellectual to which one frequently returns. In a narrower more regularly apologetic sense *Mere Christianity* by C.S. Lewis has proved to be both a very intelligent introduction to and defence of Christian faith. However the outstanding Anglican intellectual of our times must surely be Archbishop Rowan Williams of Canterbury, despite his sometimes opaque style and occasional misjudgements as in his recent reference to the introduction of some elements of Sharia law into the British system. Not unlike the misjudgement of the highly intellectual Pope Benedict XVI in his reference to Islam and violence in his address to the University of Regensburg a couple of years back.

The term intellectual was always more at home in French culture and among French writers. Two of the outstanding Catholic intellectuals of the twentieth century were Gabriel Marcel and Jacques Maritain. Simone Weil may have been even more influential on Catholic thinking. She was never actually baptised but had become very deeply Catholic. A later but very significant figure was Michel de Certeau, although unlike his earlier Jesuit confrere, Teilhard de Chardin, he did exercise great influence outside Europe. All these differed greatly in their interests. Marcel's existential personalism helped develop Catholic dialogue with contemporary philosophical movements while deepening Catholic understanding of the human person and both the dignity and the fragility of its existence. Maritain's revival and renewal of the philosophical tradition of Aquinas introduced it to modern thinking about human rights, a more complete humanism and even philosophical thinking about the arts. Simone Weil was at once the most practical of philosophers, working in factories and espousing certain Marxist views and the most metaphysical. Her direct public engagement as a thinker and worker is likely to be an inspiration to fresh generations of Catholic thinkers.

Maritain worked mainly in the United States and developed his thinking on one of the major concerns for Christians in that nation, the separation of Church and State. The distinction between state and society which he emphasised restricted the state's capacity to control citizen's lives and opened the way for his analysis and promotion of human rights, among them the right to religious freedom. This was a key breakthrough for Catholic thinkers at Vatican II. However the main architect of the Council's Declaration on Religious Liberty was American Jesuit, John Courtney Murray, who had been banned from publishing on this issue by the then Holy Office, (now the Congregation for the Defence of the Faith). Murray was undoubtedly one of the great Catholic intellectuals of his day. In a quite different domain Dorothy Day's writings and engagement with the poor, while not of the same intellectual depth as that of Simone Weil, gave a power and direction to Catholic social thinking and action which anticipated the work of the Latin American liberation theologians in the later 1960s. Subsequently, Gustav Gutierrez, Jon Sobrino and others offered a new basis for intellectual investigation of the faith in society with their insistence on prior engagement with the poor. The priority of praxis and the option for the poor has had enormous influence on all Christian action and reflection from feminism to black theology, from South Africa to South America to Asia.

Before the Catholic liberationists, Protestant theologians like Reinhold Niebuhr had, out of his experience as pastor in Detroit during the depression, made serious intellectual and practical contributions to social theology. His brother Richard and others were also engaged in this project of what Reinhold called Christian Realism in politics. A quite different line was later pursued by theologians such as John Yoder (Mennonite) and Stanley Hauerwas (Methodist) whose social emphasis concentrated on peace as the way to justice. In this they opposed the Niebuhrs' line but were in agreement with Catholic thinkers and activists such as Dorothy Day and the Berrigan brothers.

Beyond politics American theologians such as Paul Tillich and Jesuit critic, William F. Lynch entered into serious engagement with culture and the arts. Indeed Richard Niebuhr's work, *Christ and Culture* remains something of a classic in this area. Daniel Berrigan is a poet as well as a peace activist and his poetry had the kind of intellectual impact on society good poets always have. Thomas Merton belonged to this family of thinkers and writers also.

Fine novelists such as Flannery O'Connor and Walker Percy, while not propagandists, let their Catholic background have its own impact, as have later novelists like Mary Gordon. This extended discussion of American thinkers and writers seemed justified in the light of that country's vibrant intellectual life in recent decades and my own exposure to it. Yet there is much that must be passed over in the American Churches and still more in the intellectual life of Churches around the world, including Ireland. However it would be unfair to pass over the contribution of literary critic, Peter Connelly of Maynooth, who made a critical contribution to the debate on book censorship and suffered in consequence. Other Irish people who showed intellectual courage in face of authority will emerge in the following sections.

THE INTELLECTUAL IN THE CHURCH

In the previous section the focus as announced was on dialogue between the Catholic-Christian intellectual and the wider society. In this section the emphasis will be on the role of the intellectual in relation to the Church(es). The distinction is not always valid as the example of John Courtney Murray would have illustrated. And it applies more obviously to the Roman Catholic Church with its closely structured unity than to many other more loosely organised churches. However it is a helpful distinction in many ways and prompts some consideration of further attributes befitting to the intellectual with this primary vocation. Of course all the attributes and qualities of the true intellectual already discussed are still required in this instance. And the additional ones listed here apply in their own way to all intellectuals.

The first of these attributes is courage. All intellectuals have need of it from time to time. In the Church and particularly in the Roman Catholic Church with its strong tradition of authoritative teaching and of teaching authority it is particularly necessary. It should however be a thoughtful courage arising out of personal conviction and awareness of ecclesial or social need. Thoughtfulness in this sense is never calculating self-service and the audacity to speak the truth should not be tainted by arrogance. Speaking the truth in love is more than a Christian or Church requirement but it is certainly that. To conscience first and then to the Church, as the Newman phrase has it. Indeed the courage to speak is demanded by fidelity to the Church itself in such circumstances. Courage and fidelity are true marks of the intellectual's activity in the Church. They do not guarantee the truth of that speaking or its reception if true. The negative reaction of Church authorities or other Church members to the faith-filled and courageous intellectual contributions of theologians and others within the Church should be accepted, even when not offered, in a spirit of dialogue. Retiring into the role of victim is no more acceptable within the Church than the adopting of the role of victimiser. In the light of the Cross, the Christian, intellectual or no, should recognise that such roles are no longer appropriate. That does not mean that either role has simply ceased to exist within the Church.

In the theological and pastoral developments finally adopted at Vatican II, the critical role of Church intellectuals, mainly theologians, was properly recognised, although many of them had been censured in the decades preceding the Council. Rahner and Congar, Courtney Murray and Chenu had all experienced the journey from suspect outsider to approved insider as the Council Fathers worked through the Council agenda. Of course the Council was still only a stage in the historic journey of the Church as a pilgrim people. There were further distances to travel and need of the insights of other theologians and intellectuals in that continuing journey. Some of these have also suffered for their courageous search for the fuller truth. Edward Schillebeeckx, Hans Kung, Charles Curran and a range of liberation and other theologians have had to endure disapproval by Church authorities without wavering in their fidelity to truth or Church. It will ever be so as both authorities and intellectuals struggle honestly both to protect, develop and promote Christ's Gospel truth.

In Ireland the difficulties have been less apparent but then so have the developments. However, theological and scriptural scholar-intellectuals like Gabriel Daly, Seán Freyne, James Mackey, Terence McCaughey, Dermot Lane, Vincent MacNamara, Donal Dorr, Denis Carroll, Seán Fagan, Patrick Hannon, Linda Hogan, Geza Theissen and many others have contributed enormously to the thinking and knowledge of the Irish Church despite the occasional negative reactions. In other disciplines and intellectual spheres the work of Brendan Devlin, Margaret MacCurtain, Patrick Masterson, Mark Patrick Hederman, Michael Paul Gallagher, John O'Donohue, John Moriarty and Peter Connolly have left their intellectual mark on Church and society. The intellectual life of the Irish Church, if often lacking in drama, has not lacked for substance.

THE PROMISE OF DAVID THORNLEY

My association with David Thornley began shortly after I started to teach at Maynooth in 1960. In the mid-fifties I had been a member of a socially and politically concerned group of young intellectuals and others called Tuairim. On my return to Ireland after I had finished my further studies,

I reconnected with the group. David was a prominent member, if not already its chairman. We quickly became friends.

In the following years I became involved with a society for Catholic students in TCD known as the Laurentian Society. With many concerns in common our friendship developed. At one stage he lectured on politics in Maynooth, ironically as substitute for the very conservative Jeremiah Newman who had become president. Unfortunately I was away on sabbatical leave when he died and so missed his funeral. For that and other reasons I am delighted to have this opportunity to pay tribute to him.

In intellectual, academic, media and political terms David Thornley died far too young. However his many achievements in so many areas indicated what in later and more mature years he might have accomplished. In the context of this essay on the role of the self-consciously and socially engaged Christian and Catholic intellectual, his gifts and ambitions might be best handled as promise of what is still possible and necessary in Irish life. He lived in what is now considered a narrow and conservative cultural, political and religious ethos. His commitments and activities were directed to breaking out of that. However, whether he was lecturing in Trinity College (or for a short time in Maynooth), presenting television debates, speaking in the Dáil or singing in the Westland Row Church choir, David kept very different strands of Irish life, including the Catholic strand, in communication. The critics of the 'narrow' ethos of that time are often blind to the narrowness of the dominant ethos of today where religious, and particularly Catholic, concerns and resources are unheard or unread in public debate. The promise of more fruitful communication and dialogue which David Thornley among others embodied for a short time could and should be revived for the health of the nation as well as of the Church.

Enda McDonagh was Professor of Moral Theology in the University of Maynooth from 1958 to 1995 where he still lives as Professor Emeritus. He is a priest of the Archdiocese of Tuam and was ordained in Maynooth in 1955. He has a doctorate in Divinity and a doctorate in Canon Law. In the early 1960s, he founded the InterChurch Association of Moral Theology and in 2007 he was appointed Ecumenical Canon of St. Patrick's Cathedral, Dublin. He has published twenty-three books in theology and related subjects and contributed to many more.

9

'HE BOXED LIGHTLY IN THE INTERVIEWS BUT INTENDED

TO LAND A PUNCH': DAVID THORNLEY AT RTÉ, 1966–69

MUIRIS MAC CONGHAIL

It was Gunnar Rugheimer, the second controller of programmes at RTÉ television (1963–66), who spotted David Thornley's potential as a television broadcaster after seeing David on an edition of *The Professors* in early 1966. *The Professors* was a television programme put into the schedules to trawl the common rooms of the universities in the hope of identifying new broadcasting talents and to open up academics to the idea of television and to share their wares, so to speak, with the Irish viewer.

In the early summer of 1966, Rugheimer had put together his draft schedule for the coming autumn and I was assigned to originate and produce a weekly television programme on Irish politics. The programme was to centre on events within Dáil Éireann and on the activities of the major political parties. As most viewers had never been in the Dáil, one of the programme's roles was to introduce the people to the procedures and proceedings of both houses of the Oireachtas. Indeed, another of the programme's roles was to introduce the viewers to their elected representatives and for that purpose to invite various deputies to participate in the programme. With the exception of President John F. Kennedy's address to both houses of the Oireachtas in the early 1960s, microphone and camera entry into our parliament was not allowed, or even foreseen, then as a possibility, and was to be opposed by members of the Oireachtas for many years. Indeed, the very idea of politicians appearing in debate with each other was not, up to 1966, to be countenanced on the national airwaves. The history and practice of the older Radio Éireann, having been a section of a government department, imported itself into the practices of the new television service, even though RTÉ was established as an independent statutory authority.

In that summer of 1966, I was instructed by Rugheimer to enter into negotiations with David Thornley – which I did when I opened up the idea of his presenting a programme to be named *Division*, a parliamentary term which I had chosen as the programme title, with the division bells as the opening-title sound. My colleagues talked me out of the bells.

We met at lunch in the then Russell Hotel at the corner of Stephen's Green and Harcourt Street. I remember well that sitting in the same restaurant were Charles Haughey, Patrick Hillery and Brian Lenihan, each a minister in the Lemass government. On inquiry, the waiter told me that the trio dined regularly there. Haughey and Hillery nodded towards David.

I told David about the project, and he was interested in it until the subject turned to his proposed involvement. It was one thing, he said, to turn up on *The Professors* and wing it with good talk but another thing altogether to make himself available to the planning and programme transmissions involved. He questioned me closely about the nature of the work and the time involved. He made it clear that, if there was a question of any conflict between his teaching, his students, his membership of the Westland Row Church choir, his interest in the Feis Ceoil, his boxing and his other commitments, including Tuairim, and what I was proposing, he could not join with me in *Division*. David made it clear that, in his view, the kind of work involved in *Division* would be tantamount to a second full-time job, and he was doubtful if the Trinity College authorities would, or could, allow for such an undertaking.

I tried desperately to paint another, less demanding, role for him, even though I knew that what he had said was accurate and realistic. We looked over at the political trio, and each of us may have thought of what life on television would be like with them. I played down the demands of the job; in fact, I most certainly understated the demands on my way through the latter part of our conversation. David was very anxious and concerned that if the job were to be done, then it was best that it should be done well. He told me of his plans to write seriously of politics and political culture and that the ephemeral nature of television would be a distraction to him in his work. I urged him to think of the possibilities involved in getting to a wider audience in his teaching and laboured that point: 'break out of Trinity and into Ireland'.

I may even have referred to the Thomas Davis lecture series on radio, to which David had contributed a lecture on P. H. Pearse. I suggested to him that *Division* was more likely to achieve the aims once set for the Davis series, if only by dint of its access to a far larger audience. In short, I was trying to work on his ego, while the young Fellow of Trinity College concentrated on the substantive issues.

We walked across Stephen's Green, still talking about the project, and agreed to meet sometime later in the summer – when he and I would both be in Clifden – to confirm or reject the plan. I cannot ever remember talking about money, or David asking about it. Shortly after the lunch in the Russell, I got a note from the contracts officer in RTÉ, Gerry McLaughlin, pointing out that the lunch was too expensive for someone of my rank. I think it cost some £16 with wine.

David gave me his essay 'Irish Identity', published in the Dominican journal *Doctrine and Life* (Vol. 16, No. 4, April 1966), and wrote a humorous inscription on it for me 'with the compliments of the Archbishop of Dublin'. David was both a believer and intellectually committed to a robust examination of Roman Catholicism in Ireland. He saw a model in Hans Küng and his writing in the *Council and Reunion*: 'faith in the Church to faith in a machine; in a word, when letter replaces spirit'. David wrote: 'Irish Catholicism, lay and clerical, has no mandate from God and no guarantee from the inevitability of history or sociology which would allow it to opt out of soul-searching, which is the unique task of the universal Church in the second half of the twentieth century.'

David and I met briefly in Clifden and he told me that we should meet again in September and that he had lots of ideas about the programme. Without committing himself absolutely, that was enough to go on. The autumn schedule was fast approaching and here I was without a principal presenter for *Division*. At our Russell Hotel meeting, David had inquired about books on television and about television presentation and interview techniques. I had told David that there was precious little in the way of worthwhile material but that I would try to find something. I gave David several titles out of the BBC lunchtime lecture series published in 1962 and 1963. These for the most part dealt with BBC editorial policy, including one by Donald Edwards on BBC news and current affairs.

When next we met at RTÉ, David had with him a copy of the Broadcasting Authority Act, 1960. He had been up and down through the Act, and his copy was annotated with pencil: at that stage, and for as long as I worked with him, David used a fine leaded propelling pencil and a rubber. His concern, and our conversation, centred on Section 18 (1) of the Act:

> It shall be the duty of the Authority to secure that, when it broadcasts any information, news or feature which relates to matters of public controversy or is the subject of current public debate, the information, news or feature is presented objectively and impartially and without any expression of the Authority's own views.

David said: 'So, the Authority has no views . . . Does that mean that we, you and I, have no views either?'

David was concerned that any role which he might have would in his terms be that 'of a eunuch in a political harem'. He wondered whether in those circumstances just being a television presenter, with all of the time demands involved, could justify his having to reduce or abandon part of his teaching and his student contact, particularly in his '1913 and working-class movements' seminars at Trinity College.

Towards the end of the first year of *Division*, David was invited to write an essay for a special edition of *Administration* (Vol 15, No.3), devoted to RTÉ. In that 1967 article, David had by then worked out part of the answer to the question posed by Section 18 (1) of the Broadcasting Act referred to above. It is a very considered response and worth reciting here:

> Of course the performers on the programme are themselves positive contributors to balance or imbalance. They face one of the problems of all journalists – the responsibility of deciding whether or not to exercise an editorial function – but in especially difficult monopoly circumstances. [There was then no other broadcaster in the state.] The most obvious instance is where the chairman of a debate signifies, directly or by innuendo, his agreement with one of the participants. Is this legitimate? But a more pressing temptation is where a theme is not being brought out in a discussion because one of the protagonists is falling down on his job. Has the chairman the right to raise the issue, even if by doing so he helps one party and hurts another?
>
> If the chairman is responsible and does not show a consistent bias over a period, the answer is surely yes. The fundamental role which governs this issue, and indeed many more in political broadcasting, is that the politician does not have the right of intellectual privacy. He practises a public art which involves the obligation to communicate to the electorate; if he is permitted to evade that obligation by his antagonists, a monopoly-mass communication medium can scarcely shrug its shoulders and become a consenting party to the evasion.

The expression of this fundamental principle, with the 'consenting party' bit at the end, is so finely and explicitly stated that I am still moved by its challenge to broadcasting, and even more so in the fabric of today's tawdry broadcasting. I have used David's essay in the core of my teaching at the Dublin Institute of Technology because its application is to be applied not only to broadcast journalism but to all forms of journalism, in print and electronically. The mellifluous and magisterial composition of 'the Thornley principle' reminds me of the writings of Sir Hugh Greene (*The Third Floor Front: A View of Broadcasting in the Sixties*, 1969), late director general of the BBC, who after all had spent all of his life in broadcasting. What David had achieved here after such a short spell with RTÉ was a mature dialectical analysis of the problem and, having identified the problem, a resolution. I wish that I had written it.

But of course the principles as then enunciated were to be the guiding radar on which all interviews were to be mapped, not only by David but also by other broadcasters on *Division* and subsequently on *7-Days*. David was to set the tone and form in political broadcasting on RTÉ in that period.

I knew that David was rather taken by the reputation of Robin Day (or certainly by his bow tie), then the principal presenter of the BBC *Panorama* programme. I found Day pompous and full of himself. I was rather glad to be able to tell David that an editor of *Panorama*, Frank Smith, who had trained with me in the BBC, told me that Day believed that the only important thing in a *Panorama* interview was his (Day's) questions! David laughed, and we both agreed that the reaction to what was being said in the course of an interview had to be heard and that subsequent planned tactical questions must flow from what was said, or more often not said.

David's preparation for interviews was a robust and detailed examination of the words of the person to be questioned: this was done on cards, in pencil, with every move plotted on paper. Then came a session with me, in which David would wind himself up, or I would wind him up, and we would rehearse both his questions and the likely answers, and build on that process to a conclusion. David was very nervous about broadcasting, no matter how much he may have become accustomed to it. He boxed lightly in the interviews but intended to land a punch. His anxiety would be even greater when he questioned somebody that he liked. I remember a interview by David during the Wicklow by-election of 1968 with Brendan Corish, leader of the Labour Party, on the matter of Labour's then stance against coalition with Fine Gael. Was Labour afraid to go into government? When Corish (prepared by Brendan Halligan) suggested that Labour would get there by itself, Thornley recited the facts of Irish electoral possibilities. Corish weaved and ducked his way but was up against a stone wall. Corish asked after the interview 'What kind of fellows are you, giving me such a hard time?' to which David said: 'It was my producer [me] who made me do it.'

I still have David Thornley's essay on the 'Development of the Irish Labour Movement', published in 1964 in *Christus Rex: Journal of Sociology* (Vol. XVIII, No. 1), in which David had marked up again the points from his own writing to be used as a background to the interview. In that by-election in Wicklow, Labour voters, contrary to advice from the Labour Party, gave their second-preference votes to Fine Gael, thus giving Fine Gael the seat and defeating Fianna Fáil, the government party. David wrote in the course of that *Christus Rex* essay, originally written as a lecture to Tuairim in 1963: 'The [Labour] party has left few traces upon Irish social or industrial legislation; it has maintained a depressingly small representation in the Dáil. Unique among European States, Ireland has conducted her politics for the last forty years almost without controversy over those issues of social and economic policy which are the theme of politics elsewhere.'

By the autumn of 1967, *Division* had been joined with *7-Days* in a twice-weekly current-affairs programme, *7-Days*, and the demands on David's time for broadcasting had increased enormously. I had become editor of the new *7-Days* programme. I relied on David not only for his contribution to the increased output but also for his advice: we had become close friends. I had learnt so much from him, in particular on how to present editorial summaries of programmes – what we proposed for the editorial systems then in operation at RTÉ. David also helped me to write defences of programmes broadcast; this was necessary both within RTÉ structures and indeed without. RTÉ was a windy editorial place, with labyrinthine structures and double-edged axes everywhere.

In his *Administration* article, David wrote: 'How does political television affect the practising politician? How can it be impartial, informative and also entertaining? Perhaps the most fundamental difficulty – which a television station faces in attempting to meet these obligations – is that there is an essential contradiction between the nature of party politics and the role of a communication medium, especially in a monopolistic situation. Politics is a game in which only one contender can win at any particular time. The politician therefore logically views the communication medium as the cockpit of contention; he is consequently only totally satisfied with it when he is able to use it to gain advantage over his adversaries. A "good" station is a subservient one; a "good" programme is one from which he emerges victorious. This is not depraved, but wholly natural; it has some unfortunate consequences.'

Some of the unfortunate consequences were that Fianna Fáil, the government party, led by Seán Lemass, had not expected that RTÉ television would mount programming that would question government policy. Being so long in office, the members of government had become unaccustomed to close questioning either in parliament or in the press and had in fact become used to the idea of the national broadcaster being available for use by government in the dissemination of government policies without comment.

In the autumn of 1966, when *Division* was started, the National Farmers Association mounted a major public campaign as a result of differences between themselves and the Minister for Agriculture, Charles Haughey. Haughey had agreed to appear on *Division* with the NFA leader, Rickard Deasy, and then Haughey withdrew his consent; the programme went ahead without him, leading to controversy and the withdrawal by Fianna Fáil from any future edition of the programme. Mr Haughey and I had a bitter exchange on the telephone. The withdrawal by Haughey and the 'blacking' of *Division* by Fianna Fáil was not resolved until the election of Jack Lynch as leader of Fianna Fáil and Taoiseach in November 1966. Jack Lynch agreed to appear on *Division* and to be interviewed by David Thornley; this was the first major interview given by the newly elected Taoiseach. The 'Haughey difficulty' was resolved in another way. After an edition of *The Politicians*, a monthly televised political debate on which Charles Haughey appeared on behalf of Fianna Fáil as the new minister for finance, Haughey invited both David Thornley and me to a late supper in a Dublin restaurant. Haughey was accompanied by two Fianna Fáil deputies, Flor Crowley and Lorcan Allen. Haughey gave David and me a hard time. We defended ourselves with some vigour over the NFA programme and our decision to proceed without him. Haughey said we were insulting to him and in defiance of him, and who the hell were we to appoint ourselves to such a position of power without responsibility. I have to say that Haughey was quite taken by David Thornley and his manner of argument. I could hardly say that Haughey was flattered by Thornley's company but he certainly enjoyed the robust nature of our conversation and when the time came to leave, Haughey invited both David and me to join him at his house. Haughey offered us a lift in his state car but we decided against the lift and told him that we would drive. David drove a yellow Sunbeam sports coupé and we decided to leave the car at Trinity College and take a taxi. On arrival at Charles Haughey's then house at Grangemore, Raheny, the whole house was alight, the hall door was open, and as we arrived at the doorstep, we could hear Charles Haughey calling us into the house and down the stairs to a basement. There we discovered Mr Haughey sitting in a wine cellar, in which he was delighted to show us his wine stock. He selected some wine and upstairs we went to a drawing room, where we sat and talked. Haughey spoke at great length about a range of subjects. He enquired of me about my father and his painting and spoke at great length to David about history. Haughey was in command of each of the topics which he raised and I was impressed by the evidence of his reading. Then he reached over to a bookcase, from which he took down David's book on Isaac Butt, and he asked David to sign it. Haughey spoke at great length about Butt and listened very carefully to what David had to say. 'Of course both of you had been professors in the same university,' said Haughey to David. It was a relaxed 'papal audience' in which Haughey performed as a tolerant and genial host, and most courteously. It was as if the previous conversation in the restaurant had not taken place. It was only when David spoke about the great failures which he saw in de Valera that the hooded eyelids of Haughey became apparent. The audience was at an end but for one thing: Haughey gave each of us a bottle of wine, which he had brought up from the cellar when we had first arrived. 'There is only one thing wrong with that wine,' said Haughey. 'What's that?' said we two. 'The name on the bottle,' said our host. On examining the bottles, we noticed that both bottles were vintage Lynch-Bages. I don't know how long our wine survived . . .

This is certainly the best view I ever had of Charles Haughey, and that before the arms trial and his descent into tyranny and decline.

The aftermath of the election of Jack Lynch as leader of Fianna Fáil in November 1966 continued to create difficulties for broadcasting, particularly in *7-Days* – so much so that both George Colley and Charles Haughey measured RTÉ output in the matter of their own appearances. In the first Fianna Fáil ard-fheis following Lynch's election, both Haughey and Colley and their supporters complained about the coverage of their speeches. Kevin McCourt, then director general of RTÉ, discussed the matter with me and said: 'Well, it seems that not only must we keep a balance between the parties but in the case of Fianna Fáil a balance between the members of that same party.'

At Christmas 1967, a report from an all-party committee chaired by George Colley, TD, was released with an embargo for Saturday 23 December 1967. This was Christmas Eve for all intents and purposes, and the embargo was meant to – and did – exclude the last Friday edition of *7-Days* before Christmas: there would not be another edition until the new year. Nor would there be any serious newspaper coverage of the report until the new year. The Colley committee essentially proposed that the then (and now) electoral system be changed from proportional representation in multi-seat constituencies to a straight vote in single-seat constituencies. This had been signalled by Kevin Boland, the minister for local government, at a Fianna Fáil ard-fheis in the previous autumn, and Fianna Fáil had been arguing for change. Indeed, the leader of the Opposition, Liam Cosgrave, had leanings towards a version of that system also.

I decided that, without breaking the embargo, it would be possible to address the issue of abandoning PR: Fianna Fáil under de Valera had tried this once before, in 1959, when on one and the same day de Valera had stood for president and the Fianna Fáil government had initiated a constitutional referendum on the electoral system. Dev won, and the referendum was defeated.

We decided that an analysis could be done as to what might happen in a general election were a single-member constituency with a straight (non-PR) vote to be introduced. Professor Basil Chubb and David Thornley, with Ted Nealon of *7-Days* and using figures supplied by the political-science department of Trinity, prepared a report for the programme. Chubb could not be present on the programme night and so David Thornley and Ted Nealon presented the report in the form of a lecture, with graphic slides. The results of this research and presentation suggested a Fianna Fáil landslide: Fianna Fáil 93, Fine Gael 44, Labour 8 and others 9. One of the interesting features of the proposed new system would be that, with only 40 percent of the votes, Fianna Fáil would win 65 percent of the seats.

All hell broke loose after the programme, and for those viewers who had not seen the programme Basil Chubb and David Thornley wrote an article for the *Irish Times* based on the programme's figures.

RTÉ was very nervous about the programme in advance, and David and I had to discuss the script in detail with J. A. Irvine, then head of administration in RTÉ, who asked to read both the Colley Report and our script. I had to argue the issue as to whether we were breaking the embargo, and David and I had to deal with the programme's projections.

Irvine was a fair-minded man but he knew there would be trouble in store and said as much, wondering all the time about Fianna Fáil's wisdom in trying to push the change in the electoral system again, and so soon after their last attempt. David took Irvine through the figures twice before we left the meeting. We were both exhausted.

In February 1968, the labyrinth of editorial controls was to change in RTÉ, with the transfer of *7-Days* from the Programme Division, on the decision of the director general, Kevin McCourt, to the direct control of the head of news. The change in editorial control was the direct result of pressure from Fianna Fáil and their close and powerful supporters, who were well placed after long years of political patronage. The change brought about considerable industrial unrest, and RTÉ was seized with confusion. Kevin McCourt rang me and asked if David Thornley and I would meet with him privately and confidentially to discuss a number of matters and to see if some resolution could be brought about.

We met privately in the Shelbourne Hotel; as it happens, in the 'Constitution Room'. As it transpired, McCourt had given notice to the RTÉ Authority and was due to retire in April 1968. McCourt wanted to know if his earlier departure would bring some factor into play and resolve the industrial-relations issue under a new director general. McCourt had made it plain to both David and me that the chairman of the Authority, Todd Andrews, had developed strong editorial views in the matter of news and current affairs, and that this was making life difficult for everybody.

David and I went over the recent programming, including the PR programme, and McCourt listened to David with great interest. I am only sorry that David had not met with McCourt before. In my mind, I could even dream of David becoming director general, but I knew that would have to wait . . . Our advice was that McCourt should go, and quickly, so that a new director general could come into place. Our advice, which we had formed in advance of our meeting, was that were McCourt to remain, RTÉ might fall asunder in a sort of civil war fuelled by ideology, ambition and personal dislike. Goaded by a frenzy which had occupied the place, the government might then assume the editorial direction of the national broadcaster – something for which, inevitably, it had prepared itself. It was a very dangerous situation.

In October 1968, David Thornley was to chair the debate on the PR referendum between Jack Lynch, Liam Cosgrave and Brendan Corish. It was the first time that the three leaders of the political parties had ever appeared together in debate on RTÉ television; the debate was transmitted simultaneously on RTÉ radio.

David was to leave RTÉ in the spring of 1969 as we moved towards a general election, in which he became a Labour deputy for Dublin North-West. He had won the highest number of votes ever achieved in a general election by a Labour candidate in the greater Dublin area, according to Ted Nealon.

Early in January 1973, in the run-up to the general election of that year, David called in to see me in the GPO, where I was now working in radio. RTÉ had been through a devastating period, with the removal of the RTÉ Authority in November 1972 by Gerry Collins, TD, then minister for posts and telegraphs. Collins was, I am sure, delighted finally to deal the body blow to RTÉ – a blow from which RTÉ has never, and can never, recover. (The British government under Tony Blair dealt a similar blow to the BBC with the Hutton Report of January 2004.) News and current affairs are no longer the essential items to be protected in public-service broadcasting, and therefore editorial independence is no longer the backbone of public-service broadcasting.

David had come to discuss with me what might be done to overcome the damage done to RTÉ. He left a short draft memo of some four typed pages with me; the memo was dated 29 January 1973 and initialled 'DT'. The memo opened thus:

> Most previous attempts to secure independence of broadcasting have concentrated upon legislative control of the medium. This I believe to be impossible for two reasons.
>
> (a) The conflict between politicians and broadcasting is in-built in the nature of the medium. Continental experience has proved this. No government, whether socialist or otherwise, will voluntarily abdicate control of the communications media if is possible to exercise it; and
>
> (b) There is no Act of the legislature which it would be impossible to circumvent given sufficient ingenuity.
>
> The memorandum of the television producers at the time of the suspension of the RTÉ Authority falls upon both of the above grounds. Dáil experience in relation to the Offences Against the State (Amendment) Bill, 1972, supports this.

All my experience in television and its politics, and all I have read about broadcasting practice in other countries, convinces me that the only guarantee of independent television rests on the experience of the editorial staff involved.

David Thornley's draft memo then went on to suggest that a two-channel arrangement for television (one social and one commercial) be established. The social channel was to be financed completely by the licence fee, with no advertising, and the commercial channel was to be financed by advertising, and in that regard to allow the newspapers to 'buy into' broadcasting. Thornley saw that if the newspapers were allowed into broadcasting, this 'would allay their fears about their deposition from primacy in the medium of communication'. Furthermore, that legislative controls and press councils, which contained an in-built censorship factor, would be restrained by that combination of social and commercial channels.

In one of his last essays, possibly the last, before he left broadcasting, David wrote of de Valera in *History of the 20th Century: Empire into Commonwealth* (No. 46, London, 1969): 'and so, ultimately, the career of this remarkable man was already, by 1939, marked with a quality of failure which it never lost'. David inscribed on the cover: 'My last descriptive piece? With affectionate memories going back to the Russell in 1966.'

David's contribution to public-service broadcasting, his care for and thoughtfulness about it, brings me to lament its present condition.

Droichead Adhmaid, 28 Iúil MMVIII

Muiris Mac Conghail was originally a schoolmaster and holds a degree in Celtic Studies. He joined RTÉ in 1964 and trained with the BBC. He was a producer of Division, *a weekly televison programme on RTÉ, 1966–1967, where David Thornley started regular television broadcasting. Subsequently he was appointed editor of a twice weekly current affairs programme,* 7-Days *on which David Thornley worked with Mac Conghail from 1967–1969 when David was elected to Dáil Éireann as a Labour Party deputy in June 1969. In 1971 Mac Conghail became Head of Features and Current affairs in RTÉ radio. He was spokesman for the Labour and Fine Gael government formed in March 1973. In 1975 he rejoined RTÉ where he became Controller of Programmes, television, 1977–1980 and 1983–1986. He taught in the School of Media, Dublin Institute of Technology, from 1993 to 2004.*

10

THE KENNEDY REPORT

DR MARY HENRY

In the middle of the nineteenth century, legislation was brought in by the Westminster Parliament to cover the treatment of children neglected by their parents or guardians, abandoned, or involved in crime. Institutions to house these children were established throughout England, Wales, Scotland and Ireland. These were the industrial schools and reformatories.

The Irish Roman Catholic Members of Parliament insisted that the institutions established in Ireland were set up on a denominational basis and that those for Roman Catholic children were run by Roman Catholic religious orders. The industrial schools and reformatories were supported by state funds but there was no accountability in Ireland for the spending of the money allocated, which was on a per capita basis. Discipline in the schools was harsh, children were segregated by sex, families were split up, and little education was offered. Neither was there much training or preparation of the children for the outside world, although they had to leave the schools when they were sixteen and fend for themselves.

The children worked very hard in some schools, in laundries and on the institutions' farms, to help support the community. They had little contact with the outside world. Over the years, children who had been involved in crime were put in the same institutions as those who had poor school-attendance records or had been abandoned or neglected; as a result, there were no proper rehabilitation efforts.

Progress was made in updating the running of the schools by means of legislation. These laws were not extended to Ireland. When the new Irish Free State was established, nothing changed in these institutions

126

except that the small number of Protestant ones were put into the hands of voluntary committees. There were few or no inspections, no accountability for state funds, and little interest in the institutions from either subsequent governments or the general population. Subsequent disclosures by many of the children in recent years reveals that, if anything, the treatment of the children got worse over the years.

In the 1960s, a small group of courageous and fair-minded citizens objected about the widespread use of corporal punishment in schools in general in Ireland, and in these segregated institutions in particular. Senator Owen Sheehy Skeffington was one of the most outspoken of these citizens, and David Thornley identified with the views of this group, as did Dr Noël Browne and others. Martin Reynolds, an architect with the Board of Works, made an inspection of St Conleth's Reformatory in Daingean, one of the most notorious of the reformatories, and was so appalled by the conditions there that he campaigned to have it closed.

There began to be some public disquiet on this issue, and in 1968 an eleven-member committee was set up by then Minister of Education Donogh O'Malley to inspect industrial schools. The committee was chaired by District Justice Eileen Kennedy. It has been suggested to me by Bruce Arnold, who wrote an article in the *Irish Independent* on the issue, that the setting up of the committee was a direct response to the adverse comments made in a report on the schools in the early 1960s by the OECD following an inspection undertaken as part of the check on educational credentials of countries which were seeking entry to the EEC.

There were many shortcomings in the composition of the Kennedy Committee. It was weighted heavily in favour of those who ran the schools and the government departments which oversaw them. Some considered that the Kennedy Report concealed the true situation in the schools. The report recommended broadly that the whole child-care system should be geared to preventing family breakdown and that the admission of a child into residential care should be considered only as a last resort. The institutional system then in place should be abolished, it was proposed. Children from one family should be kept together; others were to be housed in group homes. These group homes were to contain children of both sexes and diverse ages. Special schools, with trained staff, should replace the reformatories. Staff in all institutions should be trained in child care, and suitable buildings should be used. Education of each child to his or her highest potential was essential, and after-care should be available. (It was recognised in the report that after-care in the schools was practically non-existent.) The administration of child care should be transferred from the Department of Justice to the Department of Heath. All laws relating to child care should be updated and incorporated into a composite Children Act. The age of criminal responsibility should be raised to twelve years. Payment should be made to the institutions in the form of a yearly capital grant, and an independent advisory body with statutory powers should be established to ensure that high standards were 'attained and maintained'. It was also recommended that research into child care in Ireland be carried out.

The committee also recommended the immediate closure of St Conleth's Reformatory and the remand home Marlborough House in Glasnevin, where very young children were kept. Marlborough House had no educational facilities, and the building itself had been condemned as unfit for human habitation years before. The house was described as 'completely unsuitable, with deplorable conditions' and the institution as 'purely custodial'.

Although in the report it was frequently noted that the members of religious orders who ran the institutions, with no special training, were not doing a good job, the report did not recommend that these should be replaced with trained laypersons. It became clear in later years, when the full exposure of the treatment of children in these institutions was made public, in the interim reports of the Commission to Inquire into Child Abuse, that this was a mistake.

As I have written, there were those who thought that the investigation would not have taken place were it not for the damning OECD report on the institutions. Certainly, the results of the educational tests undertaken by children in the schools at the request of the committee were appalling when compared with those of children in general at the time. Educational backwardness was rampant. Applying standard IQ tests then in use showed that 51.5 percent of the children in the institutions were assessed as being of average or above-average intelligence, compared to 85 percent of the population at large.

There is a minority report from the representative from the Department of Justice on the subject of St Patrick's Institution (which was, and is, part of the Mountjoy Prison complex). This was, he wrote, a place of detention for young offenders, many of whom had multiple previous convictions, and some of whom had committed very grave offences. He admitted that the institution had its shortcomings but said that the fact must be faced 'that there are inherent limitations to what can be done in any institution where the average period of stay is no more than four months, where a substantial proportion of the inmates are educationally backward, and where a significant proportion are of below-average intelligence'. This looks remarkably like blaming the inmates for their own situation.

To this day, some of the recommendations of the Kennedy Report have not been acted upon. For example, the age of criminal responsibility was not increased from seven to twelve years, as recommended, but only to ten years, despite the fact that the equivalent in all other European countries was much higher. The recommended Children Act took thirty years to come before the Oireachtas, in the form of the Children Act, 2000.

After the initial debate on the Kennedy Report in the Dáil, the interest of most politicians in this issue appears to have waned. David Thornley was one of the exceptions. There were few votes on the issue of industrial schools, but on 25 March 1971 he asked the then Minister for Education, Pádraig Faulkner, when the recommendations of the Kennedy Report on industrial schools would be implemented. The minister's reply was as follows:

> As part of the consideration which is being given to the report, it was necessary to call for the views of interested bodies on the recommendations contained therein. Most of these views have been received and are being examined. It is hoped that all the views will be received shortly and that the examination of them will be completed without any undue delay. In the meantime, action is being taken to implement many of the recommendations in the report.
>
> (i) The Remand Home and Place of Detention at Marlborough House, Glasnevin, is being replaced by a new Training School at Finglas under the control of the De La Salle Order. This school, which will be open next September, will serve as a short-term place of detention where instruction and training will be given by a specially qualified staff.
>
> (ii) Tenders will be invited shortly for the erection of a new, modern-style training school on a sixty-acre site in County Dublin to replace St Conleth's, Daingean.
>
> (iii) An intensive course in child care will be held next July for the senior members of the staffs of reformatory and industrial schools.
>
> (iv) Plans are being prepared for modern group-home units, each to cater for approximately fifteen children, which will be erected at selected industrial schools.[1]

Dr Thornley then asked the Minister if he realised that 'District Justice Kennedy had expressed her own extreme dissatisfaction about the conditions under which she is compelled to operate'[2] and that a national newspaper had that morning reported that industrial schools run by the religious orders were refusing admission to children sent to them in order to try to force some action from the government. (The article was almost certainly a piece by Nell McCafferty on the front page of the *Irish Times*).

Mr Faulkner replied that the newspaper reports were untrue, and there follows from the Dáil report details of vacancies for children in the schools run by the Sisters of Mercy, a correction of the report as to who would run the Finglas detentions centre, a shifting about regarding responsibility for committals to industrial schools (not the Department of Education but the Department of Justice, through the courts) and the promise of accommodation for those committed, which was the responsibility of the Department of Education.

Dr John O'Connell took up the baton from Dr Thornley and asked a question regarding the possible closure of Letterfrack Industrial School, which had been threatened by the principal of the school. The minister passed the buck to the brothers who ran the school, saying that they had to give six months' notice of closure and that, since he had not received such a letter, he was not going to discuss the issue with the Brothers.

After this, we go back to Dr Thornley, who again tried to get more information from the minister regarding places in industrial schools. To give the minister his due, he did provide some more information, but he seemed to have very little himself.

David Thornley had a deep commitment to the welfare of those who were imprisoned, and on 6 July of that year he asked the minister for Justice, Desmond O'Malley, about children before the Metropolitan Children's Court, Dublin. He asked about the number of applications there for legal aid which were granted, about how many children were before the courts on criminal charges, about school-attendance offences, and about 'how many children before the Metropolitan Children's Court, Dublin [have been] in need of care and protection under the Children Act 1908 during the last ten years'.

Mr O'Malley replied giving the statistics but, frustratingly, he announced that 'statistics are compiled in relation to the number of cases that are heard by the court rather than the number of persons who appear before it'. In other words, a child who was up on ten charges would look like ten children: how could one possibly make proper provision for children with figures like that? And then, even worse: 'Statistics are compiled in relation to the numbers of cases that are heard by the court rather than the numbers of persons who appear before it. No statistics are available classifying the offences dealt with by the court or seg-regating cases that involve offences from those that do not.'[3] In other words, school mitchers, those involved in criminal activity, and those neg-lected and perhaps left in danger were all lumped together.

The figures for the years 1967 to 1970 had apparently been given on 17 June 1971 to another parliamentary question, so the minister gave the figures for the six years before that:

Year	Cases[4]
1961	14,413
1962	11,924
1963	11,818
1964	9,956
1965	8,882
1966	10,777

How one could make any sense of these figures is difficult to know. Moreover, the minister disclosed that 'The figures include cases against adults who are charged jointly with juveniles and also cases against adults who were summoned in respect of school-attendance offences'. There was no breakdown of the figures to show which cases involved only chil-dren, but he thought that 'it may be taken that such cases represented the great majority of the total'.

Minister O'Malley did try to bring some more sense to the statistics by producing the figures for applications for 'committal' and 'actual com-mittal' over the last ten years, which can be seen on the following page.

He had to admit, however, that there was no breakdown of the fig-ures to show how many had been committed for destitution, lack of proper guardianship or the commission of offences. As for the legal-aid scheme introduced on 1 April 1965: two applications were granted by the court in that year, and one in 1966!

David Thornley must have been as horrified by this ridiculous lack of information (how could one plan or implement any reforms without more facts) as I am, because he was on the trail again on 8 July with Mr

Year ending 31 July	Applications	Committals[5]
1961	464	318
1962	535	292
1963	529	249
1964	388	164
1965	430	202
1966	384	155
1967	261	115
1968	229	73
1969	173	68
1970	193	61

Faulkner. Dr Thornley asked about the numbers and ages of boys in industrial schools and at what ages they had been committed. The minister obliged by giving the figures for the girls as well. Three of the boys were eight years old when they were committed – for what 'offence' we do not know.

On 13 July, David Thornley asked the Minister for Education about appeals to sentences in industrial schools and enquired as to who was responsible for making sure that the child attended the court for his appeal, and for paying any travelling expenses that were incurred. Mr Faulkner said that the school ensured that the boy went to the court and the expenses were covered by his department.

Nearly a year later, on 17 May 1972, there is a sense of déjà vu in the Dáil. Dr Thornley (with Dr John O'Connell) had tabled a question asking the Minister for Education 'if he will indicate when the recommendations of the Kennedy Report with regard to the provision of facilities for children requiring residential care will be fully implemented'.[6]

They also asked what were 'the total number of facilities for children requiring residential care that are currently available and in operation; the number of outmoded facilities in which the work of reconstruction and adaptation has begun to bring them up to the recommended standard; and in how many cases provision has been made to begin reconstruction and adaptation.'[7] Mr Faulkner replied: 'The building of the first of the group units at a number of residential homes is about to commence shortly. Provision of further such accommodation will be made as soon as the first units are completed and experience has been gained in relation to them. I cannot at this stage indicate when a general programme of the provision of such accommodation would be completed.

'The total number of reformatory and industrial schools – the residential institutions for which I have responsibility – is 32, and the number of children in these schools totals about 1,700.'[8] There followed some discussion on what 'shortly' meant.

The next day, 18 May, Dr O'Connell and Dr Thornley were back on the issue of child residential care, asking where the new group unit already under construction for children requiring residential care was located. 'Moate' said the minister, and he gave the intended location of other such units: Rathdrum, Tralee, Drogheda and Killarney.

Finally, on 18 May 1972, the thorny subject of Marlborough House (which, as already noted, had been described as unfit for habitation) was discussed. Dr O'Connell and Dr Thornley sought statistics on the daily average number of boys there, and the average weekly committal rate.

In 1970, Judge Kennedy had recommended the immediate closure of Marlborough House, as Mr Edward Collins pointed out in the debate. The minister admitted that the average number of children committed each week was three and that the average number remanded weekly was twelve. He later said: 'No further committals will be accepted from 22 May 1972' (which was four days later) and that Marlborough House would be 'phased out altogether in a short time'[9]. There was then a further discussion about what a 'short length of time' meant. Dr O'Connell suggested two months, but the minister declined to give a definition.

(Apparently the same minister had said a year before that no further boys would be admitted there, but as we can see, this had not proved to be the case.)

Let me admit that there have been some improvements over the last thirty years. The Court Service statistics are now much more reliable and informative, thanks to radical reform and updating in the last decade. The

Family Courts, held in camera, are reported on, in an anonymous way, with the permission of the participants in the cases. This gives the public some idea of the problems faced by families and how the court attempts to resolve them. There are less children in state custodial institutions.

But what about the repeated complaints by judges in every court, not just the Children's Court, about the lack of facilities and support staff to deal with the children who come before them? What about the need for a constitutional amendment to enshrine the rights of the child in our Constitution? Various ministers, including the former Taoiseach, Bertie Ahern, promised one, but now we are told that legislation will do. If he was here today, David Thornley would find that, nearly forty years after he spoke up for children in the Dáil, he still had plenty to do. What a fine contribution he would have been able to make to the final report of the Commission to Inquire into Child Abuse, when it eventually appears!

My thanks for research to Niall O'Brien, Leinster House library staff, and to Bruce Arnold for advice

Mary Henry graduated from Trinity College, Dublin with degrees in medicine and modern English. She has a long involvement with Trinity and now chairs the Association and Trust. She represented Dublin University in Seanad Éireann from 1992 to 2007. She knew and admired David Thornley both inside and outside college.

NOTES

1 Official Report, Dáil Éireann, Volume 252, 25 March 1971, Questions–Oral Answers, Industrial Schools Report, Column 1450
2 *ibid.* Column 1451
3 Official Report, Dáil Éireann, Volume 255, 6 July 1971, Questions – Oral Answers, Dublin Children's Court, Column 544
4 *ibid.*
5 *ibid.* Column 455
6 Official Report, Dáil Éireann, Volume 260, 17 May 1972, Questions – Oral Answers, Industrial Schools Report, Column 1949
7 *ibid.*
8 *ibid.* Column 1950
9 Official Report, Dáil Éireann, Volume 260, 18 May 1972, Questions – Oral Answers, Child Residential Care, Column 2153

11

OUR LOST COMRADE

BARRY DESMOND

APRIL 2008

When David Thornley wrote his first major article about the Labour Party in the *Irish Times* prior to the 1965 general election, this talented thirty-year old and handsome TCD historian wrote a thoughtful analysis of the history and future of the party. He posed the question:

> To some extent Labour is the victim of a vicious circle. Perhaps the lesson of coalition is that power corrupts and the big devour the small. But power is also the proper goal of politics; legitimately ambitious men will not be permanently attracted to a party which preserves an honourable station in limbo.

Four years later David, now a national TV star who made a considerable impact in the hey-day of the *7-Days* public affairs RTÉ programme, joined the Labour Party. As he assessed the political scene in 1965, he wrote, again in the *Irish Times*:

> Can Labour capitalise on the new Ireland, where the political language is of planning, programming and the social services? There is little doubt that the party has good hopes that within the decade it may hold, say, twenty-five seats and the balance of power.

It was on RTÉ that David and his fellow academic, Basil Chubb, illustrated their decisive findings on the proposed abolition by Fianna Fáil of the electoral system of proportional representation in the 1968 referendum. I was Chairman of the Labour Party during that long and controversial campaign and the Chubb-Thornley findings were a blessing to us in our victory over Fianna Fáil and more particularly over Kevin Boland, the ruthless Minister for Local Government, who was determined to bring in the single seat first-past-the-post constituency system, thus cementing Fianna Fáil in power.

In the early sixties in TCD, when David participated in the setting up of the Fabian Society, he described himself as 'a Liberal Christian Socialist'. He was certainly sufficiently Christian to be asked in 1964 by the reverend editor of the *Christus Rex* journal in Maynooth College to provide a major article on 'The Development of the Irish Labour Movement'. He wrote:

> There are, for Labour, a number of hopeful signs. After years of bitterness unity has finally been restored to the trade union movement. A new leader has been elected, in Mr Corish, to speak for the Labour Party; one of his first actions was to sponsor an appeal to all the elements of the democratic left to make common cause with the party in the Ireland of the sixties.[1]

After a decade of campaigning in the elections of Noël Browne, who had joined the Labour Party in 1963 with Jack McQuillan, it was no surprise when David joined the party in the run-in to the 1969 general election.

David and I were born in 1935 and we were both first elected to the Dáil in 1969. I recall our first few months in the House. One scene in the members' restaurant stands out – as I felt self-important having lunch with fellow deputies Dan Spring and Michael Pat Murphy, Dan cried: 'Jesus, Barry, boy! Will ye look at that smasher in the hot pants!' as a most attractive woman entered the room. 'Shut up Dan!' I exclaimed, 'That's Petria Thornley.' 'Fine girl she is!' complimented Dan. 'Lucky man, the doctor!' chirruped Michael Pat.

David had topped the poll in Dublin North-West with 8,446 votes. He was in the big winners league – only Líam Cosgrave, David Andrews, Garret Fitzgerald, Paddy Burke, George Colley and Charles Haughey exceeded 8,000 first preferences in Dublin. David's fellow Labour running mates were no slouches. Mick McEvoy and Tommy Watt were local full-time officials with the ITGWU and WUI and Mick Hooper was also a local activist. But they were no match for David, who charmed the ladies of the Navan Road, sang in the local Church choir and at the Corpus Christi procession. He was in excellent RIAM voice. In the event these three fellow candidates could only muster 3,091 votes between them, bringing Labour's vote in the constituency to an exceptional 38 per cent of the poll! David was now a distinguished addition to the new influx of 'the Trinity intellectuals' into the parliamentary Labour party. David, Conor Cruise O'Brien and Justin Keating had the Dáil, and perhaps they themselves thought the country, at their feet!

Within a month of our election to the Dáil, all hell broke loose in Northern Ireland with the 'Battle of The Bogside' and the arrival of British troops. By November, 1971, thirty-three members of the British Army, with RUC men, two from the UDR and, more ominously, seventy civilians were dead, mostly from Provo bombs. Charles Haughey was dismissed from government by Jack Lynch in May, 1970, amid allegations of illegal arms importation. He was famously acquitted at the arms trials. Although David was never a member of the IRA or the Provisionals, we rapidly learned that his sympathies now lay with republican aspirations. The general secretary of the ITGWU, Michael Mullen, an ex-IRA internee, who was Labour's deputy in Dublin North West prior to his union promotion, exerted a major influence on David. It was said, perhaps unfairly, that this Surrey-born, London and TCD-educated don, wished to prove that he was more Irish than the Irish themselves. In any event he sided in the Parliamentary Party with Steve Coughlan, Dan Spring, Jack Fitzgerald, Seán Treacy, John O'Connell, John O'Donovan and the leader in waiting, Justin Keating, in the outbreak of anti-Unionist and anglophobia hysteria. Brendan Corish, Brendan Halligan, Michael O'Leary, Seamus Pattison, Liam Kavanagh, James Tully, Senators Dominic Murphy, Tim McAuliffe, Evelyn Owens, Fintan Kennedy (President of the ITGWU) and myself held the line. Our anti-IRA majority on critical occasions between 1969 and 1973 was narrow. Without the calm courage of Corish, the steely determination of the Chief Whip, Frank Cluskey, and the ICTU support of Fintan Kennedy and Stephen McGonagle, we would have fallen apart. Conor Cruise O'Brien was masterful in the Dáil and in the party in excoriating the rampant sectarian Provoism of the period. Unfortunately on many occasions Conor could not resist trailing his coat in front of his parliamentary colleagues causing endless problems for Brendan Corish. But, to his great credit, Corish defended his appointment of Conor as spokesperson on Northern Ireland time and time again. The party had one further major blessing. The son of James Connolly, Roddy, was elected Chairman of the party in 1971 and gave major support to Corish and Cruise O'Brien.

And for David, where did it all go so tragically wrong? He had supported the principle of coalition at the 1970 party conference and voted for the fourteen-point programme with Fine Gael in 1973. In the 1973 general election he was returned to the Dáil with a reduced vote of 5,023. Dublin North-West was still solidly pro-Labour with 25 percent of the vote. But in his first four years in the Parliamentary Labour Party, he had become unpredictable. This was epitomised by his staunch defence of Deputy Steve Coughlan at the 1971 annual conference following Steve's anti-semitic comments in Limerick. He also appeared at the Mater Hospital in December, 1972, and supported the release of the then Provisional Chief of Staff, Seán MacStiophan, who was on a hunger and thirst strike for fifty-seven days and who lost face with the movement when he gave it up in 1973. Seán had failed the martyrdom test!

David wrote an irate letter to Brendan Corish on 13 August, 1971:

> When Connolly went into the GPO he sought to coerce, physically, not merely the Ulster Unionists, but about one-third of the population. Was he wrong? Every one of our Ard Fheises (sic) takes place under huge blow-ups of his picture. Is this consistent with a reversion to the policy of Redmond?

About this time, I beg to notice that David seemed to suffer from acute mood swings. I would meet him in the Dáil corridors and rooms we shared in the mornings when David yodelled in great voice and sang snatches of church hymns if he had been to mass in Westland Row. By late afternoon depression had set in. And then he began to drink. Even in those early days one had an ominous anticipation. The Dáil is one of the worst possible environments in which to suffer from such conditions. David's temperament was entirely at odds with this cruel trade. It was only years later I was informed that David was a diabetic.

Unfortunately, by December 1971, David was now supporting the murderous IRA campaign. Matters came to a head during a Dáil debate, to our utter embarrassment and fury. Michael O'Leary had denounced the brutal assassination of the Northern Ireland Senator John Barnhill by the Official IRA and demanded government action against the perpetrators. David rebuked his colleague in the Dáil and said that the murder had been 'excessively deplored'.[2] We were shocked. David, in defiance, produced Dan Breen's *My Fight for Irish Freedom*, a gift he had received as an eight-year-old child. It was all so appallingly sad. In 1971 in an RTÉ interview he laid down another marker:

I would certainly find myself in closer affinity with the views of Neil Blaney than I would with some of the people who sit on the official Labour Party benches.[3]

When David was challenged if his speeches implied tacit approval of the IRA, he replied, 'I deplore violence in the North and I am sorry it has proved to be necessary.' During the same debate in the Dáil on 16 December 1971, David was quite explicit in his support of the Provos operating from the Republic. He declared:

When Irishmen go across the border to carry out armed attacks on Unionist installations I am now going to place them in the same category as criminals.

David was not a lone voice in such incitement. There were at least another score or more members of the Houses of the Oireachtas who shared his extremism. It was a stark reflection of these times. At least David was no 'sneaking regarder'.

David had a very traditional and simplistic historical interpretation of the role of the embryonic trade union and labour movement in the Rising and post-1916. When David spoke to his constituency colleagues in 1971 in Liberty Hall, he denounced:

The betrayal of socialism was neither by Connolly nor even de Valera; it was by the successors of Connolly in the Labour leadership who disowned him at the Whit Congress of the TUC in 1916, who declined to follow his policy of full but separate commitment to republicanism in the Citizen Army, who rejected the appeals for aid from Liam Mellowes in 1922, and who spurned the Republican Congress in 1934, thereby driving frustrated Irish socialist republicans into the IRA.

There was in fact no disowning of Connolly at the 1916 ITUC meeting that Whit. There was intense puzzlement as to why Connolly had gone with the IRB in the Easter rebellion. There was shock at his execution. But the sympathy was muted because he had after all, without consultation with his trade union colleagues, joined the IRB, jointly planned the Rising and availed of Liberty Hall for the Citizen Army, only half of whom (about one hundred) were members of the ITGWU. Trade union and labour supporters were overwhelmingly non-involved in the Rising, North and South. The residue of the 1913 lock-out failure, the departure of Larkin to America, the destruction of Liberty Hall and the economic impact of the War were also matters of grave importance in the eyes of delegates at the 1916 Congress. The great majority of those in jail, post-Rising, were not trade unionists. David's denunciation of those trade union and labour leaders 'who rejected the appeals for aid from Liam Mellowes in 1922' was also entirely misplaced. The great majority of those leaders in 1921–22 supported the Treaty and did their utmost to persuade Mellowes, de Valera and O'Connor to give up their armed attempts to take over the democratic Dáil.

Likewise David grossly overstated the role of the Republican Congress in 1934. It was the orthodox IRA which opposed the Congress and brought about the split in this body after eighteen months. To hold the ITUC and the Labour Party responsible for the division between those who wanted an immediate workers' republic and those who wished to set up an anti-de Valera popular front was entirely facile.

The January 1972 Party Conference in Wexford had as its centre piece the policy document on Northern Ireland as ratified by the Administrative Council three weeks earlier. The position of Conor Cruise O'Brien as spokesperson on Northern Ireland was, in effect, on the line. In the debate David argued that 'some republican teeth' should be inserted in the document and that both IRA groupings should be included in negotiations for a solution. Seán Treacy moved a composite motion calling for the removal of Conor Cruise from his spokesmanship. He said that he could no longer support 'a brand of spineless, supine, unprincipled shoveenism which is anti-Irish and anti-Labour!' Brendan Corish and myself vehemently defended Conor. Corish laid his leadership before the delegates. The party chairman, Roddy Connolly, warmly praised Corish and condemned the IRA. Ultimately, sanity and party solidarity prevailed and the policy document was adopted. The no confidence motion on Cruise O'Brien was withdrawn. David and Seán Treacy were, ever so politely, sidelined.

On 15 June 1972, David landed himself in further hot water. At a meeting in the Mansion House organised by the Citizens for Civil Liberties on the topic 'Special Courts and the Citizens' Rights' he criticised nine Labour deputies, including Brendan Corish, for voting for the Prisons Bill. This bill had been introduced by the Minister for Justice, Desmond O'Malley, following a major riot in Mountjoy Jail when the Provos and other prisoners attempted to wreck the prison. The government had no option but to seek statutory powers to transfer the prisoners to military custody. David said that the party had gone 'temporarily berserk' and talked of 'the whiskey politics' of the Dáil. He pointed out that when people accused him of breaking the rules of the House 'it was just like breaking the rules of the brothel'.[4] We were in despair about David and the future of the party.

However, it is important to note that David was not the sole dissenting voice in the body politic against the introduction of the Prisons Bill and also Part 5 of the Offences Against the State Act by proclamation. Lynch, Cosgrave and Corish shared the stark view that the security situation of the State had come under serious threat. There was a body of political and legal opinion that this fear was overstated. At the Mansion House meeting the eminent Seán MacBride said that:

> We were arriving at a situation in which the Government may, through its Attorney General, exercise a selective choice as to whether or not somebody was to be tried by the ordinary courts with the usual safeguard of a jury. Even the British authorities in the North had not yet reached this stage of selective justice as to modes of trial. The Government had frankly resorted to internment and had just dispensed with any trial in certain cases.[5]

The well-known civil rights solicitor, Con Lehane, at the same meeting said that:

> It is an invasion of our democratic rights that the Executive should arrogate to itself the power to deprive some accused persons of their right to trial by jury while according that right to others.[6]

Only eight deputies in the House voted against the Prisons Bill. Brendan Corish said that his party regretted that the government would introduce the Special Criminal Court as a method of dealing with illegal organisations. Jack Lynch was fortunate in his promotion of Desmond O'Malley as Minister for Justice who was unwavering in his opposition to the IRA and their minority of ultra-republican sympathisers in the Dáil.

During this period David held the pivotal position of Chairman of the Organisation Committee of the party. Eric Doyle, William Conroy, John O'Connell and myself were the other members. A meeting of the Committee was held on 10 August 1972, at the request of Conroy and Doyle. I reported to the members the extraordinary behaviour of David during the mid-Cork by-election the previous month. He had attended a William O'Brien Fianna Fáil function attended by their candidate, Gene Fitzgerald. David had also been offered the use of the Fianna Fáil platform and equipment by the Taoiseach, Jack Lynch, during a by-election public meeting. He caused consternation in the campaign of Labour's outstanding candidate, Senator Eileen Desmond, who had lost her seat in 1969, by denouncing the prospect of an exchange of second preferences between Fine Gael and Labour. The local Director of Elections for the Party demanded that Corish withdraw David from the campaign. I wrote on 8 August in the *Irish Times* after the election that David's contribution was 'adolescent and irresponsible' and I was duly censured by the Administrative Council for this criticism. So was David for his statements. In the event Jack and Gene romped home on the first count with almost 20,000 votes, a record. Matters had come to a head and my proposal that the Administrative Council be requested to replace David as Chairman was adopted. I then knew the full meaning of the words 'Cruel to be kind'. Eric Doyle was terrified that David would kill himself in his sports car, going around the country to party meetings.

Following the mid-Cork by-election the party leader, Brendan Corish, in late August 1972, decided to reshuffle his 'front bench'. There were two significant decisions. David was removed from the spokesmanship on Education and demoted to that of Posts and Telegraphs. Michael O'Leary, a firm supporter of Corish, replaced David. Corish retained Conor Cruise O'Brien as spokesman on foreign affairs and as an indication of his approval of the O'Brien policy on the North his brief also included the Common Market. A week later while David was on holiday in Wexford, he attended the Fianna Fáil Campile Cumann dinner dance at Fethard-on-Sea. He was warmly welcomed by Brian Lenihan, Minister for Transport and Power.[7] Corish was not amused.

By the time of the election of the National Coalition government in February 1973, David had well and truly burned his prospects of the appointment to the Cabinet portfolio he coveted – education. But the party's hierarchy was in an acute quandary as to what to do with three Dublin deputies, the now more unpredictable David, the loner John O'Connell and a seriously disappointed Barry Desmond. I had been pencilled in by Corish for a portfolio (his meeting notes with Cosgrave are in the Irish Labour History Society archive) but when Frank Cluskey gave an assurance to Brendan that he would give up alcohol if appointed as Parliamentary Secretary, I was dropped. I was far too independent-minded to even ask Corish for a post. The solution to keep me out of the government's hair was to send me to the European Parliament. The Deputy Leader and Minister James Tully came to our home and exerted great pressure on Stella to accept my 'promotion'. So did Mary Davidson, the retired General Secretary of the party who was very close to Stella. There were no national elections to the Parliament due until 1979. We refused to bite the exile and David was then nominated to fill the MEP vacancy. Liam Kavanagh was the other nominee. It was to be David's death warrant. Alone in Brussels, Strasbourg and Luxembourg, the airports, the endless invitations to political and lobby functions were open temptations to alcoholism. David was dead within five years. His final tragedy was yet to unfold.

However, there was one major beneficiary from the election of the National Coalition government. Seán Treacy was now a very truculent supporter of David, an adamant opponent of Cruise O'Brien and a thorn in the side of Corish. He was nominated as Ceann Comhairle and he took to the role like a duck to the water. He was utterly pompous and held this position until 1977. When Eileen Desmond was appointed Minister for Health in 1981, Seán was appointed MEP, a position he held until 1984 when he resigned from the party in bitter opposition to the Family Planning Bill introduced. He was again most fortunate in his reappointment as Ceann Comhairle by Haughey in 1987.

In April 1976, James Tully, the Deputy Leader of the party, reported to the Administrative Council that the parliamentary party had voted by 21 votes to 3 to withdraw the whip from David 'because of his participation in an illegal meeting organised by the Provisional Movement'. Pat Carroll reported that David's Cabra constituency organisation wished to be disassociated from his action. He said that 'it seemed to them that the end result would be a loss of a Labour seat in the Cabra constituency'. On 29 April 1976, Brendan Halligan, General Secretary, notified Dr. Manfred Michel, Secretary General of the Socialist Group in the European Parliamentary, that David no longer represented the Labour Party. However, because of David's serious ill health at that stage no further action was taken. By May 1976, David was completely at odds with the Labour ministers in government. In the Dublin Regional Council's newsletter he wrote:

> I thought we had leaders, especially the Marxist, Deputy Keating, who would exact the maximum bargain. I was wrong. I plead innocence – no defence in law, I know. The lure of the Mercedes is apparently greater than I realised.[8]

It was all very fraught in the now three-seat Dublin Cabra constituency in 1977 when David lost his seat. It was a chaotic campaign with

Labour's 6,035 votes (24 percent) divided between three candidates, Cllr Pat Carroll, 2,817, David 1,615 and Michael Mullen, Junior, 1,603. David lost his deposit and was joined by fellow casualties Conor Cruise O'Brien and Justin Keating who also lost their seats. As a consequence of the loss of his Dáil seat David was no longer an eligible Irish MEP and, in effect, suffered a double blow. With the loss of his Labour Dáil seat our overall representation in the European Parliament fell from two to one seat.

***

We were all deeply shocked and upset following David's death in 1978 at the young age of forty-two. An intellectual and historian of great charm and wit, David was not the first such academic to be seduced by the lure of political power and ultimately to be destroyed by its electoral demands and temptations. He was, in his own way, another victim of the Northern upheaval. His TCD colleague, D. R. Lysaght, wrote in his memoir in *Magill*:

> In his last *Irish Times* article, David portrayed himself accurately as Hamlet. Like Hamlet he had two conflicting personae: the radical intellectual and the academic establishmentarian. To his credit he ended by supporting the first against the second. In doing so, he destroyed himself.

As an avid Munster rugby supporter, every time I read the magnificent analyses of Gerry Thornley in the *Irish Times* I thank David. I deeply regret that we, his fellow comrades in the political turmoils of the seventies, did not make a greater effort to save his health and to have him witness the transformation today in Northern Ireland.

While David professed to be an ardent socialist republican, he maintained 'This is not to equate the Provisionals with Pearse, still less Connolly'.[9] At the same meeting in Liberty Hall, he went on to assert:

> No thinking socialist could wish to join a movement led by the Provisional IRA. Their motives and sources of funds are at least suspect, and they possess no social philosophy whatever. In historical terms, they belong to the 'simple soldier' tradition of Sean Russell rather than the Republican Socialist tradition of Mellowes, O'Donnell and Gilmore – the tradition with which any Labour man should wish to be identified.

Barry Desmond was elected a TD for the Labour Party in 1969 for the constituency of Dun Laoghaire. He served as Minister for Health in the Fine Gael–Labour coalition government of 1982–1987. He was elected an MEP for Dublin in 1989 and was a member of the European Court of Auditors from 1994 to 2000.

NOTES

1   *Christus Rex*, page 20, Vol. xviii, 1964
2   Dáil Debates, 16 December 1971 and 17 December 1971
3   RTÉ, GIS transcript, 1971
4   *Irish Independent*, 21 July 1972
5   Ibid
6   *Irish Times*, 16 June 1972
7   *Wexford People*, 1 September 1972
8   Labour's Dublin Regional Council Newsletter, May 1976
9   *Irish Times*, 8 September 1971

12

'I WAS PROUD TO CALL HIM A GENUINE FRIEND OF MINE':

A PERSONAL MEMOIR

SEAMUS SCALLY

Even now, it is very hard to believe that David Thornley died thirty years ago, at the very early age of forty-two. Personal memories of him are still very firmly fixed in my mind. I was contacted some months ago by his daughter, Yseult, with a request to write an article for the book which she is preparing to write. I readily agreed to do so.

My memories and observations are entirely personal. I write as a son of a small farmer in County Roscommon, one who emigrated to England at the age of eighteen, worked there for twelve years, studied at the London School of Economics as a result of a TUC scholarship, joined the British Labour Party in the 1950s and in 1963 returned to Dublin, where I joined the Irish Labour Party, eventually retiring as general secretary. I also write as someone who was, and is, a committed Christian.

David's father was a Welsh agnostic socialist. His mother was an Irish Roman Catholic republican. He was born in England and was a convert to Roman Catholicism. He studied in London and later in Trinity College, where he became a professor and fellow in 1964 in the Department of Political Science.

Later he joined RTÉ as a presenter of the then current affairs programme *7-Days*. He was a brilliant presenter and was extremely influential during the 1967 referendum campaign on changing our PR voting system. In the late 1960s, he joined the Labour Party; however, he had been involved in left-wing fringe groups for many years previously. These would meet in dingy basements and included the 1913 Club. He was very much involved in internal debates in TCD on socialist policies and philosophy.

He was elected in 1969 in the Dublin North-West constituency to the seat formerly held by Micky Mullen, who was later to become general secretary of the ITGWU. He was re-elected at the 1973 general election and lost his seat in the 1977 general election. In 1973, he was nominated by the Labour Party as one of its representatives in the European Parliament and served with distinction until his untimely death in 1978.

David was a colourful person, cheerful, a most engaging conversationalist, with boyish enthusiasm and great sincerity. He had a very sharp brain and was a first-class historian. He was also fiercely independent and very reluctant to accept the type of discipline which must exist in a political party. David was controversial, loyal, very generous, and extremely proud of his considerable achievements; he was very tolerant, despised fascism and commanded great affection and respect. He was fascinated by the dirty side of politics, which could often be very nasty.

I spent hundreds of hours in his company when he was chairperson of the organisation committee of the party as we travelled all over the country. He loved meeting party members and listening to their views and hearing details of intrigue and the infighting of personalities in the constituencies. However, he did become frustrated and bored by life in Dáil Éireann. He had a romantic and naive view of politics. His tempestuous spirit led to great disillusionment. He could get quite depressed as political events unfolded, and he told me that he was inclined to drink too much alcohol when in that mood. He was not fully prepared for the daily grind of constituency work which is an integral part of the life of a TD.

The events of the early 1970s in Northern Ireland tortured his soul. My years living in England brought me into contact with many second-generation Irish people and many converts to Roman Catholicism. I was always of the view, and still remain of the view, that the explosive mix of the fervent republicanism of his mother, his reading of Irish history – the role of Padraig Pearse, 1916 – together with the zeal of the convert, weighed heavily with him. His belief in free speech, with all viewpoints having the right of expression, even where he disagreed with those views, created an explosive conflict in him.

I fully understood how he felt, but did not agree at all with his analysis. We discussed those current issues thoroughly and agreed to disagree on them. His commitment to the principles of socialism was 100 percent. He had great compassion for the underdog, the marginalised, those who were oppressed in any way, and for all minorities.

In conclusion, I want to state that I thought that the decision of the party to send him to the European Parliament was fundamentally flawed from a human point of view. It meant in practice that he had a lot of travelling to do, with plenty of spare time in the evenings away from his Irish home. The generous expenses available to him made alcohol more easily available. I noticed that he had put on a lot of excess weight on my frequent visits to the European Parliament on party business.

I was aware of how certain people had helped him in some difficult circumstances there. However, I was not at all aware of the seriousness of his medical condition. I visited him in Jervis Street Hospital shortly before his death.

I was proud to call him a genuine friend of mine. I enjoyed his great sense of humour. In my opinion, he should not have got involved in practical politics, as he was temperamentally unsuited to Irish politics. His academic career would have ensured a continuation of his influence on further generations of Irish university students. He had unique talents in the Labour Party at a time of other, different, magnetic talents.

Seamus Scally was born in County Roscommon and has a B. Econ. from the London School of Economics. He is a qualified accountant and was Deputy General Secretary of the Labour Party from 1971 to 1980 and General Secretary from 1980 to 1983. He worked for former EU Commissioner Richard Burke from 1983 and 1985 and served as a special advisor to the Ministers for the Environment and Social Welfare in the 1982–1987 coalition government. He is a former board member of the ESB and currently serves on the board of Crosscare.

13

David Thornley in the European Parliament

Fionnuala Richardson

David Thornley interviewed me for my job with the Socialist Group in the European Parliament in January 1974. That was the first time that I met him directly. However, along with most other politically interested people of the time, and as an active Labour Party member, I was very much aware of his role as a Labour Party TD, and even more so of his role as a political commentator, in particular with regard to the key role he had played in the PR referendum of 1968. I had also heard him speak at party conferences and other party meetings.

David was appointed to the European Parliament in June 1973, along with Liam Kavanagh; they replaced Conor Cruise O'Brien and Justin Keating, who had been appointed ministers in the 1973 Fine Gael–Labour government. Members of the European Parliament were then appointed by the national parliaments – and the European Parliament was run on the basis of the parliamentary traditions of the founding member states.

In those days of the appointed parliament, members tended to be elderly statesmen who had served party and country in the past and deserved a dignified end to their careers. Indeed, the Socialist Group of the time had two former colonial Governor-Generals – one French and one British – and several former foreign ministers. In addition, there were still many members who had fought in the Second World War – on both sides. These, of course, sat in political rather than national groups, working together with people they had once fought against, and on issues of ideological significance siding with their political comrades rather than members of their own nationality. This aspect of European integration –

149

the breaking down of old animosities and the creation of opportunities for working together, thus bringing about a situation where Europeans would never again kill one another – no longer seems relevant to younger people, and in Ireland it never was as telling an argument as in the original member states.

The British Labour Party did not take its seats in the European Parliament until after the UK referendum in 1985, so for a large part of David's time in the Socialist Group, he and Liam Kavanagh were the only English speakers in the group. They were also the youngest members of the group. It was not easy for them to integrate into the group in the early days, particularly as they were often called home for crucial votes in the Dáil – sometimes missing debates and votes which their Socialist Group comrades regarded as being equally crucial.

Their problems were little understood in Dublin, and briefings and support were rarely forthcoming. The Labour Party – in coalition with Fine Gael – had little by way of resources to provide back-up, and had more pressing problems to deal with. Media coverage of the parliament's activities was monopolised by Fianna Fáil, members of the small political group the European Progressive Democrats. In opposition at home, their members in the European Parliament, mostly former ministers and now senators, were relatively heavyweight.

In addition, as merely two members of a large group of fifty members (the numbers seem minuscule now compared to the present parliament), they found it harder to be nominated as rapporteur on any significant reports, or even to be assigned much – or indeed any – speaking time in debates of relevance to Ireland. David made this point in a debate on agricultural prices in September 1974. In addition, the media picked up the message from Fianna Fáil that they were the only ones who could protect Irish interests, particularly in relation to agriculture – which in those days was perceived to be the *only* Irish interest – and also that the Socialist Group, as representatives of consumers, was opposed to agriculture. This was not the case, however, as the French and Italian Socialist Group members were as supportive of the Common Agriculture Policy as the Irish ones: it was one of the issues upon which the parliament tended to split along national rather than ideological lines. (On a report on the EAGGF – the European Agriculture Guidance and Guarantee Fund – in June 1975, David abstained in the vote, expressing the view that the European Parliament did not understand the problems of the small family farm. The French Socialist members also abstained, largely for the same reason.)

In spite of the difficulties, David contributed to the work of the European parliament in a variety of areas. In addition to being a member of the Bureau of the Socialist Group, and attending the meetings of the group, he served on the parliamentary committees on Economic and Monetary Affairs, on External Economic Relations, and on Cultural Affairs and Youth. He participated in the work of the committees – a major part of the parliament's activities – collaborating with his socialist colleagues on some issues and with other Irish members on others.

He was rapporteur for the External Economic Relations Committee's three reports on regulations increasing the Community tariff quota for certain eels under the Common Customs Tariff (December 1973 (two) and September 1974) and on regulations extending the period of application of council regulations on the import into the Community of certain fishery products originating in Tunisia and Morocco (January 1974). David was not enthusiastic about the subject – something which he made clear in a brief, witty speech. However, there was a disgruntled Italian member who would have benefited in his home village from being rapporteur on eels. This was an example of the complex system of national weights and balances in the group: David was entitled to a report, but as a new member from a very small party would not be entitled to one of political significance, nor one which was commensurate with his abilities. The Italian, as an insignificant member of his grouping, would not get any report.

On the Cultural Affairs and Youth Committee, David worked with the other Socialist Group members of the committee on various issues. I was the staff member responsible for this committee for the group from the time I joined the Secretariat in March 1974. David jointly tabled a motion for resolution on education in the European Community, tabled with other committee members (July 1975), and an oral question with debate on European schools (May 1976), with other Socialist members of the Committee on Cultural Affairs and Youth. However, he was not completely in agreement with the other Socialist members on the issue of the Youth Forum in June 1974. He supported an amendment by Senator Michael Yeats concerning the representation of youth organisations from smaller countries on the Youth Forum. They were concerned that the proposals contained in the report would be against the interest of organisations from smaller countries. He was able to support a compromise amendment by fellow Socialist Cees Laban which resolved the dilemma.

David made several interventions in the European Parliament in addition to those mentioned above. He spoke on regional policy several times and was spokesman for the Socialist Group on the Delmotte Report on the Regional Fund in November 1974. He spoke on the sugar industry in April 1974, supporting Jim Gibbons – especially his objection to the vote being held in the absence of the French members. He expressed scepticism about the British Conservatives' concern for the Third World and sugar-cane production.

Through oral and written questions, he raised a variety of issues: employment in the motor vehicle assembly industry (October 1973), migrant workers ('Immigrant Workers in EC: statistics re. disparity in incomes between migrant and indigenous workers', May 1974, and 'Increase in British migration towards the Continent', May 1975), recognition of diplomas of Irish universities in the UK (June 1974), women's issues ('1975 International Women's Year and state support for divorced, separated or deserted women', December 1974, and 'Legal rights of women who are divorced, separated or deserted by their husbands, in view of the new members states who have not yet acceded to the Convention of 27 September 1968; Article 220 of the EEC Treaty', June 1974).

He lost his Dáil seat in 1977 and thus could not have been reappointed to the parliament: in any event, he was no longer a member of the parliamentary Labour Party and had not been active in the Socialist Group for some time prior to the general election.

I often regretted that I had not known David earlier, when he was at the peak of his career as a university lecturer and television and political commentator, and when he was operating in a social, cultural and political environment consistent with his formidable intellect, qualifications and abilities.

Fionnuala Richardson joined the Socialist Group Secretariat in March 1974 and was Deputy General Secretary of the Socialist Group from 1980 until her resignation in 1988. Since then she has been Director of Education in the People's College in Dublin's Parnell Square.

14

DR DAVID THORNLEY, TD:

AN INTELLECTUAL IN IRISH POLITICS

MICHAEL D. HIGGINS, TD

Dr David Thornley ends his introduction to Basil Chubb's *The Government and Politics of Ireland* with a quotation from W. B. Yeats:

> Parnell came down the road, he said to a cheering man:
> 'Ireland shall get her freedom and you shall still break stone.'

His choice of these lines from Yeats is significant. It acknowledges the poet's awareness of how change in the single dimension of landowner-ship would still leave an underclass breaking stones. As to Yeats's dark prognosis and his response to it: this is work for another day. In the case of Dr David Thornley's introduction to Basil Chubb's textbook, it is his correct assertion that much can change – including landownership and the development of an independent administrative system – and yet great social cleavages remain that is important to our understanding of the complexities of Irish politics.

There is a strong sense of continuity in this introduction from Dr Thornley's earlier, seminal work on the period 1868 to the outbreak of the Land War in 1879, where he deals with the brief hegemony and fall of Isaac Butt and the rise of a new leader, Charles Stewart Parnell. The earlier work addressed the tension that arose between the themes of land, religion and nationality. More importantly for our purposes, it also dealt with the prospects and limits of a parliamentary resolution to such issues, and the more general issue of the balance between parliamentary advocacy and public agitation.

The different forces struggling under the very broad umbrella of nationalism did not share a single project. There were many such projects. It was felt, by their proponents, that some of these projects could be accomplished within a Union with Britain; others felt that such issues required a more radical solution. Later in the century, the different tactics of Michael Davitt and Charles Stewart Parnell would seek an uneasy accommodation among those who comprised the Land League and their successors. Both, of course, were aware of a new dimension to the land issue, the threats from native predators, in the shape of graziers who invoked both nationality and religion to cover their acquisitive greed, which led to the destruction of their neighbours. Sending a son or a daughter into the Church could be used as an excuse for the acquisition of untenanted land on a rental basis.

The issue as to the power of Parliament to redress Irish grievances has been there for two centuries. An excessive faith in what could be achieved by such means in the second half of the nineteenth century, and in a more fatal sense within a Union, would lead to the fall of Isaac Butt. The times required a radical conversation with the multifarious voices of Irish society, some stressing tenure, some amnesty from persecution for what was perceived to be the prosecution of a legitimate cause, others for the replacement of what was suggested to be an alien Church by its Roman alternative. The outcome of this latter struggle would decide the control and structure of education for a century to come. Dr David Thornley's account of all of these tensions has been regarded as invaluable to students of the nineteenth century.

When Dr David Thornley took a decision to contest a Dáil seat on behalf of the Labour Party, he was far more aware than most others of both the complexity of the themes which comprised Irish politics and also of the fact that no clear ideology combined the different themes which the Irish State had inherited. Such inherited themes, while carrying a resonance that might be on occasion international, or even universal, would continue to be mediated by the absence of ideological clarity, or even at times moral conviction and courage.

He would also have been aware of the structures of Parliament itself, which, while it had changed since the time of his doctoral thesis on Isaac Butt, was still limited in terms of the change it could achieve. Important, essential in a democratic sense, but carrying the structural limitations of the Westminster model, it was the arena he chose, and one in which, rather like Isaac Butt, he would experience frustration, loss of hope and personal decline. The life one brings to politics carries of course those elements of one's previous occupation that can be rationally anticipated, but also those aspects of personality that are called on to respond to affirmation or rejection, companionship or loneliness.

What is it that attracts a person of such intellectual brilliance to the burning lamp that is the world of parliamentary politics? As to that journey from imagining the alternative to political action, in a recent paper I quoted from a lecture given at the University of Bristol in October 2005 by Ruth Levitas, where she spoke of 'the education of life' and the centrality of utopian thought and method in socialist discourse and practice:

> All of us have a debt to someone none of us ever met, the German theorist Ernst Bloch, born in 1885. Bloch's major work, the three-volume *The Principle of Hope*, was partly written in exile in the United States in the 1930s, revised and published in the 1950s after his return to the German Democratic Republic, and translated into English in 1986.
>
> Bloch argues that human experience is marked by lack and longing, giving rise to a utopian impulse – the propensity to long for and imagine alternative ways of being. Crucially, however, he said that this longing cannot be articulated other than through imagining the means of its fulfilment. You cannot identify what it is that is lacking without projecting what would meet that lack, without describing what is missing. In this sense, everything that reaches to a transformed existence can be considered to have a utopian aspect. His examples range across myths, fairy tales, theatre, new clothes, alchemy, architecture and music and religion, as well as the more obvious descriptions of social utopias. Bloch's work demonstrates that if we understand utopia as the desire for a better way of being or of living, then such imaginings are braided through human culture, and vary from the banal to the deeply serious, from fantasising about winning the lottery (whether or not one has a ticket) to a (sometimes) secularised version of the quest to understand who we are, why we are here and how we connect to one another. The generic utopian content lies in the attempt to grasp the possibility of a radically different human experience, even though it is sometimes embedded in forms of fantasy that are easily dismissed as wishful thinking, or is often oblique or fragmentary.

The alternative society cannot, of course, be left to the realm of imagination, however. As Levitas further pointed out in relation to Bloch's works:

Bloch does not give equal endorsement to all manifestations of utopianism. Wishful thinking is the beginning of transformative agency, but it is only by the education of hope that this move can take place. Bloch challenges the dichotomy between the real and the imaginary. Utopia is a form of anticipatory consciousness. His key concept is the 'not yet', carrying the double sense of *not yet, but*, an expected future presence, and *still not*, a current absence. But that which is 'not yet' is also real, since reality for Bloch must include the horizon of future possibilities – possibilities which are always plural, and which are dependent on human agency for their actualisation. Bloch said: 'The hinge in human history is its producer.' Or, as Alan Titchmarsh put it: 'We have to put the "heave" in heaven.'

I am indebted to Professor Tom Moylan, the Director of the Ralahine Centre for Utopian Studies, at the University of Limerick, for drawing my attention to Ruth Levitas's reflection on the work of Ernst Blochs, and much more.

Dr David Thornley's early activities at Trinity College, and his involvement with the campaigns of Dr Noël Browne and Jack McQuillan, indicate that this transition from 'lack and longing', through 'utopianism' and 'the education of hope' to action had already occurred for the young academic.

Beyond such an intellectual and moral motivation, there is always of course the personal and psychological search for fulfilment: the need for an audience, the engagement with them, the ability to move them and to respond to them. To live in the public world is necessarily no mere pursuit of recognition; it is an act of sharing driven by a sense of urgency to communicate what is perceived to be good or necessary beyond any satisfaction of the self. Yet it also constitutes the space where a personal life, with all its challenges, hopes, prospects and disappointments, is acted out.

Basil Chubb's 1970 book *The Government and Politics of Ireland* was for so long the basic text in third-level colleges that Dr David Thornley's introduction to it is possibly that piece of his work with which most students of political and social science are familiar. It is a long introduction – forty-two pages – and really constitutes a work in its own right, considering, as it does, so many of the conflicting themes of Irish history in an elegant, scholarly and accessible way.

The issues of nationality, religion, land and politics are present – issues that are neither congruent nor even compatible. It is, however, when such issues coincide, Thornley suggests in his introduction, that great public manifestations appear and the possibility of radical change emerges. That such moments may be fleeting and emerge, it seems, only to be lost – the existing order reconfigured for a renewed economic exploitation, political manipulation and cultural domination – is perhaps avoided as a testament to hope, and belief in the possibility of alternatives. Dr David Thornley's quotation from Yeats was apt.

Yet this quotation also remains apt and, on reflection, acknowledged a foreboding. Yeats's lines of warning and prophecy, even despair, had, of course, been preceded much earlier by the statements of the political activist and leader Matt Harris as he addressed Land League meetings in Counties Mayo and Galway. The land would be got for some, he felt, but the agricultural labourers would die, emigrate or, if they survived, eat in the barn. Moments of change are neither comprehensive in terms of the themes included in the change, nor essentially ethically inspired, in their achievement.

Dr David Thornley's introduction to Basil Chubb's *The Government and Politics of Ireland* also leads into Chubb's consideration of the contested concept of 'Irish political culture'. The chapter in the book which follows Thornley's historical introduction offers a discussion of the British influence on Ireland, nationalism, the dying peasant society, authoritarianism, party loyalty and anti-intellectualism. Chubb traces these elements in a context that it suggests are defined by three cleavages: the nationalist cleavage, the cleavages of an industrial society, and those of town versus country.

While staying short of a critique of clientelism, Basil Chubb set up what was to be a dominant theme in analysing Irish political discussion as to the role of the TD. He suggested a dichotomy between the role of representative and legislator. The electoral system of proportional representation and multi-seat constituencies had lent particular weight to the importance of constituency service due to intra-party competition. The monopoly of the Right to introduce legislation on the part of the government, the control of the public service residing in the hands of the government and the absence of a committee system meant that working in the constituency was how one managed to remain in public office. Chubb had published an earlier article entitled 'Going about persecuting civil servants' which outlined the typical activities of a TD.

At different stages of his political life, particularly during his days as chair of the Organisation Committee of the Labour Party, Dr David Thornley held such a generous view of the branch membership, and indeed the public, as led him not merely to exaggerate their values but to seek to become one of them. I recall his beautiful voice rendering an Italian aria in the bucolic setting of a pub after a branch meeting. While it has been claimed elsewhere, I do not recall such a repertoire ever having been discarded in favour of republican ballads.

As hope of preferment faded, he was later to place an ever greater value on the company of those outside Dáil Éireann. His inherent gregariousness brought him into contact with many of those for whom life did not hold much hope, who indeed lived lives of quiet terror. While the move from the Apollonian realms of an academic setting to the more Dionysian realms of pints and bets on horses was made with a certain amount of humour and self-mockery, which I clearly recall, I was, however, also conscious of the tragic nature of this journey and the loss that was entailed, not only in terms of a political contribution but, much more important, to those who loved him.

Even though there was still recognition at this time for public and political oratory, this would later decline as speeches were shortened, time was shared and the power of press offices increased. Getting a slot for speaking was in the gift of the party whip, who in turn felt a particular obligation to the leader of the party and, to a lesser extent, the spokesperson in a particular area. This meant that being out of favour conferred a kind of imposed silence on 'difficult' members.

The Labour candidate for Dublin North-West was well aware of this context. The risks were always there, but the popular acceptance of personality, ability and commitment to the values of socialism and labour had the happy result of his heading the poll after the election of 1969 and joining a group of people within the Labour Party whose ability and brilliance could not be contested.

In *Isaac Butt and Home Rule* – his doctoral thesis, published by MacGibbon and Kee in 1964 – Dr David Thornley had sought to untangle the theories relating to late nineteenth-century Irish life and politics. His was an original insight in terms of uncovering the multi-dimensional, multi-layered and opaque nature of nationality and nationalism. Such an insight, however, seems insufficient when one reflects on the debate on this theme at the time of his entry to the Dáil. Dr David Thornley supported the idea of coalition at the Labour Party conference of 1970, and the later fourteen-point programme for government with Fine Gael in 1973. He thus had become a focus of criticism for sections of the Left within the Labour Party. It was, however, on the issue of nationalism and the role of dissent that he was to encounter his greatest difficulties. In the atmosphere of the times, there was no space for the nuanced difference between the genuine aspirations of nationalism or anti-imperialism on the one hand, and the campaign of the IRA, which was murdering and maiming British forces and civilians alike, on the other.

The threat of IRA violence was perceived to be such that there was a real threat to the existence of the Irish Republic itself. At the meetings of the parliamentary party, divisions opened up between Dr Conor Cruise-O'Brien, the spokesperson on Northern Ireland, who forcefully presented what he saw was an emergency situation and made the case for the defence of an order perceived to be under immediate threat, and Dr David Thornley and some others, who held back from such unconditional criticism of the IRA campaign and blurred the distinction between IRA violence and the legitimate project – and memory – of nationalism.

In retrospect, it is possible to look back on the 1970s and seem to discover, along with the appalling consequences of IRA violence, the 'counter-terrorism' campaign brought into existence to confront it in Northern Ireland on the part of the British authorities. Such a counter campaign can be shown to have its incubation period in some otherwise 'respectable' British academic settings.

In short, there was no middle ground. There was neither a mood, nor space, for historical context or liberal freedoms which could be abused, and thus meetings were held on such curtailments of civil liberties as were deemed necessary by government but were viewed as a cause for concern by civil-liberties groups. In fairness to those who voted for the legislation, they placed on record at the time their deep regret that they had concluded that such measures were necessary. Nevertheless, the concern of those who wished to keep the principles of personal freedoms intact was equally genuine and was held with an even greater intensity.

From his entry into the Dáil, and membership of the parliamentary Labour Party, Dr David Thornley's relationship with the leadership of the party was fraught. It would get worse, leading to his losing the whip in April 1976 as a result of his appearance on a Provisional Sinn Féin platform ostensibly called to defend freedom of speech. I was one of the three members of the parliamentary party who voted against the removal of the whip from him, on the basis that his intention had been to sustain the principle of the right to dissent in the public space. I gave the example of Jean-Paul Sartre selling the Maoist newspaper on the streets of Paris. Even though he disagreed with the political aims and tactics of Provisional Sinn Féin, he felt that they should be allowed a place in the public space, and in public discourse, to air their views. (Years later, I would encounter this argument when I decided to seek Cabinet approval for the non-renewal of the Prohibition Orders under section 31 of the Broadcasting Act.) He sent me a note after the vote simply saying: 'Thank you for your words, the reference to Sartre was flattering but apt.'

Dr David Thornley's involvement in the event was something of a fiasco. Some of the organisers were against his appearance on the platform, and all, it would appear, were agreed that he should not be allowed to speak. No space could be allowed for liberal sentiment, not to speak of what was perceived to be soft support for nationalist sentiment accompanied by a condemnation of Provisional IRA violence. In addition, the newspaper reports contained accounts of booing from the audience at Dr Thornley's presence. However motivated, the arrival of Dr David Thornley on the platform was construed as certainly opposition to the government, and by some as support for the Provisional IRA.

The whip was restored to Dr Thornley before the 1977 election, but this was a difficult election for all candidates other than those of Fianna Fáil, as Jack Lynch had bought the election with a manifesto which promised such measures as the abolition of domestic rates. Moreover, the publicity surrounding the at times eccentric, and increasingly erratic, behaviour of Dr Thornley, combined with a lifestyle that contributed to rather than mitigated his medical predisposition, had taken its toll. Dr Thornley lost the election. His vote, and that of Labour in the constituency, had significantly declined in 1973, and he failed to survive in the electoral atmosphere of 1977.

John Horgan, in his book *Noël Browne: Passionate Outsider*, suggests that Dr Thornley was ill by the 1970s – an undiagnosed diabetic by the mid-1970s. 'He was at this stage an undiagnosed diabetic and this, combined with his political lifestyle, was a recipe for disaster,' wrote Horgan. I believe myself that Dr Thornley had such an illness as placed him at risk some years earlier.

What is clear in his work on Isaac Butt is that Dr David Thornley had a feel for the intricacies of parliamentary work in the House of Commons in the later nineteenth century. The detail of amendments used to advance or frustrate an issue certain for defeat, but valuable in terms of the degree of support or hostility it would reveal, is handled with great skill. The detail of the intrigue within the parliamentary ranks of the Home Rule movement is of a similar high level. This was a route that he would not himself travel, however.

Quite simply, Dr David Thornley knew the limits and possibilities of the parliamentary system. A university lecturer at twenty-four, an associate professor and fellow of Trinity College at thirty-four, his work on the intersections of history, politics and the Irish social sciences in general indicated a brilliant academic career already begun. While many, not necessarily as talented, were happy to settle for the rewards of only a part of such achievement and its possibilities, he was not content and was anxious to become more deeply involved, to become a legislator, to make a difference. While he was familiar with the estimation Isaac Butt had of the parliamentary process, he was also aware of its shortcomings and ultimate failure. He did not throw himself into the requirements of a slow, tedious progression through Dáil business. At any event, the position of a government backbencher would be perceived by him, quite correctly, to be as close to parliamentary impotence as one can get.

In 1965, he had written of the dangers, but also of the opportunities, of participation as a minority partner in government. Power, he had written, is also the proper goal of politics: legitimately ambitious men will not be attracted to a party which preserves an honourable station in limbo.

Such a view would be at odds with the atmosphere leading up to the 1969 election. While Dr David Thornley believed that there was much that could be achieved in holding the balance of power, others who were joining, or rejoining, the party believed that we were at a moment when the great popular will would sweep away the conservative parties, as had happened to the Irish Party at the beginning of the twentieth century. I clearly recall such a view prevailing at a heady event in Liberty Hall, when Dr Conor Cruise-O'Brien announced that he would be a candidate in the 1969 election for the Labour Party.

Significantly, before that election, Dr David Thornley and Basil Chubb had provided an extraordinary service for democracy. In 1968, just a few years after television became available in Ireland, they were able, as political scientists, to analyse the consequences of changing the voting system from proportional representation (single transferrable vote in multi-seat constituencies) to a first-past-the-post system. The result was a popular rejection of the Fianna Fáil government's proposal.

Dr David Thornley was by now a well-known broadcaster, talented, informed and handsome. He had entered the public world and, insofar as he had written of his belief in the future of the Labour Party, had connections with the trade-union movement. He saw no contradiction between being a trade unionist and a first-rate academic in an Elizabethan institution, and it was logical that he would in time become a Labour Party candidate.

There is then, I believe, much earlier, in *Isaac Butt and Home Rule*, an indication that Dr David Thornley would cross the bridge to the public world, as Hannah Arendt might have put it, and that he knew not only what it promised, but what it threatened as well.

To have written so well of the pressures on Isaac Butt that arose from the need forced on him to practise his profession as a lawyer, the transition from academic life to that of a parliamentarian was well understood by Dr David Thornley. Nevertheless, in the telling of the consequences of Butt's absences from Parliament, however understandable, Thornley stresses both the importance of the parliamentary vehicle and the popular unhappiness about the neglect in relation to the opportunities it offered. In his study of Isaac Butt, Dr David Thornley gives little time to Butt's lifestyle, even his tendency to dissipation – not unconnected to his indebtedness – which created difficulties for Butt and his disorderly and unpredictable parliamentary bunch of Home Rule supporters.

Much earlier than the work on the 1968 referendum, Dr David Thornley had written an article for a Tuairim pamphlet published by its Dublin branch entitled *The European Challenge: Its Social, Legal and Political Prospects*. This article shows him to be not only an able pamphleteer but also an optimistic pragmatist. He introduced his article, entitled 'Political Prospects', as follows:

> The movement towards European unity starts off with one tremendous asset upon its side – its power as an emotive concept. The idea of Europe is older than Gladstone, older than Dante, older than Charlemagne; as old, perhaps, as Rome itself. All of us subscribe to it, to a greater or lesser extent. To Arnold Toynbee, the scholarly weakness of Western historical writing is its great pre-occupation with self: history is a process that started in Italy, religion an emotion born in Palestine, politics and exercise in self-contemplation first undertaken in Greece in the fifth century BC. Before me, the barbarian; after me, the deluge; in between – Europe.

He went on to suggest that 'far below this barrage of idealism exists a working political institution. It is run by practical men – professional civil servants, professional economists, and politicians.'

What follows is an incisive analysis of all the options for Europe, from carefully protected national sovereignties to federalism. The dangers of technocracy are considered, and a detailed discussion of not just Irish and British membership, but also of enlargement in general in terms of decision-making, is made. The article ends with the conclusion:

> To the political scientist, the coming together of Europe is one of the greatest developments of twentieth-century politics, if it succeeds – and it surely must if politics as we know them are to endure – and the pattern which it painfully and pragmatically works out must become the unit of political organisation for many years to come. For these reasons, the great debates of Europe have more than a passing political interest; they are undoubtedly determining the form which politics will take for the future. No one can, or should, resist the fascination of this great argument.

Unfortunately, when Dr David Thornley came to European politics, his health had failed, and while he was to throw himself into committee work, the demands of travel, and of a lifestyle that was now becoming more transient, would hasten his untimely death.

To have the impulse to go beyond the role of narrator, to be seduced by the urge to contribute to the public space of one's own times, is easy to understand in somebody who instinctively operated from the values which Dr David Thornley had, and which were revealed in his popular writing. There is in his academic work, too, a mischievous pleasure in describing the excitement, the confrontations, the music of the bands, the banners, and the clash of factions at such events as the centenary celebrations in Dublin of the birth of Daniel O'Connell, which ended in a great fiasco, with the gas lights being turned off and the organisers walking away from the banquet as crowds called for a speech from Isaac Butt. I am left with the impression that Dr David Thornley had a fine sense of fiasco, and a sense of humour that enabled him to appreciate the black humour of some of those fiascos which he himself created.

It is tempting on reflection to see how much Dr David Thornley took from the subject of his biography into his own life. Indeed, in a similar way, one might might discern much of the pessimism of Edmund Burke in Conor Cruise-O'Brien's magisterial life of Burke, entitled *The Great Melody*, translated at times into Dr O'Brien's political vision. David's life was too short, and we cannot but speculate on what a contribution he might have made had he, for example, been given the opportunity of reforming the education system.

To have delivered one's talents into the public arena with generosity is an achievement in itself. The poet Paul Durcan, in his poem 'In

Memory of Dr David Thornley', written just a week after David's death, ends with the lines:

> Thinking of you, you, you,
> I both heard and saw
> In a rosebush the chuckle of a thrush.

Those of us who knew him will want to hold on to such an image, hoping that such a wry chuckle in reaction to absurdity and the futile contradictions of possibility unrealised represents the triumph of what is human over tedious and predictable circumstance.

Michael D. Higgins, TD was Chairman of the Labour Party from 1977 to 1987. He was first elected to the Dail for the constituency of Galway West in 1981. He was Minister for Arts, Culture and the Gaeltacht from 1993 to 1997, was elected President of the Labour Party in 2003 and is the party's spokesperson on Foreign Affairs. He is honorary Adjunct Professor at Large in Political Science and Sociology at the National University of Ireland, Galway. He is also an author and poet.

PART TWO

DAVID THORNLEY'S ESSAYS

15

IRELAND: THE END OF AN ERA?

DAVID THORNLEY

Any discussion of change over the last century, or the last fifty years, in Ireland, should have firm roots in sociological survey of group habits and attitudes. It should take into account factors not merely like changing patterns of employment, but like changing patterns of leisure. Shifts in population density, axes of communications – these are obviously basic to the problems. But so also are issues like class structure. How far are British or European, or American patterns of class division and of transfusion from class to class, reproduced in Ireland? Has the balance of classes in Ireland undergone any substantial change in the last fifty years? In the last twenty years? And with this inescapably go questions of cultural change. How far has Ireland developed an identifiably indigenous culture? And how far are its cultural values borrowed from British or European or American cultural mass-production?

In fact, of course, this survey must of necessity possess, at best, an interim justification. It will not be able to answer all or even most of these fundamental questions. It will fail to do so for two closely related reasons.

In the first place, the compilation of statistics is relatively an infant science in this country. Faced with the challenge of increased economic competition we are being compelled to catch up very quickly with our continental neighbours. Inevitably, we must concentrate first upon those areas of the unknown where our most immediate pitfalls may lie. These naturally tend to be in the field of economics. In so far as statistical patterns are emerging which can be correlated over the last twenty years, they lie in this area. But equally, a considerable amount of expert interpretation of recent economic development in Ireland is readily available. This study would fail, even in its limited purposes if it were to attempt to recover such territory. Beyond, then, passing references to factors like changing employment patterns, it will endeavour to avoid strictly economic issues.

This essay is then primarily concerned with what might be called sociological and political change – changes in manners and methods, in attitudes and in thinking, changes in the human animal rather than in the infrastructure in which he is set.

Here we have a much more neglected field, and one in which a contribution could most usefully be made. Unfortunately, the neglect is a well-founded one; it is based upon an almost total lack of the essential data upon which firm conclusions can legitimately be drawn or projections made. If modern economic planning is a relatively youthful science in this country, professional sociology of the kind engaged in so enthusiastically in America and to some extent in Europe is even less widely practised. There are few 'profiles' of community areas; there are no studies of power, still less of class. Within the last two years the belated advent of television to a rural community presented a unique opportunity to study changing cultural patterns in a context of universal validity. Full advantage was scarcely taken of this opportunity.

This lack of data has, of course, never inhibited the drawing of emotional conclusions and the pronouncement of generalisations. The clichés of nationalist amateur sociology are second nature to us all; phrases like 'Irish culture'; pious self-congratulation on the relative non-existence in Ireland of 'materialism', whatever that is. Rightly or wrongly, we are daily given the clearest of pictures of our way of life. We are shown a country which has somehow managed to combine uniquely a revolution in its attitudes to growth and productivity with the preservation of the simple, unsophisticated and familial virtues of a rural and deeply Catholic community.

In fact, of course, this is nonsense. Remarkably little is known of the social breakdown of the country in which we live. One has only to think of the prevailing flood of 'fashionable' popular sociology in other countries to realize this dearth in Ireland. In England, Michael Young on the meritocracy, Shank's *Stagnant Society*, and Sampson's *Anatomy of Britain*; in the United States immensely popular works on social values and class attitudes by people like Whyte, Packard, and Wright Mills.

Nothing at all of this kind has been attempted in the Irish context. And yet, in fact, are not Irish executives more subject to the stresses familiar to American 'organisation man' than to Joycean self-analysis or Gaelic nationalism? Have the problems of Irish trade unionists not far more in common with those of the Woodcocks (of which they are scarcely widely knowledgeable) than those of the Connollys and Larkins whom they ritually revere?

It is, in short, salutary to stress at the outset the fog of ignorance which surrounds this subject. We are only beginning to produce good native studies of our formal decision-making institutions like the Oireachtas and of the state-sponsored bodies. As far as this writer is aware, we have not a single study of the informal decision-making bodies like pressure groups, and virtually none of community 'elites', a vital subject in the analysis of power. We have no large-scale study of class structure in Ireland. Finally, and to an Irish Catholic trained as an historian, incomprehensibly, we have not as yet any professional study of the Catholic Church in Ireland as a social and political influence – only scattered works of polemic like Mr Blanshard's.

Of its very essence, this essay cannot be anything like the integrated study which is really needed. It can only be another piece of intuition prone to all the shortcomings of subjective reasoning. Its most useful function is perhaps less to provide the answers than to point to the really big questions. Having attempted to limit the potentialities of this essay in advance, one may perhaps attempt to set this concept of 'change' within some kind of contextual framework. The concept of change carries with it an implication of historical relativity. Change, in other words, from what?

This is the point at which to offer counsels against exaggerated assumptions. In many ways the picture of an 'Irish way of life', characteristically national, rural, Catholic, and unsophisticated is not merely a myth now, but always was a myth. It is a mistake, albeit an attractive one, to presume some concrete nineteenth-century yardstick. Nineteenth-century Ireland bore many of the signs of British provincial civilization. Dublin, the days of its Georgian glory ended by the Act of Union, probably resembled Manchester more than it did itself of the previous century. To Dublin theatres like the Royal and the Gaiety came actors like J. L. Toole and singers like Therese Tietjens and Lilian Nordica when they had exhausted the potentiality of the London season. It was as easy at least for the upper middle class to commute to and from London as it is today. Irish had already ceased to be the spoken language of any significant proportion of the people. The old O'Connellite repealer, W. J. O'Neill

Daunt, who lived in retirement on his small estate in Kilcascan, County Cork, wrote in his diary for 18 March 1872:

> The gradual dying out of the Irish language in this part of the country has often given me a pang. In my young days, and indeed much later – up to the time of the potato famine – Irish was the pre-dominant language at fair and market, in the field, in the kitchen, in the country shop, on the top of the public coach; the language of Catholic sermons, and of prayers before Mass. The last time a class of children were instructed in Irish catechism was in 1865.

With the Irish language died out the folk tradition of Gaelic culture in speech and song; it was not to return until it was self-consciously and synthetically revived by the work of Anglo-Irish intellectuals like Yeats and Dowden in the field of literature, and Hughes and Harty in that of music. Dublin was in short very much like the provincial tuppence-half-penny-looking-down-on-tuppence city which provoked the diverse antagonisms of Joyce on the one hand, and the Gaelic Leaguer on the other. Daunt continually bewailed the decline of architectural standards, writing in 1873 of a 'frightful excrescence' in Westmoreland Street. It was, after all, a pre-revolutionary Dublin Corporation which sanctioned the abomination of the 'loop-line' over the Liffey. Far from being the home of Catholic morality, Dublin suffered the social consequences of its status as a mid-Victorian garrison town. In between its nationalist rhetoric, the *Nation* newspaper, throughout the 60s and 70s lamented the fact that it was impossible for a respectable woman to make her way unmolested down Grafton Street late in the evening. North of the quays lay the brothels of Joyce's night-town.

Again, long before the television set, the pace of emigration, both permanent and (sociologically as interesting) seasonal was making the ways of New York, London, Birmingham, and Glasgow the criteria of popular mores. Between 1841 and 1911 the population of Ireland declined from over eight million to less than five-and-a-half million. Most of this emigration was from the rural areas of the south and west. Can one imagine that the unity of parish community life escaped this unparalleled shock only to wilt suddenly before the alleged stresses of modern times?

This essay opened with a warning about the lack of data from which one can legitimately assess change in Ireland. It is equally necessary to point to the dangers of exaggerating the extent of change by inventing some pre-machine, pre-television golden age of social stability. It never existed. Ireland changed violently between 1600 and 1700, between 1800 and 1900. And, like Oscar Wilde's Oxford, it has never been what it used to be.

That warning is by way of a corrective. Having made it, one can legitimately admit, however, that the Ireland which existed just before the advent of the state, bore certain unifying characteristics. It retained, despite the inroads of the famine, a predominantly rural society whose industrial sector in the period between the union and the turn of the century was fractional and localised in a few areas. It remained an unsophisticated and sternly (if superficially) moralising society. 'Looked through a novel by Ouida', noted Daunt in 1875. 'The hero is the quintessence of vicious frivolity, and the authoress seems to be a w—.' In the rural areas even more than in the cities it was a society in which the closeness of community links was emphasized by the rigidity of religious and class divisions. O'Connell in the Emancipation and Repeal movements had made the parish clergy the natural leaders of their communities. It was a position that was never to be lost, but only eroded by the weakening of parish ties themselves. It is difficult to exaggerate the political role of the nineteenth-century clergy. 'If you should happen to meet with any Catholic elector,' the Bishop of Ossory told the men of Kilkenny in 1868:

> I cannot believe you will – who would not vote for John Gray – who would even vote against him – say nothing offensive; but you can conscientiously tell that voter that he is committing grievous sin in so doing, because he thereby co-operates in continuing injustice to his religion and his country, which is a very serious sin indeed.

In class the divisions were similarly clear and difficult to pass over. The big house dominated the village; the gentry were mostly Anglo-Irish and Protestant; one landlord like the Marquess of Conyngham could own 150,000 acres of his country. In Dublin the grip of Protestants upon commercial power was reflected not merely in the endurance of names like Pim, Dockrell, Eason and Switzer but in the fact that unionist candidates could still secure election there well into the twentieth century.

The clarity and unsophistication of class and religious divisions reflected itself in a succession of clear-cut political crises. Catholic Emancipation, Repeal, the Famine, tenant rights, Fenianism, disestablishment, the Land War, and Home Rule successively taught the masses where their political duty unanimously and excitingly lay. At the end of the century the name of the dead Parnell was enough to explain most of the divisions of constitutional politics; Joyce's 'Ivyday in the Committee Room' catches all the shining masochism of the last decade of Victorian Irish politics.

In short, it seems that tentatively and provisionally one can draw some kind of relative yardstick for subsequent change from nineteenth-century Ireland. It was a period marked by intense and dearly demarcated divisions of class, politics, and religion. But, at the same time it was itself a period of transition, a period already subject to the crosscurrents of emigration and cosmopolitan influence.

The effect of the first fifty years of this century, containing as they do the first thirty years of independent statehood, was to remove some of these historic characteristics but equally to enhance others. The old class structure broke down. Under the stress of the Land War, the successive land acts of the late nineteenth century and early twentieth century, and the social tensions of the period from 1919-21, the Anglo-Irish aristocracy disappeared as a force of numerical, social or economic significance. Secondly, the effect of the success of the physical force movement was to create, through organs like the literary revival, the Abbey Theatre, the Gaelic League, and the Gaelic Athletic Association, a synthetic cultural nationalism of which little trace can be found before, say, Sir Samuel Ferguson. Finally, and most obviously, there was the equally self-conscious stimulation of Irish industry, with its necessary consequences upon the employment patterns, the standard of living, and the social conditions of the people.

On the other hand, many of the factors which have been picked out here as characteristic of 'nineteenth-century Ireland' survived into modern times. To the pattern of emigration to England and to America, the political fact of statehood has been an irrelevance. If the population no longer drops as momentously as in the last century, this only implies that it has been stabilised at a figure little more than a third that of 1841 and little more than a half that of 1871. Ireland still, at least until a few years ago, exported virtually its entire natural increase. Politics, until very recent times, remained equally dominated by the stereotypes of crisis-nationalism. The revolutionary movement, the civil war, the cry to 'open the gaol-gates', the Economic War, the Border, even the last World War, 'emigration' itself, were issues to which the historical past rather than the present or the future provided the definition of electoral loyalty. Even industrial change had the emotion of Sinn Féin's economic nationalism as its foster-parent.

Thirdly, the character of popular religion, the importance of which can scarcely be exaggerated in a state 95 percent of whose citizens are Catholics, was affected little by political change. The shock of first revolution and then civil war, with the formal if temporary censure of half the country's political leaders, was somehow absorbed by the enormous resilience of the folk-church. When the dust had settled the parish priests were scarcely less the leaders of their communities than they had been in pre-Fenian times. Indeed, the vacuum left by the old aristocracy drew them, if anything, still closer to the centre of community decision-making. Their social and cultural eminence automatically brought them to the chairmanship of cultural, athletic and economic community organisations. The British government had historically recognised their status by tacitly incorporating them in the local management of its national education system. The twentieth century still found them playing a significant part in social and political life. In the field of social philosophy, Ireland, indeed, arguably goes through a period of retrenchment from 1920-50. Labour is much less socialist in the constitution of 1952 than it was in its programme of 1918 when it called for the 'democratic management and control of all industries and services by the whole body of the workers' and 'the ownership and control of the produce of their labour'. Fianna Fáil is arguably less socially radical in the immediately post-war era of the wages standstill order and the anti-communist scare which had precipitated the temporary splitting of the Labour Party into two sections, than it was in 1927 or 1932.

Of necessity, this essay has so far taken some of the character of a cautionary tale. It does not however seek to suggest that no change, or even little change, has taken place in Ireland in the last fifty years. What it does suggest is that folk attitudes to social and even political change are fundamentally flawed. They start from a semi-mythological concept of the past which may never in fact have existed – a kind of 'Once upon a time, and a very good time it was'. This they lay against a concept of the present similarly coloured by class, political and religious biases. For change to be accurately evaluated two constituents are vital. The first is that the past should have been rationally and objectively explained by historical scholarship. The second is that the present should have been professionally explored by sociology and political science. Despite much devoted work, and recent progress, none of these disciplines as yet prevails sufficiently widely in Ireland. Change is popularly conceived of as a struggle between religion and 'materialism', between country and town, between parish and dormitory suburb, between 'national culture' and cosmopolitanism. This study has so far endeavoured to argue that such contrasts are invalid because the antitheses are partly false, because the extent of change has been in certain aspects exaggerated and coloured by pessimism and wishful thinking, and finally, because the process of change has been a continuous one, and one which is affected as much by, for example, a century-old force like emigration as by the superficial political revolution of national statehood. Even the most cursory study of the development of say, local government or education immediately reveals a continuity barely touched by the coming of the new state.

It is, however, a sterile pastime to criticise the popular mythology of change, unless one is prepared to try to provide some alternative evaluation. To this task the remainder of this essay is devoted. After the criticisms which I have already made, I would be naive in the extreme to propound alternative 'turning-points' and historical moments-of-truth as substitutes for those which I have already attempted to discredit. But without accepting either the historical climacterics of the Whig historians or the blast-offs of Mr Rostow, it is possible to argue that a significant acceleration in the pace of change is discernable in the last fifteen years. And five good reasons, of both a positive and a negative kind, can be put forward for the ascription of a special significance to the years 1948-51.

In the first place, the year 1948 saw the first fundamental shaking of the citadel of Fianna Fáil. Much that was good was accomplished in those sixteen years of Fianna Fáil hegemony and it is not within the province of this essay to make value judgments about Irish politics, but one can fairly state that from 1932 until 1948 Fianna Fáil could, rightly or wrongly, view itself as a 'National movement', as the heir to the continuity of Sinn Féin, assigned to history with the working out of the national will. Since 1948 the realization has been ever more dearly forced upon Fianna Fáil that it must in the future access its performance by the criteria not of a national independence movement, but of a twentieth-century political party, whose overall majorities must not be waited for but worked for.

Secondly, in 1949 the passing of the Republic of Ireland Act saw the beginning of the end of Fine Gael as the heir to the anti-republican vote. Until that year it had been the party for which the middle-class white-collar voter who had never, perhaps, been wholly enthusiastic about the guerilla methods of the committed republican minority, could give his political loyalty. It had been the party to which the ex-Unionist could turn as the second-best-bed of order and propriety. The Republic of Ireland

Act, and to a lesser extent the Mother and Child Controversy of 1951, imposed upon Fine Gael a similar obligation to that newly-forced upon Fianna Fáil – the obligation to re-define itself by the social and economic criteria of modern politics rather than the constitutional criteria of nationalist history.

Thirdly, 1948 witnessed the last really effective intervention in Irish political life of a characteristic form of radical republicanism. Clann na Poblachta, a brand new party born in that seminary of social and republican ideas, the internment camp, scored a remarkable triumph in winning 175,000 votes and ten seats in its first election. It was a success only partially explicable by electoral boredom; the Fianna Fáil vote fell by only 40,000 as against the 1944 election; those of Fine Gael and Labour rose. No one, probably, will ever be able to tell precisely where those 175,000 Clann na Poblachta votes came from. But a survey of that election does suggest that the new party drew the basis of its strength from two historic sources; implacable republicanism on the one hand, and on the other a social radicalism none the less deeply felt because it was philosophically unrationalised. The very marriage of these two strands was in itself traditional; it expressed an association of ideas implicit in the thought of old Fenians like John Daly and later republicans like Liam Mellowes. Historically, it assumed that to be on the side of constitutional change was to be on the side of social change. This was an assumption whose illogicality had been exposed in the Thermidorean reaction of the 1920's. It was exposed again in 1951 when the new party was shattered by a social issue whose implications it was simply not equipped to contain.

But again, the circumstances in which Clann na Poblachta fragmented were, in their way, as much as an historic milestone as those of its initial success. 1951 saw what was perhaps the last of the head-on confrontations between a politician and the Church. It was a conflict which harked back to the nineteenth century – to Lucas and Gavan Duffy, to the Papal Rescript and the Plan of Campaign, to Parnell's divorce. It is impossible to believe that such a confrontation could ever again occur within precisely those terms – the Church offering an absolute *non fiat* to a political proposal; a layman remaining obdurate and suffering dismissal from power; the *Irish Times* speaking up for secular liberalism and the Ulster Unionists drawing the exaggerated historical moral that Carson was right. If a similar issue were ever to occur again, who can doubt that our greater political sophistication would allow it to be resolved in a much less extrovert fashion?

175

Finally, one may validly add to these points the reflection that it is not until 1948 that the sway of the political pendulum begins to operate in Irish elections. It has been remarked with some truth that the civil war, with all its attendant disadvantages to our country, nevertheless bequeathed it at least the form if not necessarily the substance of two-party democracy. But this statement can be qualified. It could well be argued that Ireland witnessed one-party government from 1922-32 and again from 1932-48. Since the Reform Act of 1832, no British party has enjoyed so long a period of unbroken power as Fianna Fáil. 'Pendulum' politics were only truly effective from 1948-61. It is useful to recall this; it reminds us that there is no inevitability in the future dispositions of Irish politics.

These five points may then, perhaps, be put forward as evidence of a discernible acceleration of the pace of change in the period 1948-51. The period since then seems to this writer increasingly dominated by a series of novel political factors.

The first and most obvious of these is the retirement from political authority of the principal leaders of the civil war and immediately suc-ceeding eras. Not one of the three main political parties has retained its leader of fifteen years before.

Secondly, and scarcely less obviously, political controversy has sud-denly and quietly become permeated by the explicit, if not necessarily well-understood acceptance of the principle that the maintenance of eco-nomic growth is the first charge upon political administration. This is in itself a minor philosophical revolution as against the eras of laissez-faire in the 1920s and the protection of private enterprise in the 1930s. The catalyst here has admittedly been largely external; it is the apparent inevitability of the Common Market rather than native experiment which has imposed rethinking. But whatever the reason, the economic national-ism of Sinn Féin is dead as the policy of the state. What is remarkable almost to the point of incredibility is the passiveness with which this change has been accepted inside a single generation.

These new concepts of the responsibility of the community, through the state, in relation to economic growth are imposing yet a third recon-sideration of social philosophy. It is increasingly coming to be realised that the achievement of standards of education and social welfare com-parable to those of the rest of Western Europe is not merely a matter for ethical debate and budgetary calculation. Where concepts of social responsibility could not always move the community in the past, it is now being slowly recognised that niggardliness towards health, mental illness, housing, old age, and above all education, is ultimately inefficient and wasteful of natural resources in competitive terms. This fact is not simply ironic. It provides corroboration of the warnings given earlier in this essay about the pitfalls attendant upon the application of facile philosophical generalisations to radical groups. As membership of the European Economic Community moves ever closer, there can be little doubt that the Irish state will rationally and without major controversy come to accept a degree of social obligation in these spheres which would have provoked bitter disagreement fifteen years ago; it will accept that it cannot continue to spend 6 percent of the national income on welfare services as against 22 percent in West Germany. And when it does so its motives will owe less either to Karl Marx or, I am afraid, to Catholic social teaching than to J. M. Keynes and J. K. Galbraith.

There is a fourth and final factor which frames the politics of this age. The factor is the pontificate of Pope John XXIII. It is an historical fact that the Church has been an influence in favour of tradition rather than innovation in Irish society. Hierarchically it adopted on the whole an attitude of reserve towards every nationalist movement since O'Connell, towards the land agitation, and to what have seemed to it the excesses of socialist philosophy. This was, no doubt, in the very nature of the Church, its historically inevitable and politically proper role. But the modernising tendencies of the present Pontiff and of his great predecessor, and the influence of the historic encyclicals *Mater et Magistra* and *Pacem in Terris*, have redrawn the frame of social thinking in a predominantly Catholic community such as that of Ireland. The 'air of spring' which, as His Grace the Most Rev. Dr Conway has said, blows so excitingly through the fields of ecumenism and liturgical reform, can be breathed no less in that of social reform. It would be hard to exaggerate the importance of this stimulus in a community which historically manifests so close an interrelationship of religious and political leadership.

These last four points present a picture of an exciting age, an age of rapid change. To a great extent this may be a fair picture. But is it true without qualification to speak of this as an 'age of change'? Is such language superficially at odds with the warnings against simplification presented at the outset of this essay?

There is, in fact, something of a dichotomy between the apparent scepticism of the opening of this essay and the apparent enthusiasm of its view of the last fifteen years. It is a dichotomy simply explained. In the middle of its course, this discussion shifted its emphasis from what were to some extent sociological considerations, to those of political decision-making. But there is in fact no reason at all why change in society should go *pari-passu* with change in the thinking of administrators or even of politicians. There may be change in the criteria of decision-making at the top; change in social habits at the bottom. But unless these two are bridged by the mutual education of the democratic process, communication between the top and bottom may cease. And in Ireland, where the stimulus to change is to a great extent external, something like this may in fact be happening.

The nub of the argument is this. It is easy for a minority in administration, in politics, in the Church, and in academic life, who may be to a greater or lesser extent committed to the decision-making process, to be alive to the tensions of novelty. As they read the reports of the Committee on Industrial Organisation and the bulletins from the Vatican Council, they may all too readily assume that both the material upon which their thinking is based, and the response which they make to it, are the currency of public opinion. But change is in fact to some extent subjective; it gains much of its impetus from the conviction that it is both necessary and imminently feasible. It is not enough to ask if we have changed; we must also ask if we think we have changed. And that last 'we' must not mean simply the 'elites', the 'controllers', the academics. The political society in which the holders of power lag behind the instincts of the community falls prey to revolution. But if the decision-makers respond more quickly to the challenge of change than the masses, the continuing vitality of democracy turns essentially upon their capacity to communicate their convictions to society. If the new convictions are not sufficiently strongly held and rationally understood in the key areas of party political power and administrative authority, or if the mass of the people, largely deprived of secondary, technical, and university education and congenitally sceptical of their political masters, turns a jaundiced ear to the new rhetoric, democracy in that society does not shatter in revolution. It wanes in political apathy. If the study of change in Ireland over the last fifteen years adduces evidence of a single pitfall, it is surely that. It is not enough for leaders to know what to do and have courage enough to do it. They must be able to persuade the electorate of the necessity of what they are doing. This, if anywhere, is where leadership that is otherwise good has failed in Ireland.

A corrective to a too-simplified assumption of change in Ireland might then be to re-examine, briefly, the real extent of change, not in what may now be seen as the excessively narrow context of politico-economic speculation, but at the very grass-roots of our society. To attempt this exercise is to return from the safety of the abstraction to the rash task of making sociological bricks largely without straw. It is, however,the logical conclusion to which one is carried by the preceding argument. It would be cowardice to postpone its performance. It would be arrogance not to admit, in advance, its interim nature and its intuitive shortcomings.

One may, however, put forward a few contentions for which the evidence seems reasonably incontrovertible. For example, it is clear that the historical character of Ireland as a 'rural' community is weakening slowly but surely under the impetus of economic change. Between 1957 and 1961 the number of people employed in agriculture, forestry and fishing fell from 433,000 to 409,000 or roughly 6 percent. Between 1957 and 1962 the number of people engaged in the production of transportable goods alone rose from just under 150,000 to just over 170,000, an increase of 13 percent. The Second Economic Programme anticipates that by 1970 there will be more people employed in every aspect of industry than in agriculture, and that less than 29 percent of our people will be employed on the land. It is equally clear that this trend is logically paralleled by a frightening alteration in the ratio of the population of Dublin to that of the rest of the country. The population of Ireland fell from just under 5.5 million to 2.8 million between 1874 and 1961. In the same period the population of Dublin City rose from 265,000 to almost 600,000. There are now more people in Dún Laoghaire than in the city of Limerick. And, finally, it is equally clear that within the relatively small population which the independent state has been able to retain, real standards of living are rising. Between 1953 and 1962 wages in transportable industry rose by 63.3 per cent, wages in agriculture by 50.3 per cent. In the same period consumer prices rose by 25.3 per cent. In the last ten years the number of motor vehicles on Irish roads has more than doubled. In 1970 there will be one passenger car to every eight to ten people – the same figure as obtained in Britain in 1960. Even allowing for other factors, it is evident that some, at least, of the conditions of affluence prevail increasingly in Ireland, and with them some of the problems.

When one attempts to assess the consequences of these factual changes, one moves on to less sure ground. Many more people take continental summer holidays than did so ten years before. They must bring back from the capital cities of Europe, and from its beaches, some recol-lection of the mores of races whose social attitudes stem from traditions and assumptions fundamentally different from those of Ireland. Many families have welcomed these influences to their very hearths through the medium of television. Much has been said and written on the moral con-sequences of television, and it is not within the scope of this essay to attempt an evaluation of them. But one point is relevant to the theme of change. The advent of television underlines the assumption of inevitabil-ity which now seems to have dramatically replaced the concepts of Sinn Féin where external influences are concerned. No greater barrier has ever been imposed upon any attempt at either moral censorship or cultural discrimination against foreign influences than the sheer inability of the native television network to produce enough material to fill its own schedules.

These are perhaps the most obviously striking social changes. There are others no less important which we have scarcely begun to study pro-fessionally. The drinking habits of the Irish, one of the themes of the communal existence, are undergoing a quiet revolution. Twenty years ago the typical Irish drinker was male; he stood on a stone floor, with his male friends, at a long wooden bar, in uncomfortable and unhygienic surround-ings, drinking stout or whisky; at home, his wife made his dinner and minded his children. Now the public-houses themselves are rebuilt on every side; they are deeply carpeted, darkly lit and equipped with arm-chairs; soft subliminal music plays endlessly on mighty self-changing tapes. Into these establishments come many more women, many more young people, and many more family groups. Increasingly they patronise light lagers which imported advertising assures them to be the appropri-ate family drink. More are beginning to drink wines with their meals; wines which they often buy in large groceries or in wine-shops. Will twen-ty years more see the importation of still further British and (to some extent American) drinking habits – the off-licences, the 'telly-beer' in screw tops and cans?

These questions are not frivolous. It is with such things, and not with political or economic philosophies, that the daily lives of affluent soci-eties are for better or worse filled. But a more interesting symbol of afflu-ence in this country is perhaps the increasing development of the class structure. Like most immediately post-revolutionary societies Ireland was left in the 1920s and 1930s with something of a class vacuum. The old Anglo-Irish caste had lost its pre-eminence; it had no immediate successor. In a typically post-revolutionary manner a 'hair-shirt' reaction, a contempt for the social forms of the old aristocracy, temporarily held some sway. But now a second generation, and a third, is growing up in the families of the revolutionary leaders, of the early captains of administration and of newly-founded industry, a generation which is provided with private secondary education which its grandparents scarcely enjoyed, and renews accordingly concepts of class leisure and manners.

In 1951–2 just over 50,000 pupils were enrolled in Irish secondary schools; in 1958-9 that figure had risen to just under 70,000 – an increase of just under 40 percent. This increase is explicable only by rising standards of living, increasing numbers of children in the secondary-school age group, and growing appreciation of the competitive advantages of secondary education; we are not spending substantially more on education. In 1961 public expenditure on all branches of education in Ireland was 17 dollars per head – one-third that of the United Kingdom. According to UNESCO statistics published in 1962 and covering the period from 1955 to 1957, the proportion of Irish children between fifteen and nineteen years of age enrolled in secondary, vocational, or technical schools was 36 percent. The proportion in Northern Ireland was 75 percent and in England and Wales 88 percent. At the same time it has been estimated that there may be some 30 percent more in the age bracket 17-23 in Ireland in 1966 than there were in 1961. The social waste implicit in these statistics is too obvious to need repetition. In the political sphere, it is a contributory factor in the breakdown of communication between the decision-makers and the electorate. As politics becomes less and less concerned with emotional stereotypes and more and more concerned with complex economic issues it is ever more difficult to communicate its relevance to democracy. Politics should be a channel of direct communication; in Ireland it must more often be a continuous translation service. The constituency organization of our parties, the divisive influence of PR and the nineteenth-century character of our local politics, combine to make 'constituency service' the touchstone of electoral success. J. K. Galbraith would not be elected for an Irish constituency unless he were prepared, firstly, to hack his way through the undergrowth of the constituency machine, and thereafter, to demonstrate his zeal to his constituents by devoting the greater portion of his time to the battering of the administration on their behalf with petitions which are more often than not either superfluous or improper. And it is the victims of this machine who must form cabinets. If our legislators are to be both economic geniuses and keep their seats, they must develop the rare virtue of controlled schizophrenia. At least they must do so until the state or the political parties provide them with the secretarial services of trained social workers.

Perhaps in no democracy is all the truth told to all the people all the time. But in our system the combination of economics at the top, constituency politics in the middle, and semi-literacy at the bottom, attenuates the supply to the point of night-starvation. Our people have a vague comprehension that we must be competitive now, just as we had to be protected in the 30s and 40s. But are they being educated to the full implications of this revolution? Can they be made to understand that in the competitive future the size of the economic farm unit, and the number of families which can be rooted on the land, will be determined by the criteria of the Common Market rather than the Land League? That in industry no sentimental objection can be opposed to the principle that the worker must to a great extent go where the job is rather than vice versa?

In short, in so far as any conclusive picture can be drawn, the period in which we are now living in Ireland seems to me a transitional one, a valley between two generations. The economic ideas which effectively determine our fates are new; but the party machines which must ratify them are still in great measure survivals from different epochs and different arguments. The religious ideas are new; the parish unit is itself suffering yet another assault as our people flee from the land to the great wen of Dublin; the pristine simplicity which our faith inherited from penal times is both exposed to and stimulated by the draught of new ideas, brought from the Council, and from the theologians of Europe by the press, by television, and by publications like the *Furrow*, *Studies*, *Christus Rex*, *Doctrine* and *Life*. Our culture is ever more imported and cosmopolitan in practice even as it remains Gaelic in theory; the intellectuals want to see Beckett, Genet, Pinter, Ionesco. The state subsidizes Gaelic pantomime; the masses want to see Bat Masterson and the Donna Reed show. The state has neither the money nor the resolution to thwart them, but it pays continuous lip service to the principle that it would if it could.

Finally, in politics, a devoted handful of twentieth-century men essay the painful, uphill struggle of educating their followers to the realisation that growth-rates and schools are more important than getting a boreen macadammed or fixing a road mender's job. They are confronted by almost insuperable obstacles. Their own followers see no reason to alter

182

techniques which served them faithfully in the heady days of '32. The voters, uneducated, apathetic, grasping at a little (perhaps transient) prosperity, are jaded with the prolongation of the old slogans into the present. Many cry 'wolf, wolf' as they pass the polling-booths; many enter them only to register a negative, disgruntlement vote, or express gratitude to the deputy who wrote a letter for them.

This essay has attempted, in effect, to argue three things. Firstly that the pace of change between 1922 and 1945 has been both positively and negatively exaggerated in romantic history. Secondly, that in the period 1948 to 1951 we can see the first clear suggestion that the frame in which the immediately post-revolutionary society had set was beginning to crack. Thirdly, that in the period from the publication of the First Economic Programme up to the present time, we can see the stirrings of those political, economic, and social changes which were held back by the civil war, Sinn Féin, and by the unsophistication of our social philosophy.

If this thesis is correct, we are for the first time at the threshold of delayed peaceful, social revolution. It would be foolhardy to go on to predict its course. But a number of developments seem reasonably assured. It seems certain that our island will become affected increasingly by the spread of European social and philosophical ideas, strongly tinged with Catholicism. It is reasonably certain that many of the issues of education and social welfare will slowly be transplanted from the field of emotional controversy to that of economic efficiency, and that a great deal more money will be spent on both. It does seem certain that the depopulation of the countryside will continue and perhaps accelerate, and that our social habits and our politics will take on a flavour that is ever more urban, and, as a consequence, ever more cosmopolitan. And that this in turn will sound the death-knell of the attempt to preserve any kind of indigenous Gaelic folk culture in these islands.

In politics, it seems likely that the brief era of the political pendulum will come to a perhaps temporary end. It takes well over half a million votes to make an overall majority in Dáil Éireann. Only one party has secured such a vote since 1932, and in the last election that party won less first preference votes than in any contest since 1927. I do not believe that any of the three major parties can reasonably anticipate that it will make a practise of winning 550,000 votes in the elections of the next decade. If this is a correct prognosis, we can anticipate an era of coalition or minority government. But one thing seems not hypothetical but certain: the day of the movement, of the charismatic leader, is for better or worse dead. The future is with the type of politician exemplified by Wilson, Maudling, Erhardt, Brandt. Whatever palms are going will be the prize of the party which finds such leaders and convinces an apathetic electorate of their novelty and their genuineness.

Perhaps the greatest danger is that no party should succeed completely in the immediate future in performing this operation. If this is so, young talent will be siphoned off from the political parties into non-partisan political activity. There are signs of this process at work already. At what point are the really important decisions in Irish life being taken today? Few would deny that the publication of the first and second economic programmes were the most important political events of the last decade. Where were these policies hammered out? On the hustings? At the Ardfheiseanna of the political parties? In the columns of the press? In the Cabinet room? Or deep below the surface of politics, in a creative dialogue between a group of first-class non-partisan administrators and a handful of politicians who had enough courage and commonsense to recognise stark necessity when they saw it?

It is a welcome process in that it gives us good administration, and good administration gives us good decisions. It is better that the civil service should learn economics than that noone should. But if administration gives us five year plans, while democratic politics gives us an instant mix of vituperation and 'constituency service', democratic politics will come to seem a sideshow to the business of government, from which only the changeless and unchangeable minority of participants derive either amusement or profit. Amidst a record of much progress, that is a sombre possibility. If growth is to be a reality in this country, we must recognize that we cannot build an economic society for the seventies upon the basis of the social and political structure of the thirties. In the next twenty years, we are going to have to overhaul the politics and sociology of this republic, with as much objectivity as we are prepared to show in relation to economic problems.

16

Irish Government Observed

Basil Chubb and David Thornley

Last year, Professor Brian Chapman of the University of Manchester published an outspoken little book entitled British Government Observed. *It sparked off the sort of uninhibited controversy that every country benefits from occasionally. With this series, Professor Chubb and Dr Thornley, both political scientists of Trinity College, Dublin, hope to do the same.*

It may seem a truism to remark that democracy is a device by which we attempt to ensure that the maximum degree of consent is obtained from the maximum number of people in respect of the maximum amount of decision-making. It may also seem a truism to remark that this process depends upon the existence of three factors; discussion, voting and consent. Discussion, because unless the free play of argument has operated upon the controversies of decision-making, we are left without the basic requisite for the formation of public opinion. Voting, because no better device has yet been invented through which the consensus of the·community may be taken upon the terms under which it shall be ruled. Consent, because if the consent of the recalcitrant minority is lacking, the whole contingent sequence breaks down. If the minority is small, it breaks down in civil disobedience; if large, in civil war.

These may seem truisms, but in fact they contain the seeds of every difficulty with which modern democracy finds itself faced. Only in the Athenian city-state of classical antiquity, where the citizen body was small enough to participate in all the basic processes of decision-making, was the full implementation of these three principles possible. We have developed three concepts in modern Europe which condition the working of political democracy. Approximately five hundred years ago we arbitrarily invented the nation state. Approximately one hundred years ago we suddenly discovered that, previous historical practice notwithstanding, every adult, sane, law-abiding member of the national community had some kind of inalienable right to participate in the decision-making process. Approximately fifty years ago we began to have forced upon us the realisation that that process subsumed an ever-growing part of the direction of the economic functioning of society.

The full implications of that last development are still being worked out, and we shall return to them again and again in this series. But these three factors have led to one inescapable conclusion. The area of decision-making has grown so great that the mass of the people can only be invited to adjudicate upon a fraction of it.

Our concept of democracy has therefore to be redrawn. The people no longer decide their fate. At most, they decide upon that portion of their fate which is, firstly, physically susceptible to the slow processes of democratic decision-making and, secondly, intellectually within their comprehension. Neither of these categories is wholly absolute. There will, of course, be some issues so transient that popular opinion obviously cannot be brought to bear upon them; the state cannot hold a referendum every time it raises or lowers a tariff. There will, equally, be some issues upon which popular opinion is blatantly incompetent to adjudicate. The people may decide in principle if they want a state health service; they are not competent to decide if they need fluorine in their water. But, outside the obviously immediate and the obviously technical, there will be all the time a wide range of issues upon which the capacity of the people to adjudicate is a subject of hypothesis and of controversy. The range of modern politics is such that organs of synthesis are required between the complexity of atomistic, individual opinion at the bottom, and the parallel complexity of decision-making at the top. But an organ of synthesis is also an organ of selection. The mass of the people are not merely no longer able, if they ever were, to decide upon every issue of their own government. They are no longer free to determine upon which issues they will decide.

It is primarily to political parties, operating both locally at constituency level and centrally in the party councils and in the Oireachtas, that we look to provide this synthesis and to make this selection. The teleology of the political party is usually put forward something like this: 'despite the coming of universal suffrage, the participation of all the citizens in day-to-day politics is not practicable. Public opinion, in its naturally amorphous and atomistic form, is incapable of operating effectively upon the centres of power. The role of the party is to translate millions of slightly differing opinions into organised and potent forces capable of sustaining government. If the price we pay for this is the reduction of fine shadings of disagreement into direct antitheses, the price is worth paying.'

This is all true as far it goes. But it does not go far enough. The political parties do not simply convey upwards, and in the process refine, mass opinions. They equally convey downwards, and in the process select, the issues which face government. If universal suffrage made the political party necessary as a means to explain the people to their rulers, the ever-widening assumption of economic responsibilities by the state makes it necessary as a device to explain the rulers to the people. The party is not merely, therefore, a one-way channel of communication, but a two-way channel. And in the exercise of each of these twin functions it possesses a considerable area of subjective choice. At any given moment, then, the power of the people to control decision-making will not merely be affected both by the nature of the issues in question and by their readiness to understand them. It will be equally determined by the willingness and the capacity of the political party to make the issues comprehensible to the people. For example, there is a school of thought which holds that the people of Ireland are thoroughly disenchanted with the attempt to revive the Irish language and wish to see it abandoned without equivocation. If, hypothetically, this view were correct, then the three Irish parties, by unanimously declining for so long to offer them the opportunity to register that opinion, have failed in their role of organs of selection by refusing to place this issue to the forefront where it belongs. To take another example there is a school of thought which holds that the basic issue of government today in Ireland is that of economic growth. Not long ago, one of the opposition parties attempted with some success to persuade the people that the repeal of a particular piece of taxation legislation was a more fundamental issue. If economic growth is the basic issue, it might be argued that that opposition party was guilty of a perversion of its role as a channel of communication.

In short, what we are arguing at the outset is this: the complexity of the political process and the size of the political unit reduce the area upon which popular opinion can be brought to bear on a fraction of decision-making. Ideally, that fraction will be the most important fraction, the most fundamental. The prerequisites for the effective operation of the democratic process are, therefore, the same as the theological prerequisites for mortal sin – grave matter, full knowledge, and full consent. The device by which we endeavour to ensure the permanent existence of these three prerequisites is the political party which selects, conveys and obeys. But if its selection is dishonest or distorted, the grave matters are not communicated to the people. And even if its selection is honest, if the people fail to understand the gravity of the issues with which they are presented, either through the incoherence of the party machine in the constituencies and in the Dáil, or their own intellectual unpreparedness to understand it, then their full knowledge and consent are not genuinely secured.

The party, therefore, plays a dual and to some extent a schizophrenic role. It is both servant and architect of public opinion. The Dáil deputy is the servant of his constituents in that, firstly, they decide whether they will elect him or not; secondly, they express their opinions of his party's policies to him in their votes and in their personal contacts with him; thirdly, they convey to him their local grievances and expect him to do something about them. But equally he is their leader in that he and his kind determine the range of the alternatives upon which the voters will be allowed to adjudicate. Ideally, therefore, both party and people will have the wisdom and the courage to distinguish between responsibility and servility on the first level, and selection and distortion upon the second.

In practice, of course, there are forces constantly at work on both levels to ensure that these ideals are always, to a greater or lesser extent, perverted. The party is of its nature prone to oligarchical remoteness. It is not merely a minority, but a minority within a minority. 78.7 percent of the electors of Britain voted in the 1959 election. Slightly less than half of these, or roughly 40 percent of those in possession of votes, supported the Conservative party. It nevertheless won the election. Only one in four or five of the people who vote Conservative, or roughly 2.8 million people, are actually members of the Conservative party. Yet these people take some at least of the decisions which affect the lives of the other 32 million electors.

Precise figures for the membership of any of the Irish political parties are not readily available. But there are approximately 1,500 cumainn in Fianna Fáil. If one multiplies this figure by ten, the minimum number laid down in the Fianna Fáil constitution, one arrives at a membership figure of 15,000. This is admittedly an arbitrary guess, but it is as likely to be an over as an under-estimate. In other words, approximately 3 percent of the people who vote for Fianna Fáil exert themselves so far as to join it. Again, if one allows for the proportion of inactive members in any political party, the oligarchical character of the system is further illustrated.

Jean Blondel, in his book *Voters, Parties and Leaders*, estimates that approximately two-fifths of the members of the British Labour Party and between a quarter and a third of the members of the Conservative party play an active part in their organisations. If we arbitrarily borrow the higher estimate in respect of Fianna Fáil, we are left with a picture of some six thousand people playing any effective part in the reduction of the political debate to the alternatives which are offered to all their countrymen. In short, political parties in Ireland as elsewhere have failed to engage mass participation. And in turn, their tiny size in proportion to the votes which they can command at any given moment, and the small proportion of activists inside their ranks, inevitably cause them to crystallise in an oligarchical and inward-looking manner.

If, as we have argued, there are obstacles to the full and effective operation of the political parties, what of the electors themselves? If the electorate is to discuss, vote, and consent, it will, ideally need to possess three attributes. It will, firstly, be capable of understanding the issues which are presented to it. It will, secondly, be interested in deciding upon their respective merits. It will, thirdly, decide upon the basis of rational rather than irrational criteria. In fact, its possession of every one of these attributes is effectively limited by certain factors.

In the first place, the capacity of the electorate to understand the issues presented to it will be limited in proportion to the complexity of the issues themselves and the standards of literacy among the electorate. These limiting factors each contribute to the telescoping of the distinctions between the parties into simple images which most overtly take personalised forms – Churchill's cigar in wartime England; the cry 'Up Dev' in the thirties and forties – each doing duty as a substitute for rationalisation. But, equally, most people make a mental association between parties and issues. These associations do not necessarily require to be accurate; it is sufficient if they evoke images which the voter likes or dislikes. In a study of electoral attitudes made in Great Britain, Labour and Conservative supporters were asked parallel sets of questions to elucidate their ideas of the parties. For example, asked if the Conservative party stood for the rich and for big business, 85 percent of the Labour supporters replied yes as against 8 percent of the Conservative supporters. Asked if the Labour Party stood for the working class, 68 percent of Labour supporters replied yes and so did 32 percent of Conservatives. This process of telescoping has become obvious to the party leaders; it forces on them the realisation that the 'image' is all-important and that they must make a conscious effort to project the most effective image for the circumstances in which they find themselves. Thus, party projection becomes increasingly analogous to any other form of advertising based upon market research. In short, when we say that the electorate must be capable of understanding the issues presented to them by the political parties, we often mean in practice only that they are capable of being aroused by the psychological stimuli offered them.

Secondly, the electors must be interested. In practice, at least one in four are not. Only 70.8 percent of the Irish electorate voted in 1961. Even allowing a 5 percent wastage for deaths and for voters not yet on the register used, it remains true that a quarter of the people in Ireland who had the right to vote did not bother to exercise it.

Thirdly, the elector must make a rational choice. We have already seen that, in so far as he is the victim of advertising techniques, he may not be let do so. But worse, political arithmetic combined with the personal qualities of a key group of the electorate, the small percentage whose votes determine who shall rule, make it quite likely that the most important political choice of all, the choice of government, will be an irrational, not to say fortuitous, one. Between 1948 and 1961, the Fianna Fáil poll averaged approximately 571,000; the poll of all the other candidates combined approximately 706,000. In all that period the Fianna Fáil vote never rose more than 8 percent or fell more than 11 percent above or below its average. The combined vote of all other candidates never rose more than 9 percent or fell more than 10 percent above or below its average. Yet, power changed hands at four out of five elections in those thirteen years. It would be dangerous to press that argument to the point of contending that the same 10 percent of the people determine all political change; one must allow for the constant renewal of the electorate and for compensating changes of opinion in any given election. But one may perhaps fairly conclude that it is a small minority of the people whose changes of mind effectively determine changes of government. And many of those probably make up their minds on the basis of predicates which are not wholly rationally arrived at. Indeed, recent studies suggest that the 'floating voter' is often less rather than more sophisticated than his fellows.

These are all generalised weaknesses of democracy. They afflict all democratic countries. They are, if you like, the inevitable consequence of man being what he is. But is there anything in our Irish circumstances that operates in a particularly damaging way? We think there is.

One factor particularly springs to mind here. It is the peculiar consequences of our system of proportional representation. The most obvious consequence of proportional representation is that stable overall majorities are more hardly earned and less often gained. In England in 1959 the Conservative Party secured rather less than half the votes cast, but gained an overall majority of nearly one hundred in the House of Commons. In the general election of 1951, Fianna Fáil won 46 percent of the votes cast – almost twice as much as were gained by any other single party. Owing to the weakness or fairness of our system of election, they were only enabled to take power by the support of four independent deputies. There is much to be said for the view that the very purpose of elections is to produce governments with majorities. Whatever the state of opinion in the country, and that mathematical accuracy must be sacrificed, since in any case a government's actions are not 100 percent backed by those who voted it into power nor 100 percent opposed by those who did not.

This tendency of PR towards the production of coalition or minority governments is its most publicised but not its only significant characteristic. The rural nature of much of our politics has always led to some extent to the placing of emphasis upon the personal qualities of the people we elect. PR accentuates this. Multi-member constituencies do not merely provide unrivalled opportunities for independents to enter political life; they also set candidates who belong to the same party to some extent in opposition against each other. This in turn underlines the part which personal service to one's constituents plays in getting elected and staying elected. Irish deputies tend to be resident in their constituencies, to have worked their way up through the local party machines, and very often to have served their political apprenticeship in local government.

These characteristics may not in themselves be necessarily detrimental to the production of the best kind of political representatives. But the emphasis upon personal service has two great weaknesses. First, it makes it extremely difficult for the central party authority to introduce into the ranks of its constituency candidates personnel from outside local politics who it may feel would be the best kind of people to face up to the issues of national policy. In level of education, range of experience, professionalism, and concern with national as opposed to local matters or merely conventional and largely meaningless issues, the Oireachtas seems to us to show up comparatively poorly. Of course, it is difficult to prove these assertions. Some are not demonstrable in any systematic way, while in the case of those that are, one is faced at once by the absence of data in Ireland. Let us take the clearest case, education, as example. Only 32 percent of the Irish deputies elected in 1948 had received a university education, and this is a proportion which was maintained with remarkable consistency from 1922 to 1948. The percentage today seems to be lower – less than 30. Between 1918 and 1955, on the other hand, the proportion of university graduates in the British House of Commons rose steadily. In 1959, 60 percent of the Conservatives and 42 percent of the Labour members elected had received a university education. As far as secondary education is concerned, Professor McCracken in 1948 found that 61 percent of the Dáil had received a secondary education. In Great Britain only a handful of MPs have not been to secondary school and some of these will have followed adult education courses of some sort. Nor are these figures unique to Britain; the percentage of graduates in the legislatures of the USA and of several European democracies is even higher. The second weakness of personal service is that it overloads the time of too many of our TDs with the life and death necessity to engage in competition with each other in the exertion of largely imaginary patronage, by letter-writing and petitioning of the administration. There is absolutely nothing wrong with the role of the parliamentary representative as spokesman of local grievance, rescuer from local injustice; it is one which he fills to some extent in every democratic society. But in Ireland this obligation burdens the time of too many to an extent which is out of all proportion either to the results which it achieves, or to their relative importance in the scale of priorities which faces the men who are supposed to be the final arbiters of national policy. Together these two weaknesses are almost fatal to the efficient working of the Oireachtas, particularly the Dáil.

No-one would suggest that all problems, both of decision and of communication, would cease if more university graduates were elected to the Dáil or if TDs were released from the obligation of serving the personal and local interests of their constituents. Equally, the circumstances in which the member of a legislature finds himself, confronted by the whole scope of democratic legislation, have always to some extent compelled him to be a jack of all trades and master of none. But modern developments are accentuating the weakness of parliaments to the point where it is becoming a real danger to democracy. With every year that passes the state inevitably assumes more and more responsibility in the field of economic planning and of sociological development. How many Dáil deputies are given any training either by their youthful education, their occupations or professions, or by the efforts of their parties, which would enable them to comprehend these issues, contribute to these decisions, or appraise the government's performance in carrying out approved policies?

In short then, it can be argued that the practice of Irish politics enhances the difficulties facing Irish democracy in two ways. The effects of our proportional representation system, coupled with the traumatic excitements of our historical past, have produced a situation in which our voters are slightly more apathetic, slightly less educated than in average best circumstances. But secondly, the effect of the operation of these contingent forces upon the actual machine of politics has been to encourage the maintenance of standards of under-education and of amateurishness which are no longer supportable in the 1960s. For the moment, we are saved from the more damaging consequences of this state of affairs by the fact that the necessary decisions are on the whole being taken. But this is less because of the effectiveness of our political structure than in spite of it. The irony is, therefore, that an electoral system and a party machine, both designed to impart the purest distillation of the democratic spirit, are in practice combining to offer the electors substantially less than the basic democratic minimum.

Our analysis so far of the machinery of election and representation has suggested that there are major weaknesses in the political parties. These seem to us to be overdue for a massive overhaul. They are still based far too closely upon techniques inherited from the less sophisticated controversies of the nineteenth century. These techniques may still have served to deliver the goods in the heady nationalist atmosphere of the 1930s, when constitutional issues were still at the forefront of Irish politics; they cannot continue to function indefinitely in an era of fine shadings of programming and planning, of social welfare and educational development.

The task of particularising these criticisms is made difficult by the lack of precise information about Irish party structure. While other European democracies abound in studies of party structure and methods and of the statistical and sociological breakdown of their membership, the person who wishes to find out, for example, the total number of members of the various Irish parties will scarcely know where to start looking. But this is the kind of fact which is printed in every European textbook of political science. Equally, the questionnaire approach to members of the legislature, highly developed by students of politics and psychology in Europe and America, has in the past been inhibited here by the reticence of Irish Dáil deputies, especially in relation to statistics of age, education and occupation. The party leaderships, in turn, are still too ready to accept paper statistics of new branches allegedly founded and old ones theoretically revived as evidence of vitality at the grass roots; they should look as well for evidence of intellectual vitality and of intelligent interest in national party policy. If this carries with it the necessity to accept more criticism of traditional forms and customs from their younger members, it is a small and overdue debt to pay to the realities of changed circumstances.

In organisational structure the Irish political parties, and in particular Fianna Fáil suffer from the rigidity of an American-style hierarchial, almost federal structure which makes it almost impossible for the top echelons in authority to introduce Dáil candidates from outside the local constituency machine. This in turn means that the provision of men who may one day be cabinet ministers, required to adjudicate upon the most complex social and economic issues, depends in the first instance upon cut-throat constituency jockeying for position. In such contests the weight which a potential candidate can bring to bear in a constituency convention may be the only consideration. It is common knowledge that time and again an impotent leadership has had foisted upon it a candidate whom it did not want; the leadership is thus deprived of the services of the potential cabinet minister for whose nomination it had hoped. It is also true that in such convention battles, the principle of local option in all circumstances can, in fact, cover the employment of methods which pay more lip-service to the letter of democracy than to its spirit. The genuine existence, in fact, of many branches which enjoy both a paper existence and with it the right to a say in any constituency convention called to select candidates should be more closely inspected. And it is pointless to leave this task of inspection and registration to officers of constituency councils who are themselves the products of branch election, represent a cross-section of the local branches, and share their preconceptions and their inertia. Ideally, professional constituency or, at least, regional agents should be employed in such organisational work. Their use is a common-place in other developed democracies.

The financial difficulties of their employment in Ireland may at once be pleaded. These difficulties are surely not insuperable. It is surely an anomaly that a party of the size and importance of Fianna Fáil should only recently, one understands, have increased its full-time male professional staff from two persons to three – and been criticised for doing so. If more money is needed, could not the minimum affiliation fee for branches be raised? In this way, more money would be placed at the disposal of the central authority. Secondly, a practical obstacle would be interposed in the way of those who turn a blind eye to the annual re-registration of moribund or semi-moribund branches. The paper loss of some branches, which at present exist largely on paper, should not be a deterrent from this kind of reform.

Many of the barriers which inhibit the selection of the best possible candidates for the legislature are, as we have indicated, consequences of our electoral system. It will scarcely be possible to alter this system in the near future. But even within its limits, the parties should be able to adapt their methods of candidate selection to allow much greater scope for interference from the top. Constituency conventions should be required either to submit two or three names for a single vacancy, from which the national executive could choose one, or, conversely, to choose their candidate from a list previously vetted at national level. This is the kind of point which could weigh with young men of education and ability, but no political influence, who are prepared to contemplate embarking on a political career. Any party organisation which brands such people as carpetbaggers and closes the ranks of its constituencies against them is mortgaging its own future and guaranteeing that of those of its rivals which do not.

We have tried to show that it is difficult for young men of potential cabinet calibre to take the first plunge into public life at the constituency level. But even if such a man is successful in crossing these hurdles, he soon finds fresh obstacles to his professional education as a mature national legislator. Dáil deputies are grossly overworked at duties largely irrelevant to the purposes for which they are theoretically (and according to the Constitution) elected. Until recently, they were grossly underpaid. They are given far too few opportunities and facilities to bring themselves up to date on the changing social and economic issues of modern politics. They should be provided with greatly improved secretarial services in order to relieve their time of some at least of the routine burdens of constituency service. Financial assistance should if necessary be provided by the state to this end; such help is a feature of many other democracies.

With the same end in view, political parties should encourage their members to develop specialisations by setting up committees, working parties and research teams to investigate social and economic issues and report without prejudice to their executives. They should institute refresher courses in social science and economics for their members, using outside assistance without hesitation. Parties are all too nervous of the intellectual exuberance of their own followers; if they were really far-sighted, their elders would not merely tolerate but encourage the development of 'ginger-groups', recognising that occasional excesses of indiscipline or brashness are a small price to pay for the development of intellectual vitality in the ranks.

Above all, a serious attempt should be made to use the talent of the parliamentary parties to the full. This requires a thorough reform of our parliamentary procedures. Some of the techniques used by the Oireachtas in its consideration of proposed policies and in its scrutiny of the conduct of government are very blunt and rusty. Debates are often uninformed and sometimes irrelevant and the ability of the Dáil, let alone the Senate, to elicit information about policy and administration and to appraise what they are told is, on European standards, poor. 'No European legislature is so restricted in its functions and so inhibited by lack of information as the Mother of Parliaments', Professor Chapman has written, and he added, 'comparatively speaking the Mother of Parliaments is a very weak old lady'. So, too, we think, is one of her older daughters now settled in Dublin. In particular, a serious attempt should be made to develop the use in the Dáil of parliamentary committees both to improve the Dáil's efficiency and so that fledgling members may learn the intricacies of special areas of legislation. Politics is a profession, not an art; it has yet to require any professional training in Ireland. The young man of thirty who is elected at the bottom of the poll in a five-seat constituency may be brought, by the flatness of the surrounding countryside, to a ministry or a parliamentary secretaryship inside a decade. It is ludicrous that he should arrive there with no special preparation, no expert study, perhaps little more equipment than the pious hope that the civil service will keep on turning something up for him as it did for his predecessor. Not all new ministers are, of course, similarly unprepared.

But those who bring special knowledge and a sense of purpose to their first cabinet office owe these attributes to their own drive and initiative rather than to any deliberate encouragement from their parties to think and to learn.

We do not, we should add, underestimate the difficulties of implementing the reforms which we propose. Legislatures, of all political institutions, are the most conservative; ministers will naturally be reluctant to make life more difficult for themselves; and we may be sure that the civil servants will gravely advise against it. After all, who wants a well-informed critic breathing down his neck?

While the state of Irish party politics is scarcely critical at the moment, the obligations of the future demand fundamental rethinking now. For too long we have been prepared to accept as inevitable a process of government which was conducted by a single generation and involved controversy, on the whole, over constitutional issues alone. Considering that the generation consisted of 'politicians by accident', we should be heartily grateful that it provided so many who were capable of learning the tricks of administration in the twenties and thirties, and even a surviving minority who understand the different problems of the fifties and sixties.

But this minority is passing away. The machine which it bequeathed was well-designed to secure constituency majorities for that generation, ill-designed to produce and train its successors. It is at last beginning to be realised that in the new context of the fifties and sixties something of a breakdown of communication has begun to occur between the political and administrative decision makers on the one hand, and the electorate on the other. It is a breakdown of communication which, recent by-elections notwithstanding, is scarcely bridged as yet. But there are also equally dangerous signs of a breakdown of communication between, on the one hand, a small group consisting of the key administrators in the civil service and the state-sponsored bodies and a handful of the top-rank politicians, and, on the other, the mass of the rank-and-file in the political machines. For the moment, this dichotomy has been partially concealed by the lifting of some of the fundamental issues of economic policy into what is essentially the bi-partisan sphere. The constituency organisations soldier on as they did in the thirties, while the administrators operate the levers of decision-making. But in the long-run this device is destructive of the dignity and vitality of democratic politics. Unless the political parties are prepared to overhaul their own attitudes, to attract sufficient people with ideas into their ranks, and to allow them to play a more effective and sophisticated part in the shaping of policy, Ireland will go into the more integrated Europe of the 1970s with a civil service of traditional competence, some excellent state-sponsored bodies, and a private enterprise sector which is at least beginning to learn the facts of life, but with a political machine which is out-dated in its concept of its own role, and ill-equipped to decide upon the social and economic issues which will have to be faced, still less to communicate to the mass of the people the complex motives behind the decisions it takes – or sponsors.

Over the next few years, then, the Irish political parties have got to make up their minds whether they are content to go on electing to the Dáil, on the basis of their constituency records, men who are on average less well-educated, less professionally trained, and given less opportunity to acquire the specialist knowledge which will permit them to make a positive contribution to good government than the continental counterparts with whom they are being brought into ever closer and more competitive contact. Do the constituencies of Ireland want to be represented by men capable of helping to fashion the Ireland of the seventies? Or will they continue to demand of their unfortunate representatives that they should be part-time social workers first, whose ancillary legislative and inquisitorial skills are encouraged neither by leisure nor by opportunity? It is a straight question of priorities. There can surely be only one answer. Any one of our three major parties which neglects to give that answer is running on the capital of the past and mortgaging the future. Any one of our three major parties which could find the courage to give that answer to select those people, and actively to encourage them to train themselves in their arduous profession as political legislators, could guarantee itself a place in the sun in the 1970s.

So far in this analysis, it has been argued that, although democratic theory demands the participation of citizens in their own government, in the nature of things their control is very tenuous. Its range and efficiency depend upon the degree to which political parties succeed in their dual role of educating and leading public opinion on the one hand and reflecting it on the other. It has been argued, also, that the representatives themselves, chosen in the way they are, and organised on traditional lines in the Oireachtas, do not contribute much, if anything, to many vital policy decisions, particularly in some areas of social and economic policy.

198

This state of affairs is certainly deplorable, and it is possible and, indeed, urgent for the political parties to recruit talent and to use it, instead of misusing what they do have. Nevertheless, it must be recognised that there is a lot of evidence to suggest that the role of the representative, even of the minister, may be altering in the face of the demands of society upon the modern state. A growing proportion of governmental activity is professional and can only be carried out by professionals, that is, by civil servants, local government officers and the officers of the State-sponsored bodies. There is evidence, also, that the nature of this professional activity itself is changing with the development of the social sciences and their applicability to public policy issues. Such a trend in public affairs obviously has important and far-reaching consequences and implications both for our politicians and our public servants and, hence, for democracy itself. We need, therefore, to ascertain what is the pattern and the direction of these changes.

In the last few years, in Ireland as in many other countries, there has been a growing agreement about what services public authorities should render to the public. Today, we believe in the 'welfare state' and are disposed to use public authorities to a much greater extent than ever before to tackle all sorts of social problems hitherto regarded as unavoidable misfortunes of life or the unfortunate, but inescapable, consequences of social and economic change. We now expect the government to engineer a steadily rising standard of living and comfort for the whole community. State activity today is, therefore, increasingly comprehensive.

This is well illustrated in the development of our social services. The Victorian Poor Law was replaced by a growing, but uncoordinated, collection of services (old-age pensions, unemployment and national health insurance, widows' and orphans' benefits), which in turn were extended and co-ordinated after the Second World War to make the 'cradle to the grave' network of provisions to which we in Ireland approximate today. More recently, another concept has emerged, and in its turn, is generating another policy. It is the concept – forced on us by a growing understanding of our social and economic condition – that the so-called social services 'are not an unproductive frill tacked on to the economy as a charitable afterthought, they are an integral and (in some form or other) a necessary part of our economic and social structure – a form of collective provision required to meet the needs of an expanding industrial society' (David Walker, *The Allocation of Public Funds for Social Development*, Economic Research Institute). Social services and economic policy are now beginning to be seen to be intimately bound together. For example, the pace of our economic development is to some extent governed by the amount and type of education available; hence the sudden emphasis by the government on education to repair the paring defects of our school and university provisions.

A survey of the development of state activity in economic affairs brings one to the same point. The development of the welfare state was at first lopsided on account of the inhibitions inherited from a previous era, but, with the general acceptance of new economic theories, the state came to be recognised as capable of, and to be charged with, pursuing the basic ingredients of welfare: high levels of employment and rising real earnings.

This quest has led quickly from policies of piecemeal aid and encouragement and gap-filling public enterprise to a more comprehensive approach. 'Planning' and 'development' are the key terms here; the one raised from the status of a dirty word in less than ten years, the other now graven on a brass plate on the door of one of the buildings of the Department of Finance and, thus, clearly canonised. Grappling with the problems of guiding the community to prosperity in a Europe that is becoming increasingly integrated, our planners have become more and more aware of the oneness of development. Key elements in national development turn out to be in the field of the social services, the concern of departments located physically across the Liffey from Merrion Square and psychologically just as distant in the minds of many civil servants in the 'economic' departments and vice versa.

Less widely recognised is yet another ingredient of public welfare which is the state's concern. This is the urgent need for us to care for the appearance of the country, or at least of those parts of it on which we build or have built, and for physical amenity. The middle twentieth-century industrial revolution, like its nineteenth-century predecessor, is throwing up eyesores and asphalt jungles and causing chaos and congestion in town and countryside. Public authorities already have functions and powers in this area, but public squalor is all too evident and, in respect of many private activities, these powers are largely negative. Traditionally, we do not associate public authorities with taste and beauty, but to whom else, if not to public authorities, can we turn as our best hope for securing tolerable, tasteful and civilised surroundings. That this is, in fact, recognised by the government is evidenced by the inauguration recently of an Institute of Physical Planning and Construction. But these activities, too, are intimately bound up with economic and social development. One has only to think of contemporary transport problems to see this.

Welfare is, then, one and indivisible and it is fairly and squarely on the public authorities, central and local, that we have placed the responsibility for ensuring it. While it was possible in the past for the state to attempt to solve a few of the most urgent social and economic problems pragmatically, each administrative unit, department or other, working with a fair degree of autonomy, the great range of state activities and the close interlocking of one with another make necessary a high level of closely planned and co-ordinated activity. Furthermore, the development of the social sciences has now made it possible, as the developments outlined above make it essential, for social problems to be tackled scientifically and systematically, bringing to bear all the existing knowledge and experience and using the increasing range of economic and sociological research techniques for acquiring precise knowledge and for forecasting future trends and needs. We can, and to some extent already do, apply to our public problems statistical methods, survey techniques, and analysis of one sort or another which permit the construction of policies based on facts and not conjecture.

This is well recognised and accepted in respect of some economic functions: the successive Programmes for Economic Expansion, Agriculture in the Second Programme for Economic Expansion, and the work of the Committee on Industrial Organisation and the National Industrial Economic Council all bear witness to this. The readiness of some ministers and officials in this area to investigate and learn quickly from European experience, instead of emulating British fumbling, is clearly reflected in the striking resemblance of our developing planning machinery to that of France. But, in principle, and to an increasing extent in practice, these tactics are applicable over the whole range, the limitations in each area being only those of the state of our knowledge and techniques in the relevant social sciences. Alas, the response of other ministers and other officials has been negligible and it is far from clear that they even realise the nature of the changes that are occurring or the opportunities that are there for the taking.

It is the extension of the economic and social responsibilities of the state to embrace the planning and construction of the material framework of our community, and the development of the social sciences to the point where they are indispensable tools of policy-making which have enhanced the role of the professional and made him increasingly the initiator of social policy and the architect of the community. To say this is not to denigrate the role of the democratically elected representative or of ministers. Of course they have critical elements to add to government. Above all, they have the authority, the right and the duty to the first say, the decision as to which of the many possible social problems shall be tackled next; and the last say, the crucial choice, if there is one, between this or that alternative policy. They add, or should add, that vital element in government, the voice of the consumer, the citizen. The public service is the instrument of the government that they elect, to be used as that government wishes. It is for the government and the representatives to lay down the broad objectives, to provide the drive, and to engage in a continuous appraisal of the conduct of public business, and to do these things in such a way that, in their turn, their masters, the public, can appreciate, if only dimly in the case of many of them, what is going on. But it would be foolish to suppose that they can assume a much greater part in modern government than they now play. The Oireachtas cannot itself govern; the government cannot itself devise great programmes of development. The most that can be hoped for – and should be demanded – is that each is of the calibre to do its own job efficiently and is organised and equipped in a manner to do so. This is what we have doubted.

These same developments – the great increase in the functions of governments, the advent of planning, and the need to apply the social sciences – have important consequences and implications for the structure and organisation of the public services. What has been their response? Are the consequences accepted and the implications fully worked out? Is the public service adapting itself to the extent of which seems to be required or quickly enough? This, too, we doubt.

The administrative inheritance of 1922 was on the whole a good one. The Irish Free State took over an administration in good working order, and an efficient civil service which was virtually complete as it stood and which had high standards and a proud tradition. Once the complex jumble of public offices had been reduced to eleven ministerial departments, and in some departments senior posts had been created and filled, the machine was available, fully fashioned and in working order, for governments to use. In general, that machine has continued to operate little changed to this day. It has served the country well, and has proved an adaptable instrument of government. Departments have been added here and there, as welfare services expanded and as the regulation and development of the economy became state functions. Significantly, however, there has been a growing propensity to assign economic functions (regulatory as well as enterprising) and also the administration of some social services to state-sponsored bodies, though this has not altered the status or role of the departments in any fundamental way. As far as the civil service itself is concerned, some service grades have been amalgamated, and minor adaptations have been made to meet new conditions.

To its everlasting credit, it is this machine that fashioned the first comprehensive development policies whose effects, psychological no less than material, are now so obvious around us. To an extent hardly realised by the public, it was senior public servants, encouraged by a few ministers, who in the late 1950s diagnosed the needs of the time and recognised the opportunities for the future.

Considering the extent of the changes of recent years, changes in which the administration itself has had such a large hand, it would be surprising if these institutions, created in the·early twentieth-century on late nineteenth-century models, did not need considerable adaptation. Senior members of the public service are aware of this, and some significant changes have already occurred. But both politicians and top civil servants almost always seem to be fully extended coping with the business of the day, and have little time to consider structure. Also, as Walter Bagehot observed, bureaucracies have a natural tendency to see the organisation 'as a grand and achieved result, not a working and changeable instrument'. The innovations and changes that have taken place so far suggest a thoroughly pragmatic approach to meet the most pressing needs of the moment. There seems to have been no full-scale review of our machinery of government as a whole. Moreover, the results of the examination in the Department of Finance of some aspects of civil service recruitment and training do not as yet suggest that the full implications of the changes in the content and techniques of government have been accepted.

What we are asserting is that this country has arrived at a point where the opportunity – more, the necessity – for changes that amount to more than cautious modifications of existing arrangements needs to be grasped. The existence of a planned framework within which public authorities can work and the advent of new techniques of administration and control call for more than attempts to fit new responsibilities into old patterns of working that is a feature of the reaction so far of the Department of Finance, and, indeed, of the whole civil service.

That the basic problem of organisation is recognised by some civil servants is clear enough. The Secretary of the Department of Finance has himself summarised it: 'I am not sure now that the biggest problem after all will not be one of organisation: how secretaries and other senior officers can organise their time and work so as to get away from their desks and the harassing experiences of every day sufficiently to read, consider and consult with others.' He is quite right. Increasing numbers of senior public servants are going to have to turn themselves into applied social scientists, seeking out, absorbing and using large amounts of systematic data as they elucidate social problems and plan solutions to be placed before ministers – in the economic field (business and agriculture), in education, health, social welfare, transport, town and country planning – over the whole area of state activity, in fact. They cannot do this, as too many still are expected to, as adjuncts to the job of administering existing schemes and services. The overwork and strain on officers when new legislation or new schemes are in train are obvious even to the outsider.

The solution seems to be to make *two* jobs. Senior officers should be engaged on only one of these functions at any given time, though, in the course of properly organised careers, they could and should serve periods in each, as well as in other public authorities. To some extent, this pattern is already emerging. Just as 'establishment' work, now all too slowly embracing training, has always been regarded as a separate activity, so the emergence of the Economic Development Division of the Department of Finance is to a large extent a recognition of the need for specialised intelligence, forecasting and planning personnel in the field of economic development. The establishment of the Survey of Investment in Education, which, under Mr. Patrick Lynch's direction, is attached to the Department of Education, is another example. That it was needed at all is, of course, a sad reflection on the total failure of that department to do its job, but the fact that it was set up after the Commission on Higher Education began its work is, one can hope, at least indicative of a recognition that the former is a middle twentieth-century way of investigating social problems, the latter a middle nineteenth-century method.

But is the same not necessary in other areas? Who can deny that we desperately need some systematic thought about our health services (where a select committee, an equally archaic device for mapping out new policy, at present labours); and about our social services generally where, it seems, the addition of a half a crown on existing benefits is regarded as a major administrative feat and the limit of administrative ingenuity. Agriculture is perhaps better served, for here there is at least, as in the field of economic development and physical planning, a research institute. But the existence of semi-independent research units does not, and cannot, absolve departments from their task of advising ministers, which task requires them to be in a position to appraise and apply the information coming from these units.

This line of thought suggests, perhaps, that it is necessary to make clearer distinctions inside departments between the administration of services and the function of gathering intelligence, forecasting, planning and advising on policy. Such a division as this appears to be the practice in French central government departments.

The development of an overall, planned framework (laid out at least in outline in the Second Programme and supporting documents) presents us with the opportunity for yet another radical change. At present, many, though by no means all, public services are administered or controlled in some detail by government departments. The Department of Finance controls the other central departments; which, in turn, control the local authorities, and to varying degrees, the state-sponsored bodies. Hence, some local authority and state-sponsored body proposals are scrutinized by the parent department and the Department of Finance. But are these systems of detailed control any longer necessary or useful? We think not; the less so where a department's 'administration' in fact consists of controlling other agencies which actually operate services.

Circumstances are now, or will shortly, make it possible and the time might therefore now be coming to dismantle the system of Department of Finance control and analogous controlling systems. These systems and the parliamentary procedures that go with them were devised, at a time when administrative techniques were comparatively crude, to ensure meticulous accuracy, strict parsimony, and compliance with rule in the performance of a limited range of government functions costing small amounts. This type of control appears to encourage a preoccupation with compliance with detailed rules and with justification of detail. It conduces to a defensive and cagey mentality. It can breed frustration – and sometimes has. It often leads to narrow scrutiny of new items, while continuing expenditure may escape without anyone identifying in it those items which ought to be brought up for scrutiny and possible re-examination of the policy implied in them. It is ill-suited to the efficient scrutiny of large programmes of expenditure of the type that are now commonplace.

Today, with the emergence of an overall framework of objectives and targets for public policy and expenditure, we ought to be able to relate all departmental expenditure proposals to the appropriate general programme for the area (whatever it is) for some time ahead. With targets agreed and with general limit of departmental responsibility fixed, it should be possible for departments to prepare their own estimates and to devise and implement schemes without constant reference to the Department of Finance. The Department of Finance to some extent recognises this in fact. Limits of discretion allowed to departments have been getting wider, but the extension proceeds at an uneven pace and very slowly. At most the department seems to think in terms of a cautious relaxation of limits inside the framework of the existing system when what may well be needed is a revolution in techniques. Today, we have reached the stage where economy can best be assured not by Department of Finance scrutiny of the traditional variety, but by the checking by appropriately trained and experienced officers of the quality of performance and management in the various departments, including particularly their financial control systems; a check imposed in such a way as to stimulate and evoke initiative and resolution and not to frustrate them.

The Oireachtas in its turn should direct its attention to ensuring that this is done, that significant information on progress towards agreed objectives is available and that emerging problems are quickly identified, rather than wasting its time with the traditional, and now increasingly meaningless, rituals which pass for public scrutiny and control.

Certainly there are difficulties in devising and imposing suitable tests and standards and in eliciting the right types of information. This calls for the application of mathematical and statistical techniques, modern accountancy and systems analysis and the seeking out of relevant comparisons in both the public and the private sector. However, we are not without the experience of business enterprise in these areas. It is this activity which is the modern equivalent of the traditional supply (and some establishment) work. The same arguments apply to the relationship of the local authorities to the Department of Local Government, the Department of Health and other departments with whom they deal. There is widespread agreement among public officials themselves that control over the local authorities is often far too detailed, a view echoed recently by the Secretary of the Department of Local Government himself. Certainly one does not have to talk for very long to local government officers to hear horror stories of schemes prepared by competent officers being subjected to minute examination generating much correspondence and often delay. Too often, the examination is conducted by central government officers not obviously, if at all, better qualified to judge. Perhaps, also, the same may be true of the relations between some state-sponsored bodies and their sponsor departments. These, however, seem to vary a great deal on no obvious pattern and, indeed, without the public knowing or being able to know exactly what they are. So far as these are concerned, the great need is for quite clear objectives and formal public statements of the limits of discretion for their managements and where and under what circumstances departments have the right and duty to direct them.

It is possible to pursue this type of argument even further. Could we not administer many of the services now run directly by government departments or controlled in detail by them (eg health, social welfare services, agriculture) as we do, say, transport, by means of state-sponsored bodies? Each would operate autonomously under a statute or other legal instrument which clearly outlined its objectives and would work within a long-term budget related to the overall development plan. The functions of the central department would then be limited to checking that general policies are being adhered to, negotiating the general lines of the budget and changes in objectives and controlling statutes, to co-ordination, and to an efficiency audit. A system somewhat along these lines is a feature of Swedish government, where the staffs of most departments are numbered in scores rather than hundreds (many of them housed in one single building) and where, as a consequence, detailed departmental control of the administration of public services is impossible even if it were desired. And why do we not treat our local authorities in the same way?

These are, we think, some of the ways in which our administration might be adapted to achieve not only the quality of decision-making that is now possible and necessary, but also a more enterprising administration of these services. The first moves in these directions have already been made: they do not seem yet to have been radical enough.

As the new tasks of the public services, and particularly their higher ranks, become clearer, a picture of the various professional skills needed in those who man them is emerging. Senior civil servants, county managers, and the top executives of the state-sponsored bodies are all increasingly concerned today with the problems of recruiting men of the appropriate qualifications or attributes, and with training and developing them, once they have them. Never before have these matters occupied the attention of public administrators as they do today. The tremendous demand for training and development is reflected in the growing volume and range of courses conducted by the Institute of Public Administration, by the Irish Management Institute and by administrative organisations themselves.

Much of this work is simple enough to plan and organise, the needs being relatively easily ascertained and the types of training well enough known. At the heart of the public service, however, in the executive and administrative grades of the civil service, the needs are not so easily pinpointed, nor are the necessary qualifications and skills recruited or inculcated. What is more, developments in this area so far do not suggest that the senior civil service as a whole accepts that their recruitment, training and 'executive development' procedures are in any great need of drastic reform or that the new tasks of the civil service require an officer much different from the traditional pattern. Yet it is precisely here, where the whole of our national development is planned, co-ordinated and directed, that the responsibilities have altered and increased the most. It is here, then, that we shall concentrate our attention.

A very real 'managerial revolution' has been taking place in the public services of other countries, as well as in business and industry generally, and it is producing a new type of administrator. The steps taken by some European states since the Second World War to improve their public services contrast strangely with our comparative lassitude in these matters. What needs to be done? In general, it is necessary to get a much wider recognition that what modern administration requires is:

1. A knowledge of the social sciences – economics, sociology, statistics, social administration, law, etc. – and social research techniques appropriate to the sector in which the officer works. It follows from this that the idea that an officer can be transferred to any department (which is largely a myth in any case) must be abandoned in favour of the principle of departments grouped in

sectors (financial and economic, industrial and commercial, agricultural, the social services etc.) within which there could, and
should, be real movement.

2. A knowledge of 'management', including social psychology. The
civil service has traditionally tended to regard 'administration' as
an art different from that called 'management', which indeed
some still regard as 'third-rate witch-doctory' with little relevance
for them.

3. A knowledge of one's own country and both knowledge of, and
experience in, different branches of the public service.

4. A massive investment in time and money in the men and women
who are eventually going to the top, to ensure that they get this
knowledge and experience.

It is not, of course, possible, even if it were desirable, to insist that
recruits to the general service ranks of the civil service should already
have studied management and one or more of the other social sciences.
Most of our higher posts are, and in the foreseeable future will be, held
by people who are recruited from secondary school. What one might
hope is that modern selection methods would be applied by the Civil
Service Commission to select those with the best potential to be educated and trained in these subjects. This is very far from the case at present.
The civil service selection board procedure virtually ignores modern
advances in selection techniques and in methods of assessing personality
and aptitude. More, it positively denies them. Some at least of the selection boards have no reports on the records or showing of the candidates
in their jobs, no reports on aptitude or psychological tests or interviews
(because there haven't been any) and, indeed, no reports of any kind
other than the candidate's own record of his previous jobs, if any, and a
list of his academic achievements. Selectors are not even permitted to
know the names of the candidates and cannot be told the nature of the
jobs they are going to do, because no one knows what these are or even
in which sector (financial, economic, social service or other) they will be
located.

It might be thought that the mysterious working of the instincts
of experienced men can select the best candidates. If this is so, it is a

merciful and totally undeserved blessing. With luck, the selected candidates are promising material; by design, they are raw material. They must then be trained; but are they? It is unfortunately necessary to say that, apart from so-called 'training on the job', which is often a euphemism for throwing the new man into not too deep an end in the hope that other spluttering lads will teach him how to survive, many civil servants have received little or no formal training at all. Today, a trickle are given university scholarships; another trickle are to be released to attend year-long courses in the Institute of Public Administration.

For the rest, training is measured in days rather than weeks. Thus the amount of time and energy given to training the senior men of the future is ludicrously small. If this will be thought, as it probably will, to be an overstatement, contrast the training given to the Irish administrative officer with that given to his French equivalent. In France, it is thought worthwhile to give *three years* training to people who are already social science graduates, before they are posted to their departments.

Considering the neglect of initial training, it is hardly surprising to find that planned development of careers is not a feature of the civil service. It is not surprising either that, apart from isolated instances of officers being sent away for special training, mid-career training for higher responsibilities is largely confined to the so-called 'Killarney' courses, the five week courses for officers of all services organized by the Institute of Public Administration, which are attended by a mere trickle of civil servants. The scale of these, both in respect of the time given and the numbers participating, reflect the attitude of senior officers and particularly the low priority which they give to systematic preparation for the highest responsibilities. This is in sad and growing contrast to the increasing recognition given to this type of activity by the best of the business world and the public services of Western Europe, not to speak of the military to whom goes all the credit for having invented the staff college a very long time ago.

The response of the civil service to the need for training and planned development of careers has, then, in our view, been meagre in the extreme. Moreover, systematic action to broaden the working experience of officers ascending to top positions has been negligible, despite the flicker of interest some years ago which evoked the *Report on Mobility in the Public Service*. The public service is not mobile. True, the transfer of officers from one branch of the public service to another would be awkward to arrange under any circumstances, but its benefits can hardly be denied. These go far beyond the broadening of a man's experience; they embrace also a heightened appreciation on the part of the civil servant of the problem of his customers – the officers of the local authority or state-sponsored bodies with whom he deals – and vice versa. Who can doubt that officers of the Department of Local Government or of Health or of Agriculture would benefit by a period in the field. Those whose life is spent in the field certainly don't.

The civil service is generally regarded as a profession, and rightly so. It is one of the distinguishing features of a profession that to a large extent it controls entry to its own ranks, guards its own standards and fosters its own science or art. Autonomy in these matters is a privilege rightly accorded to it, and with benefit to society: but it implies also a duty, a duty to pay constant attention to these matters and to give them the priority they deserve. Society has suffered much from the conservatism and obscurantism of some of the older established professions; this community cannot afford to suffer from the failings of its civil service, since, as we have argued, it is in their hands more than at any time before that our very prosperity lies.

As Professor Brian Chapman has written: 'good policy is a function of the quality of the information on which it is based and of the quality of the men who are formulating it.' And so, too, we may add, is good management. It is unfortunately true that on Western European standards we appear to be falling behind. In the face of the record of our civil service to date, no one can honestly say that we have suffered yet, but we are increasingly likely to do so. It would be a strange thing if those who are, for better or for worse, amongst the major architects of our community, attacked their own domestic problems more in the manner of the plumber than the architect.

17

THE DEVELOPMENT OF THE IRISH LABOUR MOVEMENT

DAVID THORNLEY

This essay is not designed as a factual history of the Irish Labour movement in this century. It is not so designed because, in the first place, it could not, in the existing state of our knowledge of the period, attempt to supply such a history. The student of politics or of history who comes to the consideration of this topic will find that a certain amount of secondary material exists for the pre-1916 period. There are, for example, several studies of James Connolly, outstanding amongst which is the recent work by Mr Desmond Greaves; there are some devoted to James Larkin, all almost exclusively orientated towards the 1913 period. There are newspapers articles and chapters in larger works, in which some consideration is given to the part played by the Irish Citizen Army in the Rising of 1916, and to the nationalist ideas of James Connolly.

But after 1916, one can almost say – nothing. We are invited to watch Captain White training the Citizen Army in Croyden Park, but when Connolly leads his men into the GPO, in an epic moment of decision, he leads them, also, out of the ken of history. These were men devoted to the militant pursuit of a specific political attitude – ask what became of them, and of their ideas; ask how the Labour movement of Connolly developed into the organisation which we know today, and your question will fall resoundingly into an historical void. For example, of the nineteen chapters of Mr R. M. Fox's biography of James Larkin, slightly less than three are devoted to the twenty-four years of his life after his return to Ireland in 1923. In Ireland and America one or two monographs on different aspects of the labour and trade union movements are in course of preparation, and with their publication something may be done to fill this gap. But at the moment of speaking the only work of scholarship which sets out systematically to trace the development of the labour movement not merely up to and into but also through and after the Rising is J. D. Clarkson's *Labour and Nationalism in Ireland*, a thesis by a graduate of the University of Columbia, some few hundred copies of which were published in 1927 and which has never been reprinted or brought up to date.

It may be asked, then, why I should attempt a task after first asserting it to be impossible. The answer is a double one. In the first place, this is a void which has always fascinated me. The riddle – how did the militant Marxist* (**It should be noted that, wherever the author of this article refers to Connolly and Larkin as 'Marxists', he is referring to the fact that they believed in class conflict, the inherent instability of capitalist economics, and in 'revolutionary' rather than in 'evolutionary' or 'gradualist' Socialism. Strictly speaking, Marxism is essentially atheistic and materialistic. This is an aspect of Marxism to which these Irish socialists do not appear to have been committed – Editor*) movement of Connolly and Larkin become the gradualist and scarcely socialist party of today, has always seemed to me a most proper and long-neglected subject for scholarly investigation, and one which in the near future I hope to attempt to unravel rather more systematically than I could ever do here. Secondly, this essay does not and could not pretend to be a definitive treatment of the issue. It does not seek to fill the void, but rather to draw your attention to it; it does not seek to provide all the right answers, but rather to devise the right questions. And insofar as it is a history, it is a history not of the Irish Labour movement, but of its political philosophy.

THE POLITICAL IDEAS OF CONNOLLY AND LARKIN

The movement, which, in the early years of this century, took the characteristic form that we associate with Irish Labour in the period, was very largely the work of two men, James Connolly and James Larkin. The characters of these two were, by a historical accident, perfectly complementary: as Mr Fox has put it: 'In the earlier Irish labour movement Jim Larkin and James Connolly represented the two halves – action and theory – which had to be brought together before something vital could emerge.'[1] Yet the traditional picture of Larkin as a pure and simple man of action, large, lovable, and uncomplicated, with no clear picture of where he was going, content to leave higher strategy to the intellectual Connolly, is an oversimplification. It may be going too far to suggest that this is a picture drawn by the hagiographers of the national struggle

213

deliberately to save themselves from present-day embarrassment. But an oversimplification it is. Both Connolly and Larkin learned their socialism in similar contexts and from the same kind of course; the goals which they pursued they held philosophically in common.

Connolly grew up, worked, suffered and learnt in the slums of industrial Scotland; his first decisive political commitment was to the Scottish Socialist Federation. At this time many disparate groups contested with one another the right to articulate the grievances of the English proletariat. The Lib-Labs, working-class associates of the Liberal Parliamentary party, competed for the growing Labour vote with the Independent Labour Party of Keir Hurdie, an association which was dedicated, very largely to the practical task of convincing the respectable English trade unionist that the distinctiveness of his cause demanded the establishment of an independent parliamentary organisation for his representatives. On a slightly more theoretical level Shaw, Wells, the Webbs and the other leaders of the Fabian Society offered one justifying social philosophy for working-class action; the Social Democratic Federation of H. M. Hyndman offered another. Hyndman, whatever his idiosyncrasies and his failure to leave any permanent mark on the English Labour movement, is arguably the only Marxist of any importance in that movement's history. He had been converted to socialism by reading *Das Kapital*, and while tactical considerations prevented him from making proper acknowledgment to Marx for his ideas – an omission which offended the latter greatly – he remained a lifelong exponent of Marx's principles. In addition to purveying theoretical solutions, however, the Social Democratic Federation also put forward candidates for parliamentary elections. These were invariably unsuccessful, but secured a respectable measure of support at different periods – not least among the notoriously disaffected Irish émigré population. Michael Davitt spoke in favour of Hyndman's candidature in Burnley in the 1890s.

The Scottish Socialist Federation was, then, from its inception faced with a number of alternative claimants upon its political allegiance. It decided at first to ally itself with the one which offered most promise of practical political success – the Independent Labour Party. It did so, however, always with the intention of informing what it viewed as an excessively opportunist organisation with sound principles of scientific, or Marxist, socialism. It was an attempt which was doomed to failure from the outset. Whether the Scottish Socialist Federation found itself, like later left-wing ginger groups, thwarted by the obdurate immediacy of

English political trade unionism, it is impossible to say; but historically, it soon found itself increasingly out of sympathy with the Independent Labour Party, and more and more attracted to the rival Marxist Social Democratic Federation, until, in 1895, it took the plunge, and formally affiliated itself to Hyndman's movement.

This, then, was the background to Connolly's early socialist experiments, and against it he developed allegiances which he was never to lose. In 1896 he left Scotland for Dublin, but he made several return visits to Scotland and the industrial north of England in the first decade of this century, and on each occasion he lectured under the auspices of the Social Democratic Federation, and spoke in favour of its candidates rather than those of the gradualist Independent Labour Party.

The immediate occasion of Connolly's return to the land that was his father's birthplace was the invitation of the Dublin Socialist Club to become its paid organiser. It was an invitation sweetened, to an irregularly employed man, by the prospect of regular payment – disillusioning in that the payment only spasmodically materialised. On his arrival Connolly found the socialists of Dublin devoted, as it seems socialists everywhere must characteristically be, to fragmentation and mutual recrimination. To restore dynamism to them was Connolly's immediate task.

The device which he adopted to achieve this end was the formation of a new and untainted organisation, the Irish Socialist Republican Party, and the publications of this body, the first of several Irish working-class movements with which Connolly was associated, serve to give an insight into his principles in this period. The Irish Socialist Republican Party was at once more militant than previous Irish – and indeed, most English – socialist organisations in two ways; firstly, in its uncompromising dedication to the principle of Irish Republican self-government, secondly, in its actual social programme. In regard to the latter, one can see, significantly, the influence of H. M. Hyndman: the initial *pronunciamento* of Connolly's new party closely parallels the 1883 declaration of the Social Democratic Federation. The new movement called for, as its immediate aims, the nationalisation of railways and canals, the abolition of private banks and their replacements by State bodies, graduated income tax, free education up to the highest level, a minimum wage, and a maximum working week. But it called also for the gradual extension of public ownership to all the necessaries of life, and it pronounced, as its ultimate object, the 'establishment of an Irish Socialist Republic based upon the public ownership by the Irish people of the land and the instruments of production, distribution, and exchange. Agriculture to be administered as a public function, under boards of management elected by the agricultural population and responsible to them and to the nation at large'.[2]

Such a programme was well in advance of that being put forward on the English hustings by the Independent Labour Party. In England, Marxism never gained a firm foothold; the Labour Party which was to emerge from the coming together of the Independent Labour Party, the Labour Representation Committee, the Fabian Society, and the trade unions, owed more to noncomformism and to the 'pure' craft unionism which Connolly despised, than it did to Marx. Connolly stands in a completely different stream; he could write, around the same period, in the Paris journal of Maud Gonne, *Irlande Libre*: 'Scientific Socialism is based upon the truth incorporated in this proposition of Karl Marx, that, "the economic dependence of the workers on the monopolists of the means of production is the foundation of slavery in all its forms, the cause of nearly all social misery, modern crime, mental degradation and political dependence".' To Connolly, Marx was 'the ablest exponent of socialism the world has seen, and the founder of that school of thought which embraces all the militant socialist parties of the world'.[3]

If we require further evidence of this divergence in principle between Connolly and the gradualist socialism of such organisations as the Independent Labour Party, we can find it, fortuitously, in the history of the development of continental European Socialism, for this was the period of one of the most famous of the revisionist controversies inside the international socialist camp. In a time of hunger and revolution, in the middle of the nineteenth century, Marxism had imparted a new dynamic to the working-class movement everywhere. But by the beginning of this century the starkness of Marx's message was already falling less happily upon the ears of many western European socialists and trade unionists. The growing impetus of remedial social legislation had begun to mitigate the worst evils of the working-man's lot; more important still it was beginning to impress upon him a positive and hopeful vision of what the state could achieve in his behalf. Marx had, on the other hand, defined the state as an executive committee for the bourgeois which must be totally smashed if the true interests of the workers were ever to be realised. Now that this same state increasingly accepted the obligation to palliate the injustices of industrial society, the logic of Marx carried less conviction. And at the very same time as socialists began to see the state not as their enemy but as a potential means to their emancipation, the gradual extension of the franchise opened up to them the practical prospect of some day gaining control of this instrument by peaceful parliamentary means.

It was against this background that the Millerand controversy was played out. Millerand, as a French socialist, decided that his principles did not at all debar him from joining a coalition ministry with members of the Radical Party. At once, a storm broke out inside the second International over the propriety of his action. To the purist Marxist revolutionaries, his was the act of a renegade; to many of the revisionists it was no more than a perhaps excessive and premature step in a direction which was in itself only realistic. The Paris Congress of the International faced, in 1900, the problem of reconciling these opposite viewpoints. It did so in a compromise resolution drafted by Karl Kautsky, chiefly remembered as the adversary of Lenin. This resolution affirmed, as a political necessity, that socialists must, in the majority of cases, accept the prospect that they could only attain power not by any dramatic *coup de main* but by the laborious conquest of the parliamentary representation. At the same time, however, the resolution implicitly dissociated the International from the specific action of Millerand by questioning the tactical wisdom for socialists of entering into coalition with bourgeois ministries. This compromise was accepted, with varying degrees of enthusiasm, by almost all the shades of socialist opinion represented at the congress; only two delegations voted en bloc against the resolution and came out unequivocally in favour of the traditionally revolutionary Marxist policy. One of these two was the delegation of the Irish Socialist Republican Party.[4] Connolly was not himself a member of this delegation; his financial circumstances – never in this period secure – probably prevented him from making the journey. But he fully concurred in its course, and at home, in the Worker's Republic, he published his criticisms of revisionism and gradualism, not merely as practised by Millerand, but also as manifested in the tactics of the Independent Labour Party in England. He believed, he said, in the fundamental importance of the class struggle, which would lead to the 'working-class seizing hold of political power and using this power to transfer the ownership of the means of life . . . from individual to public or social ownership'.[5]

In 1903 Connolly paid his first visit to America, and shortly afterwards transferred the home of himself and his family to that country, in which he was to remain until 1910. The decision to emigrate was one which he was subsequently to regret, but his inevitable involvement in

American socialist politics affords us further insight into his theoretical position. The American socialists he found divided into the customary factions; amongst them, he was at once attracted towards the Socialist Labour Party of Daniel de Leon. This body is described by David Shannon in his history of the rival Socialist Party of America as 'a small and doctrinaire sect of Marxist purists'[6] – such was the character that no doubt attracted Connolly to it, despite the sporadic flirtations of its leader, de Leon, with the somewhat deviationist policy of syndicalism. But the personalities of the two men – de Leon was opinionated, vituperative, and stubborn, Connolly merely stubborn – soon proved incompatible. After repeated squabbles the year 1907 found them in open conflict inside the party on the issue of trade union policy within the capitalist wage system. De Leon discounted the value of hard-won wage concessions; he argued that they were invariably followed by compensating rises in prices – an argument more familiar to modern students of economics. Connolly characteristically replied with a defence of industrial action based upon a restatement, in the Industrial Union Bulletin, of the classic Ricardo-Marx theory of value.[7]

Connolly's personal quarrels with de Leon did not prevent him from joining, in the meanwhile, with the latter and the famous 'Big Bill' Heywood in the founding of the equally famous IWW – the Industrial Workers of the World, or, as they were colloquially known, the wobblies. The message of the IWW was that the worker should scorn the rightwing craft unionism of the American Federation of Labour; in its place he should subscribe to the 'one big union which would unite all the workers of America not merely in the defence of their minimal rights inside the capitalist wage structure but also in the prosecution of militant and revolutionary socialism. 'The working-class and the employing-class have nothing in common . . . ' declared the opening manifesto of the new union: 'Between these two classes a struggle must go on until the workers of the world, organised as a class, take possession of the earth and the machinery of production, and abolish the wage system'.[8] 'Let us be clear', wrote Connolly in 1905, 'as to the function of Industrial Unionism. That function is to build up an industrial republic inside the shell of the political state, in order that when that industrial republic is fully organised it may crack the shell of the political state and step into its place in the scheme of the universe . . . Under a socialist form of society the administration of affairs will be in the hands of representatives of the various industries of the nation; . . . the workers in the shops and factories will organise themselves into unions, each union comprising all the workers in a given industry; . . . said union will democratically control the workshop life of its own industry, electing all foremen, etc., and regulating the routine of labour in the industry in subordination to the needs of society in general, to the needs of its allied trades, and to the department of industry to which it belongs . . . Representatives elected from these various departments of industry will meet and form the industrial administration or national government of the country. In short, social democracy, as its name implies, is the application to industry or to the social life of the nation, of the fundamental principles of democracy. Such application will necessarily have to begin in the workshop, and proceed logically and consecutively upward until it reaches the culminating point of national executive power and direction. In other words, socialism must proceed from the bottom upwards, whereas capitalist political society is organised from above downwards.'[9] As a political attitude it was a curious hybrid, looking at once backwards to classic French syndicalism, and, at the same time, curiously presaging the Leninist–Trotskyist cry of 'all power to the Soviets'.

When Connolly returned to Ireland in 1910 he had, then, added to his Marxist socialist politics a new interest in revolutionary trade unionism. There can be little doubt that both of these interests, but more especially the latter, were shared by James Larkin. Indeed, one of the developments which inspired Connolly to return to Ireland was the foundation by Larkin in 1908 of the Transport Union, and one of Connolly's first actions upon his return was to acquire membership of the union, of which he served for a time as Ulster secretary, and to the Control of which he succeeded upon Larkin's departure to America in 1914.

To Larkin, as to Connolly, trade unionism was no mere palliative of the wage system, and 1913 was much more than an attempt to secure a better deal for the workers inside the capitalist framework. The product, like Connolly, of an emigrant upbringing, Larkin too was a member of Hyndman's Social Democratic Federation, and had acquired an interest in revolutionary syndicalism before he ever left England. When Connolly returned from America, Larkin had just emerged from a prison sentence earned for him by his trade union activities. Rapidly the two men gravitated towards one another and struck up a close association. Already they had arrived, separately, at a basic identity of viewpoint. Indeed, when Larkin went to America in 1914 he quickly assumed a similar political stance and pursued similar political activities to those which Connolly had prosecuted some ten years earlier. By this stage the evolutionary Socialist Party of America had forged clearly ahead of its rivals on the left; under the leadership of men like Eugene Debs, Norman Thomas, and Upton Sinclair it seemed to offer, indeed, in this period a serious challenge for political power in the United States. In these circumstances, the majority on the American left accepted the necessity to make common cause under the Socialist Party's leadership. But for the extreme left this was conceded always with reservations; it was unceasingly wary of a bourgeois betrayal by the party leadership.

The conflict which destroyed this alliance was provoked by the spectacle of the Russian revolution. The left wing of the Socialist Party of America saw the Bolshevik triumph as the signal for the immediate adoption of a comparable revolutionary policy in the United States. The old guard would have none of it. The rebels responded by organising in New York a 'Left Wing Section' of the party, with its own dues, officers, and newspaper. The programme of the new group called for worker control of industry through workers' soviets, the nationalisation of all banks and railways and the socialisation of foreign trade. Above all, it demanded that the party as a whole should 'agitate exclusively for the overthrow of capitalism, and the establishment of socialism through proletarian dictatorship', and furthermore, that it should at once affiliate with the Russian Bolsheviks.[10] One of the leaders of this group was James Larkin.

It is easy to see, then, that Connolly and Larkin had more in common than a happy coincidence of personalities. They were both Marxists with inchoate yearnings towards syndicalist action, these latter being, perhaps, more pronounced in the more flamboyant and less clear-thinking Larkin. They were both Irish nationalists and republicans. The reasons why they saw these two attitudes as, not merely compatible, but complementary, were, however, essentially socialist. To Connolly, as to Larkin, the struggle against imperialism was justifiable not merely in patriotic terms. He had no hatred of the English as such. 'The Irish worker who starves in an Irish cabin and the Scots worker who is poisoned in an Edinburgh garret are brothers with one hope and destiny . . . ', he once said. 'The landlord who grinds his peasants on a Connemara estate, and the landlord who rackrents them in a Cowgate slum, are brethren in fact and deed'.[11] Connolly's was no emotional, wrap-the-green-flag-round-me nationalism. In an appendix to Sean O'Casey's very rare pamphlet, the 'Story of the Irish Citizen Army', (O'Casey was its first honorary secretary) there is a copy of the first handbill which the Citizen Army issued. It openly appeals to the workers of Dublin not to join the National Volunteers, who, it says, are led by men who have long opposed the labour cause, but rather to enrol in an organisation led by men of their own class. Patriotism may have turned Connolly's steps towards the GPO, but he could rationalise his decision in Marxist terms. Certainly, he had no desire to assist in the destruction of an English bourgeois State only to witness the creation of an Irish equivalent in its place; indeed, arguably, with his decision to join in the local nationalist revolution in the middle of the First World War, he can be seen as the only Marxist leader of any importance apart from Lenin to apply with complete logic Marxist teaching on the proper tactics for the proletariat in the context of imperialist war. 'The political institutions of today are simply the coercive forms of capitalist society', he wrote in 1908, rejecting, explicitly, the Fabian view of the state. 'They have grown up out of and are based upon territorial divisions of power in the hands of the ruling class in past ages, and were carried over into capitalist society to suit the needs of the capitalist class when that class threw over the dominion of its predecessors. The delegation of the function of government into the hands of representatives elected from certain districts, states, or territories, represents no real natural division suited to the requirements of modern society, but is a survival from a time when territorial influences were more potent than industrial influences, and for that reason is totally unsuited to the needs of the new social order which is based upon industry'.[12] One need hardly say that this is basically pure Marxism, with perhaps a syndicalist gloss. One need equally hardly say that it was scarcely representative of the ambitions of, for example, Joseph Plunkett. Can we not say, then, that 1916 was in a sense one of the first of this century's popular fronts? And, moreover, perhaps the only one in which it was the Marxists who got taken for a ride?

THE POLITICAL IDEAS OF THE LABOUR PARTY

All this exegesis is not, however, designed as an attempt posthumously to witch-hunt the late James Connolly. It is rather an attempt to answer a specific question, perhaps the only one of the questions posed in this essay to which, indeed, a positive answer can be given. Ask the average Irish Labour Party supporter today what he believes in, and he will most certainly not say, with Marx, the class war, the total smashing of the bourgeois state, and the establishment of the dictatorship of the proletariat. He will almost equally certainly not say, with Clause Four of the English Labour Party programmes of 1918 and 1929, the common ownership of the means of production, distribution, and exchange. It is, indeed, unlikely that he will even say the welfare state. What he is most likely to say is: I follow the principles of James Connolly. Each May, when Connolly Commemoration week is held, Dublin hears one Labour leader after another rise and make that statement. I think, however, that we have seen enough to reach one conclusion: for better or for worse – none of them does anything of the kind.

However, that is not the only issue which is posed by this evidence. It is, I think, quite clear to anyone who makes even the most perfunctory inspection of the modern Irish Labour Party, that it belongs in the broad stream of the revisionist Social Democrat parties of the continent, of men like Ollenhauer, Brandt, and Mollet. It accepts not merely the parliamentary but the capitalist system; it is content to work within this system, on Fabian lines, for, on the one hand, ameliorative social legislation, and, on the other for some limited and on the whole unspecified extensions of State activity in the industrial sphere. The word socialism almost never passes its lips. And yet – how simply we accept this development as a political fact without wondering at its origins. The attempts of revisionists like Messrs Gaitskell, Crosland, Jay, and Jenkins to end the paper commitment of the English Labour Party to public ownership were not merely bitterly opposed inside the left but widely published and watched with interest throughout the political spectrum. Forty-six years ago the Irish left was superficially more doctrinaire than that of England; its two most prominent, and still, today, most symbolic leaders were Marxists. The comparatively unobtrusive dilution of Irish Labour policies over the intervening years, can then, it might seem, be accounted for only by some remarkable local circumstances. What were they?

This, my second question, is a more difficult one to answer. But one can, at once, make some important qualifications. In the first place, the antithesis which I have deliberately drawn between the revolutionary Marxism of Connolly and Larkin and the reformism of contemporary Labour thinking, while justified, I hope, as a corrective to facile associations between the two, masks one fundamental and neglected point. *Pace*, once more, the traditionalists, one must concede that the revolutionary fervour of Connolly and Larkin was never fully representative of the movement as a whole. Larkin's practical authority was not extensive outside Dublin, and his Transport Union represented only one aspect of

Irish trade unionism. Connolly and Larkin were only two among the leaders of the Labour Party which was founded in Dublin in 1911, and established on a national basis by the Irish Trade Union Congress in Clonmel in May 1912. Connolly's intellectual commitment was much more to the older Socialist Party of Ireland or Independent Labour Party of Ireland, as it alternately described itself. This was the organisation which Connolly had joined immediately upon his return from America; it included among its leaders such men as Francis Sheehy Skeffington and R. J. P. Mortished. It was much more to the left in its policies, and much more dominated by Connolly, than the official Labour Party. Of these two, the Labour Party, or the Trade Union Congress and Labour Party, as it described itself in this period, was the ancestor of the party which we know today. It was by far the more representative of the two, and it shared neither Connolly's Marxism nor his militant and explicit nationalist republicanism. Yet this was the organisation which was called upon to reorganise the left after the collapse of the 1916 revolt and to determine its subsequent tactics in the period of the troubles and the civil war.

The importance of the Rising as a turning-point is perhaps almost impossible to exaggerate. To Connolly and Larkin, republican nationalism was all of a piece with militant Marxism; after 1916 Connolly was dead and Larkin still in America, and their spiritual heirs held very different views on both subjects. Nationalist hagiography has it that through his position as leader of the Irish Citizen Army Connolly committed Irish Labour irrevocably to the republican movement. In fact, he was in no position to do anything of the kind. The Citizen Army arose out of the 1913 strike as a counter-organisation to protect the strikers from police brutality. With the ending of the strike, as O'Casey admits, its numbers dropped enormously.[13] Many left it on account of its association with Larkin's Transport Union, still, it must be remembered, the object of the employer's odium. In 1914 it was reorganised, and according to O'Casey rose to a membership of a thousand.[14] But it was never warmly endorsed by official trade unionism; even inside the Transport Union the top level leadership were not all its devotees, and at the time of the Rising it still seems to have drawn little support from other unions.

THE AFTERMATH OF 1916

At all times, then, the Citizen Army was a small force, unrepresentative even of the average Dublin worker. According to W. P. Ryan, at its heyday it could muster no more than 118 rifles.[15] After 1916 it ceased to count as a political force; the hard core of its leaders died or were arrested with Connolly; by the time of the truce in July 1921 it is doubtful if even a working chain of command had been maintained. The Transport Union itself passed from the hands of Connolly to those of William O'Brien, an able and determined man, but moderate and unspectacular by comparison with what had gone before. With all his customary brilliance, O'Casey describes, in his autobiography, the changed atmosphere at Liberty Hall: 'Liberty Hall had been shoved back into order after the battering it had got from the guns of the Helga, but there was a woebegone look on its face, for its great men had gone, and Ichabod was its name now. It was but a hatchway now for the payment of dues by the members. Odd the building looked, disarmed of its temper and temerity, and it seemed to be ashamed of still standing there with one of its champions dead, and the other in a far-away prison. The Union's executive had gone far from the madding crowd of workers, and had taken over a Georgian house in Rutland Square whose dignified doorway, tiled hall, plate glass, pinewood counters, and stately desks gave it a presence that made it ashamed of its parent, Liberty Hall, with its raucous voice, turbulent manner, and defiance of all power inimical to the workers' cause. Here, behind a formidable desk, sat William O'Brien . . . ' Even allowing for O'Casey's intense personal commitment one can recognise, objectively, that times had changed. O'Casey's reaction was, predictably, to enrol in Connolly's old Socialist Party of Ireland.[16]

So much for the Citizen Army and the Transport Union. That the Labour Party itself should wish to draw in its horns in a context of martial law and military disaster is even less surprising. The party as a whole had never endorsed Connolly's open association with the nationalist cause; as an all-Ireland movement, resting almost as much on Belfast as on Dublin, it could scarcely have afforded to do so. With the failure of the Rising, the task of pulling the movement together again devolved upon men who had not been implicated in it, men like Thomas Johnson and David Campbell, both active in Ulster. The first Congress of the party after the Rising was held in Sligo in Whit 1916. It placed on record its affection and regret for those who had died both in the streets of Dublin and on the continent, but declined to assess the relative merit of their sacrifices. Without actually repudiating the action of the Citizen Army, the congress took pains to remind the world at large that this body had been a small and quite independent organisation, domiciled in

Liberty Hall purely as a sub-tenant. At the same time, on the level of trade union policy, the members of unions with cross-channel affiliations dug their heels in firmly against the proposal of the surviving Connollyites to press on towards his old IWW-inspired goal of 'one big Irish union'.

By no means, though, did the party at once dissociate itself from all kinds of socialism. In 1918 a statement of aims was adopted which included the intentions 'to win for the workers of Ireland, collectively, the ownership and control of the produce of their labour' and 'to secure the democratic management and control of all industries and services by the whole body of the workers'.[17] (These two provisions are notable absentees from the present constitution of the party, adopted in 1952, which nevertheless commits the party to the establishment of 'a democratic republic based upon the social teachings of its founder, James Connolly'.)[18] The party applauded the success of the Kerensky revolution in Russia, and at the 1917 congress resolved to send O'Brien and Campbell to the Stockholm conference which followed it. The success of the second, November, revolution in Russia did not at once reverse this policy of support. O'Brien and Campbell met Litvinov in London; they were told of the admiration felt by Lenin and Trotsky for Connolly's writings, and assured of Russian support for the claim of Ireland to be admitted as a full nation to the socialist International. Thomas Johnson and Cathal O'Shannon were despatched to the Berne congress of 1919; the congress passed a Swedish resolution on 'Democracy and Dictatorship' which underlined the breach between Bolshevik and democratic socialism. A rival resolution warning against 'any kind of stigma which may be applied to the Russian Soviet Republic', and seeking to leave open the door for its admission to the International was deferred; among the minority which supported it was the Irish delegation. On their return to Dublin Johnson and O'Shannon were reported as having described the Soviet Union as Ireland's 'best and most disinterested friend'.[19]

But tactically, all this militancy was probably vitiated by the failure of the movement to recognise and to put into practice what was arguably the most vital element in all Connolly's teaching. Connolly realised that Labour would have to participate wholeheartedly in the nationalist struggle as a separate and characteristic unit if it was to have any influence at all in the ultimate reconstruction of the state. Of all the factors which helped to bring about the relative decline of Labour after 1922 this was perhaps the most vital. Individual labour men were, of course, active in the republican war, and in its later years the trade union movement made useful gestures such as the refusal to transport arms and British military personnel. But as a unit, Labour made no independent contribution. In both the 1918 and 1920 elections the party stood down and called upon the electors to support the exponents of self-determination. It expressed the hope that the nation would remember Labour's sacrifice and repay it when the time came. The nation, of course, did nothing of the kind. 113 thousand men were unemployed in December 1921, not including agricultural labourers, but the civil war perpetuated the slogan – Labour must wait. When Tom Johnson led a deputation to Arthur Griffith, Griffith told him: 'I know and understand perfectly this question of unemployment'. He offered to appoint a committee to investigate it, but inside the Dáil his party consistently ignored the social proposals put forward by Labour spokesmen. The vice-chairman of the national executive, L. J. Duffy, remarked: 'One of the things this alleged freedom has brought to Ireland is the most desirable freedom to scrap everything calculated to benefit the condition of the working classes in this country'.[20] In the civil war Labour carried its official aloofness from nationalist politics into what may well have been yet another tactical blunder. The leaders of the movement insisted upon a policy of absolute neutrality, and so an opportunity was, perhaps, lost of joining up with the radical wing which undoubtedly existed in the republic camp and which was best personified in Liam Mellows.

Meanwhile, in America, Larkin, the surviving partner of the old team, had been watching these developments, not always with approval. Characteristically and logically, he broke Labour's silence during the treaty negotiations by cabling home his condemnation of the signatories.[21] Now, in 1923, he returned to Dublin after an absence of over eight years. So was sparked off a catastrophe which is the last to be considered in this chronicle, and in many ways, the one still most remembered with regret and sorrow. The Transport Union had changed too much to accommodate peacefully the explosive personality of its old founder. The incompatibility of Larkin and William O'Brien soon flared into an open struggle for power between the two men. Larkinites seized the offices of the Transport Union, O'Brienites expelled Larkin from the general secretaryship which he had technically held throughout his exile. Injunction and counter-injunction between the contending parties formed the background to the 1923 election, in which Labour lost three of the seventeen seats which it had won in the previous year when it had been the only independent element in the so-called pact election. The Larkinites were finally worsted in the courts, and left without a formal organisation. In 1923 Larkin founded the Irish Workers League, and a year later, during his absence in Russia, his followers founded the Workers Union of Ireland as a counterblast to the Transport Union.

The controversies of 1923 were not singly responsible for the subsequent weakness of the Labour movement. But they illustrate two characteristics which were to be all too typical of it in the next thirty years. One was the disunity of the trade union movement. The other was that steady siphoning-off of the self-consciously socialist elements on the left from the Labour Party, which should have been their natural home, and for whose national trade union support they should have been performing the service rendered by the Webbs and Tawneys to the English Labour Party, that is to say, the provision of the independent social policy which Irish Labour was so signally to lack in this period. Instead began that pilgrimage from splinter-group to splinter-group into ultimate disillusion which is the life story of so many Irish socialists.

There would, however, be little point in attempting here to trace the the electoral fortunes of the Labour Party from that day to this. It is, on the whole, as even Labour's most fervent supporter would surely have to admit, a record of frustration and little success. The party has left few traces upon Irish social or industrial legislation; it has maintained a depressingly small representation in the Dáil. Unique among European States, Ireland has conducted her politics for the last forty years almost without controversy upon those issues of social and economic policy which are the theme of politics elsewhere.

The Future of Labour

What chance has Labour today of becoming a significant party? No less a witness than Mr Lemass has recognised the Labour Party as potentially the main alternative to Fianna Fáil.[22] But after forty years of quiescence, can this potential ever be realised?

There are, for Labour, a number of hopeful signs. After years of bitterness, unity has finally been restored to the trade union movement. A new leader has been elected, in Mr Corish, to speak for the Labour Party; one of his first actions was to sponsor an appeal to all the elements of the democratic left to make common cause with the party in the Ireland of the sixties. How much practical effect this will have it is hard, as yet, to say; but can we anticipate the emergence of a new and more dynamic Labour Party in the next decade?

In endeavouring to answer this question one leaves, at once, the relative certitude of the historical past, and enters into the dangerous realm of prophecy. Yet there are signs which suggest that a qualified affirmative may be hazarded in reply. Of those hopeful signs, the restoration of unity in the trade union movement is, of course, the most obvious. If the Labour Party could resume the close organisational association with the Trade Union Congress which it once possessed; if it could, by a relationship comparable to that which exists between the trade unions and the Labour Party in England, gain access to the reserves of money and manpower in the unions, it would, at once, multiply many times over its political resources. Two main obstacles stand in the way of such a development. In the first place, there is the hostility of the individual trade unionist who votes for Fianna Fáil or Fine Gael. If there are many trade unionists in Great Britain who do not vote Labour, there must be many more in Ireland. But still more important: how could such an alliance be established between a thirty-two-county trade union movement and what is essentially a twenty-six-county party?

Here indeed one places one's finger on a major weakness in Labour's position. More than any other party, Labour, surely, was struck a vital blow by the loss to the Republic of the industrial north-east, the area which with Cork and Dublin had formed one leg of the urban tripod upon which so much of Labour strength in the early years of the century had been based. It is as much this, perhaps, as any other factor, which has orientated Labour's attention away from industry and towards the more conservative rural worker, until the ludicrous point has been reached in which what is historically a party of the industrial working class can hold only a single seat in the one great urban concentration in the Republic.

This peculiarity is naturally reflected in the social policies of the party. In general these have long tended to be pragmatic and unconvincing. By name and origin the party of the left, Labour nevertheless lacks a distinctive political image. For this the general sterility of Irish political debate must to some extent be blamed. Most original political thinking in the west during the last thirty years has been done to some extent in reaction against the spectre of Marxism. But in Ireland not merely Marxism, but liberal democratic socialism, arguably Marxism's most detested philosophical opponent, are stereotype labels which evoke inevitable anathema. It is questionable if political progress can ever be made while the limits of permissible debate are so dogmatically prescribed. But more than Labour should have cause to fear this vacuum on the left. Vacuums have a way of getting filled. The price which other countries have paid for the exclusion of all democratic socialist influences has all too often been the ultimate triumph of Marxism. If that were to happen in Ireland, then, at last, ironically, we could properly celebrate Connolly Commemoration Week.

NOTES

1 R. M. Fox, Jim Larkin, p. 176.

2 Programme of the Irish Socialist Republican Party, in *J. Connolly, Socialism and Nationalism*, ed. D. Ryan, p. 184.

3 *L'Irlande Libre*, 1897, quoted ibid.; Workers' Republic, 1 July 1899, in *J. Connolly, The Workers' Republic*, ed. D. Ryan, p. 41.

4 G. D. H. Cole, *History of Socialist Thought*, vol. III, part I, pp. 37-40.

5 Quoted in C. D. Greaves, *The Life And Times of James Connolly*, p.117.

6 D. A. Shannon, *The Socialist Party of America*, p. 1.

7 *The IWW, Its First Fifty Years*, complied by F. Thompson, pp. 37-8.

8 Ibid., p. 4

9 S. and B. Webb, *History of Trade Unionism*, 1920, pp. 655-7.

10 J Oneal and G. A. Werner, *American Communism*, pp. 375-7

11 Quoted in Greaves, op. cit., p. 50.

12 Quoted in W. P. Ryan, *The Irish Labour Movement*, pp. 163-4.

13 P. O'Cathasaigh, *Story of the Irish Citizen Army*, pp. 7-lJ.

14 Ibid., p. 31.

15 W. P. Ryan, op. cit., p. 250.

16 S. O'Casey, *Inishfallen, Fare Thee Well*, pp. 4-5, 6.

17 J. D. Clarkson, *Labour and Nationalism in Ireland*, pp. 325-6.

18 *Constitution of the Irish Labour Party*, adopted 18 April 1952, Part II, Clause I.

19 G. D. H: Cole, *History of the Labour Party Since 1914* (1948), pp. 98-100; Clarkson. op. cit., p. 336.

20 Ibid., pp. 441, 462.

21 Ibid., p. 343.

22 Speech to Fianna Fáil (Dublin North-Central Constituency) Annual Dinner, *Irish Times*, 5 May 1961.

PATRICK PEARSE

DAVID THORNLEY

Pearse was more than a patriot; he was a virtuous man. He possessed all the qualities which go to the making of a saint . . . it would not be astonishing if Pearse were canonised some day . . .[1]

That passage is taken from Louis Le Roux's biography of Pearse, first published in English in 1932, and to date the only full-length biography. It illustrates the virtual impossibility of writing, even today, an objective study of a man whose death elevated him into the most sacred realms of national mythology. Behind the Pearse of legend – the orator, the Gael, the child Pearse, allegedly swearing on his knees to free Ireland or die fighting the English; the man Pearse, writing a promised poem to his mother in the condemned cell – it is not merely difficult but almost blasphemous to discern a human being of flesh and blood. It is the historian's obligation to make the attempt, but in the circumstances, and at fifty years' remove, it can only be an interim one.

Patrick Henry Pearse was born on 10 November 1879 at 27 Great Brunswick Street, now Pearse Street, Dublin, where his father, James Pearse, carried on business as a monumental sculptor, James Pearse was born, according to his obituaries, in London in December 1839, and seems to have been of thoroughly English and probably Protestant stock, although be was a Roman Catholic at least as early as the birth of his first child in 1864. He came to Dublin, reputedly from Birmingham, as a very young man, being one of a group of ecclesiastical craftsmen brought to Ireland as the influence of the Gothic revival swept over post-Emancipation church-building. He worked for various monumental firms before finally setting up in independent business in 1878. By the time of his death he had attained a considerable eminence as a sculptor; his most acclaimed work was the heroic group of figures crowning the facade of the National Bank in College Green, but examples of his style are to be found in many of the churches built in Ireland in the second half of the century, and the Freeman's Journal described him as 'the pioneer of modem Gothic art, as applied to Church work, in this country'.[2]

He married twice: firstly, Emily Fox, who bore him two children before dying in 1876 at the age of thirty, and secondly in October 1877, when he was thirty-seven, Margaret Brady, a twenty-year-old Irish girl whose family came from Meath. She bore him four children, two of them sons, Patrick, born in 1879, and William James, born in 1881.

In politics James Pearse was a convinced Home Ruler, but of a mentality unmistakably that of an English radical. His one literary work was a pamphlet entitled 'England's duty to Ireland as it appears to an Englishman', published in 1886 in reply to an anti-Home Rule and anti-clerical tract of a Catholic Fellow of Trinity College, Thomas Maguire. Pearse's pamphlet shows remarkably wide reading for a man who must have had relatively little formal education, he quotes triumphantly Caius Gracchus, Tiberius Sempronius, Polybius, Addison and Thomas D'Arcy Magee to sustain the thesis that 'you ought not to force a mode of government upon an unwilling people. And you cannot forever do so whether you ought to or not.' 'I am Englishman enough to say' he declared, 'that were I an Irishman my duty and my patriotism would force me into the ranks of Mr Parnell.'

James Pearse maintained his English connections throughout his life; members of the Pearse family stood sponsor at Patrick's baptism, and it was on a visit to his brother's home in Birmingham that he suddenly collapsed and died in 1900. His body was brought back to Dublin and buried in Glasnevin. His business was carried on for some years by his younger son, among whose work is a Mater Dolorosa which still stands in Westland Row church. James Pearse, English radical, mature and opinionated, must have been an interesting father for a boy in his teens. James Pearse may well have suffered neglect in a nationalist tradition to which the source of filial inspiration must almost always be seen as maternal. At the very least he provided the mixed background not unusual to Irish patriots: Parnell's mother was an American, Thomas MacDonagh's mother English, Tom Clarke's father a Presbyterian and a soldier in the British army, Eamon de Valera's father Spanish.

Patrick was educated at the Christian Brothers' School, Westland Row, and through the old Royal University. He took his BA in 1901 and was soon after called to the bar. In 1905 he made one of his few appearance as a barrister, pleading, with Tim Healy, before the King's Bench division, the case of a Donegal farmer who had been fined one shilling at Dunfanaghy for putting his name on his cart in 'illegible', that is to say, Irish letters. Pearse's defence was described by one of the judges as 'very ingenious, interesting, and from a literary point of view, instructive', but he lost his case. He never apparently practised again, and in later years described the lawyer's craft as 'the most ignoble of all professions'.[3] His career was instead to lie in education.

In September 1908 he founded St Enda's College as an experimental bilingual secondary school for boys in Cullenswood House, Rathmines. In 1910 he decided that the house was too small and too close to the city to give full scope to his ideals. Cullenswood House was converted into St Ita's, a sister-school for girls, while the main school was moved to The Hemitage at Rathfarnham, the lease of which Pearse managed to secure with the financial backing of some friends. St Enda's now became wholly a boarding-school, and assumed the form described so affectionately in Pearse's own *Story of a Success* and in Desmond Ryan's writings.

Pearse's educational ideas were in advance of their time. The school language and games were Irish, and all other subjects except languages and the scientific subjects were taught bilingually. Nature-study was encouraged, and Irish plays were regularly performed. The disciplinary emphasis was upon trust and self-reliance. Opinions normally vary as to how wholly successful those methods proved, but such an issue falls outside the scope of this study. Two points are relevant. Firstly, the role of educationalist always remained central to Pearse's character and was to be the theme of many of his writings, of which the best-known in this context is the collection of essays between 1912 and 1914, later published in pamphlet form in 'The Murder Machine'. This work combines liberal teaching methods with unyielding nationalism. 'What the teacher should bring to his pupils is not a set of ready-made opinions, or a stock of cut-and-dry information, but an inspiration and an example; and his main qualification should be, not such an overmastering will as shall impose itself at all hazards upon all weaker wills that come under its influence but rather so infectious an enthusiasm as shall kindle new enthusiasm'. To an anxious parent who asked what be should do with a son who was good at nothing but playing the tin whistle, Pearse replied: 'Buy a tin whistle for him'.

With these thoroughly modern ideas went, however, a view of the place of nationalism in education with which some might quarrel. 'If the true work of the teacher be . . . to help the child to realize himself at his best and worthiest, the factor of nationality is of prime importance.'[4] The child was to be taught that the Irish separatist tradition began in 1169 and embraced the supporters of Edward Bruce, Art MacMurrough, Shane O'Neill, and just about everyone else who had ever taken up arms in Ireland.[5] This is scarcely the view of modern historical scholarship, but it was logically the view of a man who saw no incompatibility between the roles of educationalist and propagandist to his pupils of Gaelic and, at least from 1910 onwards, physical force nationalism. As MacDara, the hero of Pearse's most famous play, *The Singer*, published in 1915, declares: 'The true teacher must suffer and do. He must break bread to the people, he must go into Gethsemane and toil up the steep of Golgotha . . . Sometimes I think that to be a woman and to serve and suffer as women do is the highest thing. Perhaps that is why I felt it proud and wondrous to be a teacher for a teacher does that.'

However successful St Enda's may have been educationally it did not pay its way. Pearse had no head for money matters, he was sometimes unable to pay his teachers' salaries, and was recurrently saved from the school's creditors by loyal friends. Yet even this was to play a circumstantial part in the inevitable process by which Pearse's educational work gained the active support of the Irish Republican Brotherhood.

Pearse, like so many of the young men of his time, came to nationalism through the Gaelic League. His love of Irish was apparently first stimulated around the age of eleven or twelve by a female relative of his mother's who was well versed in Gaelic history and legend. The youthful Pearse studied Irish through the grammar and texts of the Society for the Preservation of the Gaelic Language, and later at the classes held by Canon O'Leary in Dame Street. As an adult he widened his knowledge by regular visits to the Connaught Gaelacht, where he acquired a cottage at Rosmuc. Pearse's Irish was largely self-taught, and although many of his works were to be written in that medium, expert opinion can always detect that he was not a native speaker. But his writings were suffused by a tremendous love of the language and of the Gaeltacht folk to whom it was the medium of story-telling and reminiscence. This quality of folk sympathy is seen most clearly in the simpler and less rhetorical of Pearse's writings such as the stories 'Iosagán' and 'Brigid of the Songs'.

Pearse's advocacy of the Gaelic revival was remarkably precocious. At the age of seventeen he founded the New Ireland Literary Society with the object of popularising Irish poetry and folklore to 'the barbarian'. His three presidential addresses, subsequently published in 1898, in his nineteenth year, show him an ardent Gaelic nationalist of a mystical rather than a revolutionary kind. 'The Gael is not like other men', he declared in 1897, just before his eighteenth birthday, 'the spade, and the loom, and the sword are not for him. But a destiny more glorious than that of Rome, more glorious than that of Britain, awaits him: to become the saviour of idealism in modern intellectual and social life. . . '[6]

Naturally Pearse was quickly attracted to the Gaelic League which, it must be recalled, was from its foundation in 1893 up to the Dundalk convention of 1915 an essentially non-political body. 'My service to Douglas Hyde,' Pearse wrote in 1913, 'began when I was only sixteen.'[7] In 1903 he became editor of *An Claidheamh Soluis*, the organ of the League, a post which he retained until 1909. Four years later Pearse was to describe the Gaelic League as 'a spent force',[8] the first stage of a revolution which was now to be brought about. But by that time Pearse was a member of the Volunteers and on the fringes of the IRB; in 1909 his resignation from *An Claidheamh Soluis* seems to have been chiefly the result of the growing demands made upon his time by St. Enda's.

Pearse in 1909 was therefore known principally as a dominant figure in the Gaelic revival movement, a writer and speaker of great force and fluency. Physically he had developed a commanding presence. He was above average height, of stocky build, with a clear and impressive profile, although according to contemporaries his facial appearance was marred by a distinct cast in the left eye. By dint of application he had become a fine orator, overcoming in the process a slight natural stammer. His oratory was of the set-piece rather than the impromptu kind, his speeches carefully memorised and rehearsed before a mirror in St Enda's. He was not yet a consistent physical-force revolutionary; as late as April 1912 he spoke from a Home Rule platform in Sackville Street, though making the reservation that Home Rule was a stepping-stone to complete independence.[9] As late as 1912 Pearse was also, according to Desmond Ryan, still critical of the Irish Republican Brotherhood as an association of 'talkers and old Fenians, past all capacity for action'.[10] These might seem incongrous sentiments for the future Commander-in-Chief of a revolution largely organized by the Brotherhood. But three factors determined Pearse's rapid progression to the centre of the republican stage. Firstly, be was a militant Gael, prepared to follow to the bitter end the promptings of his nationalist conscience. Secondly, he was a man who could move and inspire other men. And thirdly, the IRB was in the same period undergoing a rejuvenation which could cause it to appreciate the potential utility of a man with these qualities.

In the period before the outbreak of the First World War the IRB came increasingly under the control of a generation of young, vigorous men. The key figure in this process seems to have been Tom Clarke. To no single figure, Clarke, Pearse, or MacDermott can the inspiration of 1916 be ascribed. But undoubtedly the fact that Clarke, the symbolic fellow-martyr of an older generation, was prepared to throw the weight of his name behind the young men and their policy of action was a major influence in its success. These young men, determined upon a fight, were ready to·make use of congenial material. Clarke had already been enor-mously impressed by a speech which Pearse had made at an Emmet com-memoration concert in 1911,[11] and in June 1913 the IRB chose Pearse to deliver the Bodenstown oration at the grave of Wolfe Tone. Pearse, in the first of a set of orations which have passed into Irish history, fully iden-tified himself with the tradition of Tone. 'We have come to the holiest place in Ireland,' he began: 'holier to us even than the place where Patrick sleeps in Down. Patrick brought us life, but this man died for us.'[12] In the same month Pearse began to contribute a series of articles 'From a Hermitage' to Irish Freedom, the IRB newspaper, which also show a steady progression towards physical force. 'There are only two ways of righting wrongs; reform and revolution' he wrote in October 1913. 'Reform is possible when those who inflict the wrong can be got to see things from the point of view of those who suffer the wrong.'[13]

Pearse was not yet, apparently, a member of the IRB. He was still dis-liked in some IRB circles for his spasmodic constitutionalism. Many of his senior and university students resident at St Enda's, including Desmond Ryan, Con Colbert, Liam Mellowes, and Sean Heuston, were sworn members of the IRB at least eighteen months before their head-master.[14] Late in 1913 Pearse approached Bulmer Hobson with the proj-ect of a fundraising American lecture tour to rescue St Enda's from a financial crisis. Hobson wrote to John Devoy with the approval of Clarke and MacDermott recommending Pearse as 'all right and in line with us here' and St Enda's as 'the only college preparing boys for the universities that is really and intensely national in tone'.[15]

The precise occasion when Pearse was actually sworn into the IRB has been and probably always will be the subject of controversy, but the most probable date is shortly after the foundation of the Volunteers in November 1913 and before Pearse went to America.[16] Of the founding group of the Volunteers, which first met on 11 November 1913, Pearse is listed by Bulmer Hobson amongst those members who were not in the IRB.[17] But the Volunteers were from the outset effectively infiltrated by a cadre of IRB men. Elections to officer rank were used to place them in key positions, and particularly after the split with Redmond in September 1914 the revolutionary nucleus of the Volunteers was supplied by the secret organisation.[18] The overt purpose of the Volunteers was firstly defensive against conscription and partition, but at least from September 1914 the covert purpose of the IRB was to mount a rising before the war ended.

Pearse rapidly rose to a position of prominence in both organisations. He was one of the principal speakers at the Rotunda Rink meeting which launched the Volunteers on 25 November 1913, and from then on became the principal orator of the movement, his work culminating in his electrifying oration at the O'Donovan Rossa funeral in August 1915. On 6 December 1914, at the first meeting of the General Council of the Volunteers after the split with Redmond, he was appointed Director of Organization, and as such issued orders on behalf of MacNeill, the Chief of Staff. Equally, in May 1915, he was appointed, with Joseph Plunkett and Eamonn Ceannt, a member of a three-man military committee set up by the Supreme Council of the IRB to draft a plan for a military insurrection. This committee later became the Military Council and was widened in 1915 to include Clarke and MacDermott, *ex officio*, as Secretary and Treasurer of the Supreme Council and its key figures, and in 1916 Connolly and MacDonagh. In September 1915 Pearse figures as a co-opted member of the Supreme Council of the IRB. In January 1916 the Supreme Council decided upon revolution at 'the earliest date possible', leaving the timing and details to the Military Council.[19]

Two fundamental questions do, however, arise concerning Pearse's position. Firstly, why was Pearse, after only two and a half years in the IRB, and with no military experience, elected by the Military Council to the position of Commander-in-Chief? Secondly, why was Pearse prepared to place himself at the head of a rising which had little initial chance of success and which, after the failure of the arms ship to arrive, he knew could only conclude in his own death?

The first question is only partially answered by Pearse's oratorical powers. More fundamental was the position which he held as a member of the Supreme Council of the IRB and of its Military Council, and at the same time Director of Organisation of the Volunteers. Plunkett and Ceannt were also commandants in the Volunteers, but no other IRB man held such prominent dual rank as Pearse. Clarke, for example, a dedicated revolutionary continually under detective observation, had held back from the prominent role in the Volunteers which Pearse naturally assumed, and Clarke's role and that of MacDermott in the planning of the rising was necessarily little known outside the IRB.

Pearse therefore was indispensable in the link between the IRB and the Volunteers. When he issued orders for military manoeuvres, culminating in the decisive order of Easter 1916, he did so in a dual capacity. To the rank-and-file non-IRB Volunteer he was the spokesman of the Volunteer leadership. To the IRB man in the know he was the spokesman of the Brotherhood. The IRB was the agent and mainspring of the Rising, but with probably not much more than two thousand members, of whom perhaps about a quarter were militarily active,[20] it needed the umbrella of the Volunteers. Hence the protracted deception of MacNeill; hence also the key role of Pearse, whom several of the IRB leaders still regarded as a political amateur.[21]

The seven signatories of the Proclamation of the Republic, the seven members of the Provisional Government, were the seven members of the Military Council of the IRB. But the ordinary Volunteer living in 1916 when communications were so much slower than today, confused by orders and countermanding orders, about to embark upon a desperate gamble against the mightiest empire in the world, knew little of the planning of the Rising which had been perhaps the best-kept secret in Irish revolutionary history. To such a Volunteer, Pearse of the IRB seven was the most familiar figure, the name which had appeared on so many Volunteer orders since December 1914. So the duality of the secret and open organizations, and the reluctance of MacNeill, the technical head of the Volunteers, to strike, propelled Pearse inexorably to the titular leadership.

Why, in turn, was Pearse prepared to assume a role which virtually guaranteed his execution? The answer to this question most probably lies in his writings between 1912 and 1916. In this period Pearse developed the idealism of his 1897 essay to the point where he concluded that his own generation had lost the right to freedom by its decadence and servility, and could only be rejuvenated by a blood-sacrifice. This idea was broadly shared by Connolly, Plunkett, MacDonagh and MacDermott. But Pearse, in both his controversial and his dramatic writings, developed it most fully and single-mindedly. He once wrote to himself, in his short-lived journal, *An Barr Buadh*, 'Pearse, you are too dark in yourself . . . Is it your English blood that is the cause of that, I wonder?' He went on later: 'However, you have the gift of speech. You can make your audience laugh or cry as you please. I suppose there are two Pearses, the sombre and taciturn Pearse and the gay and sunny Pearse.'[22] As the Abbey actress,

Maire nic Shiubhlaigh, a sympathetic observer, recalled, inside St Enda's he was 'a quiet young man, full of nothing but the business of the school. But outside, some might have said Pearse was vain – a bit of a poseur'.[23]

He was indeed a gentle and considerate, if rather humourless man in his school and in his private life, and he was deeply conscious of the responsibilities of military leadership: 'It is a terrible responsibility to be cast upon a man, that of bidding the cannon speak and the grapeshot pour,' he wrote 11 January 1914.[24] But a month earlier he had written: 'May it not be said with entire truth that the reason why Ireland is not free is that Ireland has not deserved to be free?'[25] The right to freedom, he became convinced, could only be won in arms: 'We must accustom our-selves to the thought of arms, to the sight of arms, to the use of arms. We may make mistakes in the beginning and shoot the wrong people; but bloodshed is a cleansing and a sanctifying thing, and the nation which regards it as a final horror has lost its manhood.'[26] Of the European war he wrote in December 1915: 'The last sixteen months have been the most glorious in the history of Europe. Heroism has come back to the earth . . . The old heart of the earth needed to be warmed with the red wine of the battlefields. Such august homage was never before offered to God as this, the homage of millions of lives given gladly for love of country.'[27]

With this concept of the cleansing effect of bloodshed there devel-oped in Pearse's mind a vision of the overthrow of injustice by the sacri-ficial death of virtue. If Pearse's nationalism stemmed principally from Tone, Emmet, and Mitchel, this sacrificial concept had a strongly reli-gious, even Messianic quality. The hero of his play *The King*, first pro-duced in 1912, is a young child whose innocent readiness to give his life for his people frees them where the efforts of the adult King have failed. 'I do homage to thee, O dead King, O victorious child!' says the king at the end; 'I kiss thee, O white body, since it is thy purity that hath redeemed my people.' And *The Singer*, his last play, which is often seen as expressive of his own sense of mission, ends in the same way with the hero going out to certain death crying 'One man can free a people as one Man redeemed the world.' The same expectancy of death is seen in sev-eral of Pearse's poems such as 'The Mother', with its famous lines:

> I do not grudge them; Lord, I do not grudge
> My two strong sons that I have seen go out
> To break themselves and die, they and a few,
> In bloody protest for a glorious thing.

And still more clearly in 'Renunciation':

> I have turned my face
> To this road before me,
> To the deed that I see
> And the death I shall die.

And so, on 3 May 1916, Pearse died, as he had foretold. As soldiers, he and his colleagues were failures. The military plan was foredoomed once the arms failed to arrive, and arguably was ill-conceived from the beginning. There were already those who questioned the logic of sitting within a tightening ring in Dublin waiting to be overwhelmed. Such men were to come back from English prison camps to apply the lessons of 1916 in a more ruthless and ultimately more successful kind of war.

But whether they could have done that *without* 1916 is another question. Maxwell's firing squad made Pearse, even more than his colleagues, the inspiration of a national myth. His was in many ways a strange, divided nature. His elevation of death to the status of a first principle is uncongenial to an age less familiar with the grand gesture. In his own time he was an unrepresentative figure, regarded as an unpractical visionary by many not merely in the Parliamentary Party but in the IRB. In the secret groundwork which preceded the Rising others, specifically Clarke and MacDermott, appear to have played a greater part. But it is difficult not to feel that, by the standards of his own teachings, posterity vindicated Pearse. He had become convinced that the risings of the past had been bedevilled by a last-minute reluctance to strike.[28] In common with the rest of the IRB Military Council he was determined not to repeat that fatal hesitancy. To him to strike was in a sense to win. 'We seem to have lost,' he said at his court martial: 'we have not lost.'[29] And on Wednesday of Easter week in the GPO he is reported as remarking: 'When we are wiped out, people will blame us for everything, condemm us ... After a few years they will see the meaning of what we tried to do.'[30] And indeed, as the released prisoners came back to Dublin in the following year they were accorded a heroes' welcome. If Pearse's course was sacrificial and irrational, it had the unanswerable self-justification of success. As he wrote in his poem 'The Fool', some six months before he was executed:

> The lawyers have sat in council, the men with the keen, long faces,
> And said, 'This man is a fool', and others have said, 'He blasphemeth';
> And the wise have pitied the fool that hath striven to give a life

In the world of time and space among the bulk of actual things
To a dream that was dreamed in the heart, and that only the
heart could hold.

O wise men, riddle me this: what if the dream come true?
What if the dream come true? and if millions unborn shall dwell
In the house that I shaped in my heart?

NOTES

1 Louis Le Roux, Life of P.H. Pearse, p x
2 *Freeman's Journal*, 8 Sept 1900.
3 *From a Heritage*, June 1913.
4 'The Murder Machine', in *Political Writings and Speeches*, 1962 ed, pp.28, 33, 39-40.
5 *Ghosts*, 1915.
6 'The intellectual future of the Gael', in *Songs of the Irish Rebels*, etc, p221.
7 *From a Hermitage*, Aug. 1913.
8 'The Coming Revolution', *An Claidheamh Soluis*, 8 Nov 1913.
9 S. T. O'Ceallaigh, 'The founding of the Irish Volunteers', *Capuchin Annual*, 1963.
10 *Irish Press*, 7 Dec 1963.
11 Donagh MacDonagh, 'Patrick Pearse', in *An Cosantoir*, Aug 1945.
12 *Political Writings and Speeches*, p 53.
13 Ibid, p172.
14 *Irish Press*, 7 Dec 1963.
15 W O'Brien and D Ryan, ed, *Devoy's Postbag*, Vol II, pp 412-13 (incorrectly dated according to Hobson).
16 Rev F. X. Martin, OSA, private correspondence with B. Hobson and D. Ryan, 19, 20 Dec 1963)
17 Rev F. X. Martin, OSA, ed., *The Irish Volunteers*, p30.
18 B. Hobson, in Rev. F.X. Martin, op. cit., pp 12-32; D Lynch, *The IRB and the 1916 Rising*, pp 23, 35.
19 D Lynch, op. cit., pp 30-31.
20 Interview with D. McCullagh, 5 Oct 1965.
21 D MacDonagh, *An Cosantoir*, Aug 1945.
22 Quoted in L le Roux, *Patrick Pearse*, pp 40-41.
23 M. Nic Shuibhlagh, *The Splendid Years*, p 145 et seq.
24 *From a Hermitage*, Jan 1914.
25 Ibid, Dec 1913.
26 'The Coming Revolution', Nov 1913.
27 *Peace and the Gael*, December 1915.
28 'The Coming Revolution', *An Claidheamh Soluis*, 8 Nov 1913.
29 D Ryan, *The Rising*, p260.
30 D. Ryan, *The Man Called Pearse*, p 58.

PART THREE

SELECTED SPEECHES

19

Debate on the Department of the Taoiseach's Estimate for the year 1970, 17 December 1969

Dr Thornley:

I had intended to make only a few very general remarks but, since I was referred to by name by Deputy [Thomas] Meaney (FF), I should like to take up one or two points with reference to myself and my alleged views. There is also the general point, which bears upon what Deputy [Brendan] Corish (leader of the Labour Party) and others have said, about decorum of this House. I am a new member and I am the first to accept this. The Taoiseach's speech, if not particularly inspired, was definitely dignified. He was followed by a speech by the Leader of the Fine Gael Party which was comparably dignified and, in turn, that was followed by a speech by Deputy Corish of the Labour Party which, again, was comparably dignified. Then, from two rows behind the leaders of the Fianna Fáil Party one back-bench member stood up armed not merely with the statistics of the history of the national struggle but also with predictable references to, for example, divorce and to communism and to individual naming of people.

I happen to feel particularly strongly about the visit of the Springboks. This is my first time to speak on the Estimate for the Taoiseach's Department. I am informed that it is a wide-ranging debate covering all aspects of government policy. I did not realise quite how wide-ranging it was until I had the pleasure of hearing the recent speeches. As a citizen of a country which, for very many years, experienced exploitation, discrimination and injustice, it is not inappropriate that I and many of my colleagues in the Labour Party should be members of the Anti-Apartheid Association. Members of the Fianna Fáil Party are members of it and likewise are members of the Fine Gael Party. This is our right. For reasons of conscience, I do not feel it possible to attend the match to be played at Lansdowne Road. It will be a sincere deprivation to me because I am a rugby follower. If a journalist, in the course of his professional involvement in a trade union, took a decision that, in conscience, he should not go to a match and cover it, our point in signing that letter was to argue that he is entitled to make that decision and that no editor should be permitted to coerce him into covering it. I would defend to the last the right of free reportage of any event provided all the political content and all the innuendoes attendant on that event are taken into consideration. I would also defend Deputy [Patrick] Donegan's (FG) right to go to the match, since he is so misguided as to wish to do so. I will be outside with a picket. I shall salute him courteously and I trust he will reciprocate. I have as much right to stand outside as he has to go inside.

I do not want to go back to the hoary business of the *7-Days* team. Does the fact that I was a member of the *7-Days* team prove that it is a sort of Labour Party conspiracy? I am president of Dublin University boxing club. Does that make it a Labour Party conspiracy? I am a member of Westland Row choir. Is everything I am a member of a Labour Party conspiracy? I do not think I have to go over the hoary ground again to make the point that one can have certain political sympathies and at the same time be able to practise objectivity and impartiality as a journalist. Perhaps this is a concept Deputy Meaney is not capable of understanding. I understand it. I do not think this sort of smear tactic is really necessary.

Finally, Deputy Meaney plummeted to the point of the defence of the family unit, as if the back bench of Fianna Fáil have the monopoly of defending it. How low can you sink? Do I have to say here that, like the great majority of the members of this House, I am a follower of a religion which believes in the family unit and which does not believe in divorce; that I accept the rulings of this religion and, at the same time, I think an argument can strongly be made, in a pluralist society, that divorce should be made available constitutionally to those whose religious beliefs entitle them to think they are entitled to have it? There is nothing despicable, communist, neo-Trotskyist or Maoist in arguing that. The argument that the special position of the Catholic Church should be removed from the constitution has the blessing of Cardinal Conway. The arguments on divorce were first put forward coherently by the committee on constitutional reform. This is the kind of smear which it is useful to throw at a member of the Labour Party. If such arguments are to be discussed in this House, could they not be discussed at the level of the debate on the North of Ireland which was of a consistently high level from all sides of the House? For example, I remember Deputy [Michael] O'Kennedy's (FF) distinguished contribution. We should get away from this kind of smear or the next thing is that it will not be permissible to come into this House without wrapping a rosary beads around one's fist first, to show one's credentials. I am as dedicated to the sanctity of the family unit as Deputy Meaney and I think that goes for the majority of my colleagues and for the majority of the members of this House.

The impression was given to me that, in a sense, the Taoiseach took this opportunity to provide, as it were, a keynote speech to the nation, a sort of State of the Nation address which would carry some inspiration, some message, some total review, the kind, for example you get in Congress in the United States.

I am not being personally offensive to the Taoiseach when I say I think that what we got instead was a recital of economic statistics which could have been circulated in tabular form to the House without the loss of illumination of any kind whatsoever. I personally do not think this is adequate. I agree with Deputy Donegan. We are facing a very challenging year and I do not think this is adequate as an address to the nation, a last annual review before this parliament adjourns for the Christmas recess.

I think it would not be unkind to say of the Taoiseach that what he was doing was painstakingly reading through a civil service brief, a point which brings home yet again something which I and others have written about and spoken about – I have spoken about it in this House and will speak about it again – that is, the danger, it seems to me, of the excessive co-relation between government policy and a single stream of advice emanating from a single civil service. I do not mean any disrespect to the individual members of the civil service.

One of my favourite beliefs has always been that one of the best guarantees for the maintenance of democracy has been the existence of two sets of economists. It seems to be a function of this country very often to have only one. However, the Taoiseach gave us this brief, this recital, and it was, of course, an extremely optimistic recital as one would anticipate, and as he is entitled to present as the leader of a political party if not, perhaps, as Taoiseach of this nation. May I suggest that the amount of optimism which ran through the recital is not totally justified at this juncture.

In the four years that lie ahead in which the government have got a large and substantial majority, on which I congratulate them, we have a major debate facing us about the future shape of Ireland. The fact remains true and incontrovertible that between 1864 and 1966, 7,399,000 people were born in this country and 3,653,000 of them emigrated. This is a pattern which has not been fully reversed as yet. Will we be able to reverse it in the next four years? We have a right to approach this as a deliberative assembly because, certain incidents to the contrary notwithstanding, it remains a fact that this is a deliberative assembly, not simply a confrontation of victors and vanquished in which the victors are entitled perfunctorily to dictate the policy and the vanquished are permitted at intervals to ask parliamentary question to which they may or may not get replies.

This is a deliberative assembly and in our deliberations we suffer from the embarrassment that a vast number of question marks hang over government policy in the whole area, and in particular in the area of economics upon which the Taoiseach chose to concentrate. Within the past two years sundry commissions have been established to which Deputy Corish in particular referred. The Buchanan Report, the Devlin Report, the Fitzgerald Report spring most immediately to my mind. When members of the House press about the status of these reports they do not get clear answers. When they ask if they will get an opportunity to debate these reports they do not get clear answers.

It is impossible for us to proceed with our deliberations without knowing what these answers are. The Taoiseach emphasised, correctly, the rise in employment which had taken place in the manufacturing industry. This is in line with the estimated change in population and employment in Ireland predicted by the Buchanan Report for the year 1986 when it was anticipated that employment in agriculture, forestry and fisheries would have dropped by 48 percent, employment in manufacturing and mining would have risen by 74 percent and employment in building and services would have risen by 30 percent.

It is I think fair to ask whether this whole change in the emphasis on the pattern of Irish employment is one which this House wants to accept. We are concerned here with the status of Ireland, the quality of Irish life, and the distribution of Irish men and women, and we have a right to ask the question: Do the government accept the kind of thinking which permeates the Buchanan Report and permeates some of the NIEC reports, which seems to imply a radical redistribution of population in Ireland so that it becomes located around a few growth centres: the national capital, two national growth centres and six regional growth centres with the remainder of the country, effectively speaking, an increasingly depopulated hinterland?

When we press the government on this question we get two kinds of answer. If an election is imminent we are virtually assured that every hamlet from here to Malin Head will be a growth centre. When an election is over, effectively speaking we are told: 'The government will give you the answer in due course'. I have actually heard that marvellous phrase 'in due course' used in this House in reply to the question: 'When will the government give the House an opportunity to consider their decision upon the Buchanan Report?'

In that self-same report the emphasis is upon a whole change in population by sectors. Is this the quality of life and the kind of Ireland to which we are looking forward; a major shift of population towards the eastern seaboard and towards these certain selected growth centres? Do we want this to happen? Do we want a situation to arise in which the population of Dublin, for example, increases between 1966 and 1986 by 42 percent, a situation in which the population of the entire east of the country increases by 32 percent, a situation in which outside the main growth centres and the main towns in the rest of the country there is a ten per cent diminution in the population? Do we want this to happen?

We are not being given an opportunity to debate this. Many of us in this House would feel that we do not want it to happen and that we would much rather see a determined central effort made to preserve many of the traditional patterns of Irish living, which some deputies on that side of the House seem to think are their private preserve. What has become of that report? What is its status? Why has a condition been reached where even the economic correspondent of the *Sunday Press* – which, like Deputy Donegan, I also read – was able to write an article last Sunday asking: 'Whatever became of Baby Buchanan?' What has become of Buchanan?' We are entitled to ask.

One of the privileges of power is the right to make decisions. Deputies on that side of the House have this power and, in a democracy, it is correct that they should have it, but it is not just the right to make decisions; it is the obligation to make decisions even when these decisions are sometimes unpopular. The government are slipping up by failing to take the people into their confidence and provoke what is necessary: a major debate about the kind of country we want to live in. Do we want everything to happen by accident? Do we want a certain kind of society, a Dublin-orientated society, a rather shoddy society, a rather chromium-plated exhibitionist society to develop more or less by accident because we are largely influenced by developments in the British market?

It may seem strange that I, as a Dublin deputy and a Dubliner, should argue in this way, but I assure the House I am quite sincere. I personally do not want to live in an Ireland which, effectively speaking, consists of Dublin and a hinterland from which people commute backwards and forwards along autobahnen most of which, if the Buchanan Report is to be believed, seem to stop somewhere around the Shannon. I do not want this to happen. Nor do I believe that we won our freedom in order that the pattern of life here should develop purely accidentally. That belief does not make me a communist. That is what is happening.

In a paper published only the other day by Dr Michael Ross of the Economic and Social Research Institute, it was pointed out that Dublin enjoyed the highest income lead in 1960. It increased that lead over half as fast again in the intervening period as the average in the other twenty-five counties. It was pointed out that there had been an 11 percent growth in the population of Dublin in the last five years, three times that in any other county.

Much is often made of the fact that for the first time the population is remaining static or moving forward infinitesimally but the point is also made in the report that if Dublin is excluded from the figures for Ireland the total population figure represents a fall of 53 percent instead of a rise of 2.3 percent. If Kildare, Wicklow, Meath and Louth were excluded the decline would be twice as large, 107 percent. The pattern in those figures shows what is happening in the community. When ministers and deputies on that side of the House have finished talking about their heritage and traditions and their dedication to the small farmers, and speak as if the Labour Party had no interest in small farmers, they should realise that the country is drifting into this situation year by year – and government action is not being taken to stop it – where not merely are we an economic offshore island of Britain but the rest of the country, with the exception of a couple of growth centres, is becoming a kind of tourist hinterland, a vast dormitory suburb for the Dublin area. Again, the average income rise in Dublin was 22 percent over that of the nearest county in the same period. Next in line were the four counties which contained the largest towns, Waterford, Cork, Louth and Limerick. The five counties of Connacht plus Cavan, Monaghan, Longford and

Donegal, had the lowest income rates and the highest population decline.

We can fairly ask, as we see this country drifting away from the traditions and off-derided pattern of the Sinn Féin past, do we want this kind of Ireland? I can think of no subject which is more serious for the national agenda for the next four years, and which is not being adverted to in this House, or certainly has not been adverted to since I became a deputy; we are not being given an opportunity to debate this question, whether we want Ireland to fall into this new and unfamiliar pattern, this sort of sub-American, sub-British pattern in which small farms become a thing of the past. I confess to having a great deal of sympathy with the feelings which I know the Minister for Industry and Commerce possesses and which the Minister for Lands [Deputy Seán Flanagan] not merely possesses but somewhat inadvisedly, in view of his party, enunciates in public. Their view of Ireland is a rather different view to that contained in the Buchanan Report. The view in the Buchanan Report is consistent with the view contained in the Fitzgerald Report and is also a view consistent with the manner in which the economic future of this country is drifting along and the relatively marginal growth which is a by-product of a general pattern of western European growth. This is something on which the Taoiseach congratulates himself that it is taking place, something which is changing the face of the country even as we are looking at it. Yet we never ask ourselves the question: do we want this?

One of the functions of government is the taking of difficult decisions. Successive governments for many years have managed to evade facing up to those items on the national agenda: What kind of Ireland do we want to live in? What kind of demographic structure, what kind of farm unit do we want? They have managed to evade this, but they will not evade it in the four years ahead because the answer has to be found in that period. They have the power to make these decisions and they have the obligation but so far they have not lived up to that obligation, as may be seen in the euphoric-like, dry and listless statistics supplied by the Taoiseach. It may also be seen in the Third Programme. A very distinguished economist – it would not be fair to mention his name – once said of the different programmes that the first was all principles and did not have any statistics; the second was all statistics but left out the principles, and in the third they found that statistics would not work, so they took out the statistics but did not put back the principles, with the result that there was nothing in the Third Programme at all except a kind of descriptive summary of the aids available to develop industry. This is a very fair criticism and very relevant.

This brings me to a point which I want to treat differently to the way in which Deputy Donegan treated it, as he said he wanted to be provocative. It is the philosophy of the Fianna Fáil Party. It always seemed to me that Fianna Fáil fall into roughly four periods: the period from 1926 to 1932, when they were essentially a small farmers' party; the period from 1932–33 up to about 1938 when the major steps forward were taken to build up tariff-protected, private enterprise, and, to some extent, State enterprise; thirdly, the period of the war and the years immediately following it which were necessarily years of marking time and, fourthly, the period we face now, when we are entering into a whole new context, the context of free trade. That seems to me to be a context which the government are approaching both philosophically and economically unprepared to give the nation the guidance to which it is entitled. The traditions of the party, the traditions which get them elected from time to time, are rooted in the small farmers of the west, but the practice of the party is to acquiesce in a situation in which employment in agriculture is steadily and alarmingly diminishing, in which the whole pattern of production is going over to industry and in which we are moving towards conditions of free trade in a state of semi-unpreparedness.

In this context a great philosophical debate, a great moral debate should be taking place in this independent nation as to its future character, but it is not. One reason why it is not is because I do not believe the cabinet is united on this issue. It is fashionable to speak of divisions in the cabinet in a derogatory sense, but I do not mean to speak in that way. There is a clear-cut distinction between the kind of Ireland which the Minister for Industry and Commerce and the Minister for Lands envisage and that which some of their colleagues envisage. The hardy annual of the EEC was brought up. It may be correct, as Deputy Meaney said, that if Britain joins the Common Market we must do the same. This may seem to be the only realism. I would not suggest the members of the Labour Party were so obscurantist as to deny a hard economic fact like that. Are we preparing ourselves for this challenge? What has become of the interest that lay behind the Committee of Industrial Organisation? What has become of the interest that lay behind the Second Programme? It seems to me that these have been ground down and that the government now rely solely on exhortations. As incomes policy, serious planning, are things of the past and as a result a great question mark hangs over the jobs and livelihoods of the self-same industrial workers about the increase in whose numbers the Taoiseach boasts so much.

In the article by Mr [Raymond] Crotty in *Studies* to which Deputy Corish referred, he said:

'Perhaps the most significant fact in the whole of this report' – the Buchanan Report again – 'is that those foreign firms which were here before 1962 and which replied to the questionnaire indicated that they expected to reduce the numbers they employed by 22.4 percent in the five years 1967 to 1972. The seemingly clear-cut lesson to be deduced from this would appear to be that it is easier to attract outside firms to Ireland than to keep them here.'

If that is true in the conditions where some measure of tariff protection still survives, how much more true will it be in conditions of membership of the European Economic Community? Here I agree with Deputy Donegan.

Are we preparing for this? It is not just a question of statistics which the Taoiseach has put forward so drily and which I suppose it would be fair to say I am putting forward rather drily too. These statistics affect ordinary human beings, ordinary people in factories, who will be injured if we are unprepared to face up to this challenge just as the small farmers of the west are being injured at the moment by the refusal of the government to face up to the challenge of mounting a great national debate on the future character of this island. What are the government doing? I was able to take only a few notes of what the Taoiseach was saying, but I could not help noting one thing he said when he was alluding to price increases: 'We will expect firms to make increasing efforts to avoid price increases.'

The very note of that – expect firms to do this, expect firms to do that. What if they do not? What if they sell out to British combines? What if they do not send back the questionnaires that are sent out to them? What became of the high hopes of the CIO years? What is being done, apart from pious exhortations, to make sure that when the cold blast of full competition hits us, the honeymoon is not then over and we find exactly what we have walked into?

It is often thrown at us on these benches here that we want to nationalise everything, that we want to socialise everything, that we want to communise everything. This is completely untrue, but what I do suggest is that the version of the free play of the market which the Taoiseach's administration has followed so slavishly over the last few years is simply tantamount to an abdication in large degree of responsibility to prepare this country for conditions which will vitally affect the lives and happiness of ordinary workers. The recent changes in the IDA, belated changes, are one of the few examples I have seen of an attempt by the government to take a slightly more constructive, directive role in the development of private enterprise industry.

One does not have to be an extreme socialist to feel that it is the role of a government in a country as small and as open as ours to protect the livelihood of ordinary workers by doing something slightly more than making pious exhortations to industry to prepare itself for conditions of competition. The fact that one does not have to be an extreme socialist to believe this is shown by the fact that Deputy Donegan believes it too, and whatever else he and I have in common, I do not think either of us are extreme socialists in that respect.

As I say, a great question mark hangs over all this. We do not get any answers. We are told that when the answers are processed we shall be given an opportunity of debating them. When the government have decided what to do with the Buchanan Report we shall be given a chance to say whether we like it or not. When the government have decided what to do with the Devlin Report we shall be given a chance to say whether we like it or not. This is just not good enough. On this annual occasion when we get an opportunity of reviewing the state of this nation, we are entitled to slightly more information about the intentions of the government in relation to this country of ours.

Another point raised was again in regard to the Devlin Report. Whatever became of what was a very far-seeing idea of the former Taoiseach, the then Deputy Seán Lemass, that each arm of the civil service should regard itself as a development division? That idea seems to have died a death as well, or does a question mark hang over that as well as over the report?

Over the next few years we will have to have a great debate about the quality of life of ordinary people in this country, because when the statisticians are finished talking, when the Taoiseach has finished reading the statistics figures of change, change means one thing essentially; it means that the people in the middle get hurt; people whose jobs cease, people who are too old to be retrained for other branches of industry, the sick, the homeless, these are the people who are ground between the wheels of the free economy to which the Taoiseach's government are so totally committed.

I had a case in my own constituency – I am not trying to make a constituency plug: it is quite a sincere case – of a man of sixty years of age who was thrown out of work after forty years with a certain firm because that firm had been bought up by a British combine. His entitlement after all this was to something like £340 under the redundancy payments scheme. Owing to the fact that I was a personal acquaintance of the managing director of the firm I was able to get him another £250, what one might call a copper handshake; one certainly could not call it golden.

That man at sixty, after forty years productive service, was simply thrown on the scrap heap. Retrain him at sixty? A man who has been a porter, retrain him to be a technological expert of some kind or other? Really? That is the kind of person who gets hurt and that is the kind of person who is on the conscience of this nation and for whom the government have an obligation which, in my opinion, their bland *laissez faire* attitude to economic statistics is showing they do not accept.

Through all this we are helping to bring into disrepute the whole parliamentary system. I am not setting forward, as Deputy Meaney seemed to imply that I would, to lecture my elders and betters on how parliament should be run, but I might respectfully suggest that some of the protests to which Deputy [Liam] Cosgrave [leader of Fine Gael] referred are occasioned by the fact that, rightly or wrongly, people outside this House have got the impression that its debates are irrelevant to them, that they have no chance of winning social justice for themselves through the available channels. It would be tragic if political rights so dearly won were to be brought into such disrepute, and I think we here have a tremendous obligation to make sure this should not be done.

There are a couple of other points I wanted to make but time is running short. In general, may I just support the plea for a reform of parliament, for the greater involvement of committees and for the improvement of the entire conditions of work of the members of the Dáil?

Repeatedly on both these benches and on the Fine Gael benches pleas are made to the government for the establishment of phenomena like ombudsmen, civil bureaux, social advice bureaux and all that sort of thing. These pleas are always resisted. Questions are asked by myself, Deputy [John] O'Connell and others – indeed, Deputy [Joe] Dowling had a question about this here today – asking the government to make available to the people simple booklets on their housing rights, their social welfare rights and so on. Behind all these questions lies a desire on our part to get away from the question by which, as anyone who attends the public galleries of this House regularly is aware, this House is almost continually empty because all of us are driven inexorably to complete in writing letters for constituents about housing or about farm grants. As the Budd judgment so correctly pointed out in 1960, our function here is essentially as legislators. The very emptiness of these benches, which is not necessarily a reflection upon the quality or the relevance of what I am saying, demonstrates this point adequately. As Deputy [P. J.] Burke (FF) said in the context of the debate last night, he was not able to be here because he was receiving a number of deputations. Far be it from me to criticise Deputy Burke.

MR [LIAM] CUNNINGHAM:
There are a few committees meeting at the moment.

DR. THORNLEY:
I can see legitimate reasons why members cannot be present all the time, but people know perfectly well what I mean, and off the record every member of this House will agree there is a certain validity in what Deputy Donegan says about the peddling of illusory favours in which we compete on the whole network of the constituency clinic. This sort of thing has a slightly deceitful and shoddy side to it and every effort should be made, in the interests of the dignity of the House, to get away from it. I am not suggesting that the individual deputy does not have individual responsibility to his constituents – of course he does. What he should not do is to try to persuade them that he is capable of doing favours for them which he is not capable of doing. This goes on all the time.

The subject of Christmas cards has come up quite a lot in this session. Like every other deputy, I get Christmas cards thanking me for getting people houses. These Christmas cards embarrass me. I know perfectly well that the officials of the housing department of Dublin Corporation are not going to do me or anybody else any favours; they are going to play the game by the rules. However, we are all engaged in this great competition.

This is a deliberative assembly, not just a competitive one. I think the Taoiseach should use his majority with humility. I think he should listen to suggestions from this side of the House which are made in a non-partisan way. We are asked to be constructive often enough and I think such suggestions as the setting up of social bureaux and the greater use of the Dáil are two useful suggestions put forward from this side of the House.

254

In concluding, I shall return to my central theme. Over the deliberations of this Dáil hang a great number of unanswered questions. What about Buchanan? We do not know, we will not be told. What about Devlin? We do not know, we will not be told. What about the FitzGerald Report? We are not quite sure except for the hints we got in the course of the Health Bill. What about the university merger? We do not know and they do not know either. What about the new Ministry of Physical Planning and Development – is it on or is it off? What about reforming the constitution? We do not know. What about the whole case of Ireland? How will the population be distributed? What will the country look like in ten years time when the life of this report will already be exhausted? All these questions must be answered in the lifetime of this Dáil.

We have had the start of a very great debate on this subject and I think it is going to be a tremendously important one. Even if we were not to ask the government to answer these questions members of the EEC are going to make them answer and the British will also make them answer. The cold draught of competition will also make them answer them. They will have to get off the hook of power. I would suggest, therefore, that they approach their task with a certain humility. It is easy to deride the old virtues. I see many virtues in the old homespun, honest poverty of the Fianna Fáil of the Thirties – of the de Valera epoch. It had a certain pride and a certain self-respect about it. Whatever disadvantage this country started off with, at least it started off with a homogeneous society with a close balance between country and town. If that pattern is to be disturbed, if we are to move into a new ridge, particularly a new urban ridge, let us debate it and let it not just happen in the stealth of the night.

20

SPEECH IN DEBATE ON ESTABLISHMENT OF TRIBUNAL TO

INVESTIGATE *7-DAYS* PROGRAMME ON MONEYLENDING,

16 DECEMBER 1969

Debate resumed on the following motion:

That it is expedient that a tribunal be established for inquiring into the following definite matters of urgent public importance:

1. The planning, preparation, arrangement, production and presentation of the recent television programe on illegal moneylending, that is to say, that part of the *7-Days* feature broadcast on television by Radio Telefís Éireann on 11 November 1969, which related to unlicensed moneylenders and their activities.

2. The authenticity of the programme and, in particular, the adequacy of the information on which the programme was based and whether or not the statements, comments and implications of the programme as to the number of unlicensed moneylenders operating in the city and county of Dublin and the scope of their operations, and the use of violence, or threats of violence, to secure repayments of money illegally lent, amounted to a correct and fair representation of the facts.

3. The inquiries on behalf of Radio Telefís Éireann, and the films, tapes, statements, scripts, records, notes and other material in their possession, which relate to the programme.

4.   The inquiries on behalf of the Garda Síochána, and the
       statements, taken by the Garda Síochána, which relate to the
       programme.

DR THORNLEY:

I feel very strongly about this subject which is an extremely serious one,
one which deserves to be treated with something more than the levity
with which it has been treated in the last few minutes. This apparently
simple measure comes before the House carrying with it generalised
implications of a most frightening kind which have to be seen in a very
broad context, if they are properly to be understood in the context in
which they are placed in particular by Deputy [Barry] Desmond (Labour)
and Deputy [Garret] FitzGerald (FG).

It would be less than honest for me not to admit at the outset my former association with this programme, and I was glad to hear Deputy
[Noel] Dowling (FF) praise it as an independent journalistic programme.
I was pleased to be for once in agreement with him. There is no need for
me to speak of the journalistic integrity of the members of that team. I
had three years association with them, and while there have been no
smears as yet in this debate, except one slight innuendo from Deputy
Dowling, it has been my experience in Telefís Éireann that there are people who are Labour sympathisers, Fianna Fáil sympathisers, Fine Gael
sympathisers, Sinn Féin sympathisers – there may be even a few communists; I do not know. Similarly there are people with political opinions on
the staffs of every major newspaper in this country. This does not prevent these people from being independent journalists of integrity, and I
believe that to be as true of the 7-Days team as it is of the staffs of, for
example, the four national newspapers.

To bring in what seems to me to be the general point here, we are
launching this night a major onslaught upon the whole principle of journalistic freedom. The Taoiseach, both in his actual motion and in the
words which he used introducing it, made it quite clear that this would be
a public inquiry empowered to make people come before it and produce
documents, tapes, scripts and records. This is completely at odds with all
the standards of journalistic procedure, as Deputy FitzGerald correctly
pointed out.

Does this mean that in future every young crusading journalist in television, radio or in the newspapers will have the threat of a public inquiry
over him if he produces any evidence of a social evil which has not been

previously discerned by the government and about the existence of which they do not agree? We are initiating tonight a process which no one can win. Nobody is calling into question the integrity of the judges who will form part of this tribunal. Nobody is calling into question the integrity of the Garda Síochána. I, for one, am certainly not calling into question the journalistic integrity of the members of the 7-Days team. A chain of events has taken place here under the initiative, in the first instance, of the Minister for Justice which can only lead to a most unhappy conclusion for freedom of speech, and freedom of journalism in this country, a principle which, as I say, applies just as much to the newspapers as it does to television.

I hope I am not out of order in saying that we have, for example, in this House a man for whom I have deep personal respect, Deputy [Vivion] de Valera (FF), who is involved in the newspaper world. Would he be happy or would some of the honourable friends I have on the government benches be happy with the situation where a crusading journalist of, let us say, the *Irish Press*, could be similarly hauled before the bar of justice, compelled to reveal his sources, to flush out into the open people who had given him information in confidence, so that he could produce his work in accordance with accepted journalistic practice? It is a dangerous and a tragic step forward, and I agree completely with Deputy FitzGerald that, if we go through with this motion in its present form, it will be a bad night's work for freedom of speech in Ireland.

The point about the sworn inquiry was apparently lost completely upon Deputy Dowling. The Labour Party have no objection to a sworn inquiry into the principle of money lending and our amendment sets that out quite clearly. Obviously any sworn inquiry into the principles of moneylending would take into consideration as a part of its function the relevance of the evidence, accurate or inaccurate, of the 7-Days programme. We have no objection to such an inquiry at all. We are not trying to cover up for anybody. The 7-Days team are well able to look after themselves. There is a distinct difference between an inquiry into moneylending and the kind of inquiry we are being asked to assent to, where the sledgehammer of the legislative process of the national parliament is being brought down, not even on a programme, but on an individual transmission of one night of a programme. The hammer is certainly not being brought down on the social evil of moneylending but simply, if the terms of the motion are accepted, on one issue of one programme, just as if it was being brought down on one article in a newspaper. We object to that and we are perfectly consistent in our attitude to this in our amendment.

The intense and sincere trepidation which I feel about this motion in its present form must be seen in a broad context. Some two years ago I wrote an article on television and politics in administration in which I said that current television started off with two disadvantages – the monopoly situation where we had only one broadcasting authority and the fact that the Irish are traditionally interested in politics. This is still true but the monopoly situation of the television broadcasting network makes it all the more important that it should be, and should be seen to be, completely free from government interference or from the threat of such interference hanging over it. There is a tremendous danger in a network which is being beamed without competition into all the houses in Ireland. There is fear of the shadow of retribution of a kind unknown in any other country or in journalistic practice anywhere. When we encounter the novel phenomenon of this inquiry into this specific programme we must set it in context. The suspicions which are felt on this side of the House about the terms of this inquiry must be understood and must be taken seriously. They must be taken as relevant to our attitude to this motion in its present form.

There is a long history of suspicion and hostility on the part of the government towards independent television broadcasting. The last three years in which so many steps forward have been taken on independent broadcasting have been marked by row after row between the government and the television authority. We had the row with the NFA, the row over the Biafra programme and rows over other programmes which were never shown. We had a row over the 7-Days programme at the beginning of 1968. I am not making any imputation on any professional journalist in any section of RTÉ in connection with the transfer of the programme from one section to another. There is a long history of dislike on the part of some members of the government of the whole principle of free broadcasting in this country. It is with the memory of that history in our minds that we, on this side of the House, approach with great distrust and fear the motion put before us in its present form. Why have we this strange procedure? Some reference has been made to this. A very important point has to be made. There are clearly laid down procedures in the Broadcasting Act 1960, by which the government can make known to the authority their displeasure over a particular programme. Many of us feel that the powers given to the government in that act are, if anything, excessive. In all successive rows the government have not chosen to utilise the formal procedure of communicating their displeasure to the authority. They have relied on the telephone, the hint, and on the suggestion rather than on the direct communication. They have the power of hiring and firing any and every member of the authority at any moment. They have not used the form of procedures by which they may influence current affairs transmissions. No precedent has been established for communications between the government and the broadcasting authority. Today we have the situation where the massive sledgehammer has to be brought down and the unhappy situation created from which only one loser can emerge eventually, that is to say, journalistic independence and integrity. In this context the sequence of events is significant. Deputy Dr FitzGerald has listed the sequence of events which has built up. This unhappy tribunal is the consequence to that sequence.

I have no intention of descending to personalities. I made this resolve before I came into this House and it is one I intend to adhere to scrupulously. I will not attack anyone personally. Over the past three years there have been some ministers who were more ready to co-operate with the principle of free broadcasting than others. The Taoiseach himself was most co-operative. The Minister for Finance, a strong, and some would say ruthless man in some ways but a gifted and able man, a courteous man who, because he knows he is able to carry himself with conviction before the people on television, does not hesitate to go on it when asked and does not try to bend the medium to his own will. He is a much maligned man in this respect. I spoke in my article in *Administration* [the journal of the IPA] of the old war politician or the favourite son who find television uncongenial. It is no coincidence that it is one of the most consistently bullying and uncooperative members of the House who has initiated this process. I feel that some of his colleagues are possibly not too happy about it. Deputy Desmond quoted, quite correctly, at great length from the statement made by the then Taoiseach, Deputy [Seán] Lemass, on the 12 October 1966, to the effect that the government rejected the view that RTÉ should be generally, or in regard to its current affairs programmes completely, independent of government supervision. On 27 November 1969, I put down a question asking whether this was government policy and was informed that it was. In the light of that statement how can we view the terms of this motion with anything other than suspicion?

Let me make another point which has already been touched on. The Broadcasting Act 1960, whatever its defects, placed the burden of impartiality in matters of public controversy fairly and squarely on the RTÉ Authority. They have answered that in their view this programme was impartial. The proper procedure for the government under the 1960 act is either to fire the authority which is its creation – I am not saying it is biased, it is a rather maligned authority on the whole – or else to accept the judgment of that authority under the Act. This House has been manoeuvred by the Minister for Justice into a situation where that procedure cannot be followed and where nothing can be done except to bring to bear the full weight of public legal exposure upon the officers and servants of the authority, as they are designated in section 12 (1) – ordinary journalists, as Deputy Desmond has said, young men in many cases who will now be brought forward and asked to compete, to place themselves in competition with the police and the Minister for Justice in their methods and in their findings.

This is a most unfortunate conclusion and while we in the Labour Party supported the setting up of an inquiry of the kind we described, it remains true that the necessity for this inquiry has been brought about by the quite extraordinary, intemperate, lengthy and carefully prepared answer which the Minister for Justice gave to a question about moneylenders by Deputy [Brendan] Corish, the leader of the Labour Party – and he is the leader of the Labour Party in case anybody has any doubt about it. The terms of reference, as put, give the inquiry an almost impossible task. In many respects they are complex, confused and ill-judged and I want to address a direct question to the Taoiseach which he might answer at the end of the debate. May I quote paragraph two of the Taoiseach's motion:

> The authenticity of the programme and, in particular, the adequacy of the information on which the programme was based, whether or not the statements, comments and implications of the programme as to the number of unlicensed moneylenders operating in the city and county of Dublin and the scope of their operations, and the use of violence, or threats of violence to secure repayments of moneys illegally lent, amounted to a correct and fair representation of the facts.

As Deputy FitzGerald has pointed out, one possible interpretation that could be placed upon that, as it stands, is that the lawyers appearing for RTÉ before this inquiry would be fully justified in calling evidence to prove the extent of unlicensed moneylending in this country. This, in turn, would mean they would be fully justified in mounting a lengthy and protracted social survey of the kind which we feel is overdue. I should like to know in advance, if possible, will it be in order if they so seek, or will it be strictly and solely limited to one transmission on one night? Has this House sunk so low that it has to wheel in the whole battery of its power and the battery of the law simply on the narrow issue of an individual programme?

The Minister for Justice has prejudged the inquiry with his definitions of the programme as 'phoney' and all the other words he used on the 26 November. It is for this reason we feel that, unless our amendments are accepted, the motion as it stands at present places the tribunal in an almost impossible position because it is being asked to adjudicate a three-corner struggle between the Minister for Justice, the Garda Síochána and the 7-Days team. However, apparently only one of these is to be subpoenaed, only one must expose its files and scripts, only one is to tell of its contacts, to bring them into the public eye, to tell who briefed them. Yet the tribunal must judge between the public statements of all three – statements made in this House and circulated in the public eye, statements which would have been out of order had the Minister for Justice made them after the inquiry had been set up rather than before. This was an excellent piece of timing on his part and one which, as Deputy FitzGerald has pointed out, showed the sinister nature of the sequence of events in this whole sorry story.

Our amendments recognise that the tribunal has been placed in this impossible position. For that reason we intend to press them and I hope they will be supported. One of the Fine Gael amendments in particular recognises the unique nature of the journalistic profession and will, in turn, be supported. Why, therefore, are we in this sad position for the history of free broadcasting and free press in Ireland tonight? We are left with only one of two conclusions. I have far too much respect for some individual members of the government front bench to believe they wish to mount an onslaught upon an individual programme; yet one can only conclude either that the government as a whole have been talked into this situation by the Minister for Justice or else that much more is at stake than apparently appears.

May I make my last point on that issue – that much more is at stake. For three years I had some brief experience as what you might describe as a part-time journalist; I have, therefore, some small experience of the difficulties of maintaining independence of journalism. Freedom of speech and freedom of the press is not won in one single onslaught, nor is it destroyed in one single onslaught. What happens is that it is eroded by a process of attrition, by a dripping of water upon stone. The men in Telefís Éireann, like men in newspapers, are men of integrity; but they are only human. If they feel that the whole apparatus of Dáil Éireann is waiting behind them, then, before they make a serious social inquiry programme or mount a controversial political programme, they are almost inevitably going to say to themselves: 'Is it worth the bother? Let us stick to chamber music; let us stick to bromides, let us stick to safe programmes. Even if we win, the struggle is not worth it; it is too hard on the nerves. They have the whole battery of the government behind them, we have only a small research staff.' You are embarking on a terribly dangerous process when you do this and, in the sequence of events since the minister's reply to the first question from Deputy Corish, a whole shadow has passed over journalism. Doubts have been raised in our minds which I am extremely sorry to have to feel about a government that contains some people for whom I have respect and whom I do not believe would wish to mount an onslaught like this.

However, it did cross our minds that when the government won the last election – squarely, though I will not necessarily say fairly – the writing was on the wall for free television; it was inevitable that some battleground would be picked. Are we being very devious in entertaining such suspicions? The very nature of the battleground lends strength to our suspicions. It is not a direct confrontation on a political issue; it is not the firing of the authority under the terms of the act; it is a kind of side battle

MR. MICHAEL O'LEARY:
It is an ambush.

DR. THORNLEY:
It is an ambush, as Deputy O'Leary correctly says, whose implications are far more sinister and are simply contained in the terms of the motion as they stand before us here. Very often it is thrown at us that we are communists, Maoists, Trotskyites and all these things. I should like to remind members of the government that behind the Iron Curtain in Czechoslovakia one of the first signs of the diminution of freedom was the erosion of the independence of the television network. Do the government want to start doing that now? Do they wish to produce a situation like that of ORTF in France? I do not believe that Deputy [Jack] Lynch himself as a personality, as Taoiseach, wants to do this, and I do

not believe that some of the men whom I knew and liked in a different professional category during the last three years want to do this. The ultimate import of the form of words of the motion set out before us leads to that conclusion. There is something sinister about this motion in its present form.

This whole concept is enough to send a chill, not just down the spines of a few people in *7-Days* who, as they would be the first to admit, are not of themselves important, but should send a chill down the spine of every journalist who depends on the independence of journalism. It has got to be taken in context with the known antipathy of the government, or some members of it, towards freedom in broadcasting. It has got to be taken in context with the remark of the leader of the government party in the Seanad about academic freedom as exemplified by a certain lecturer in political science in University College, Dublin.

Deputy Dowling said it was important that the broadcasting service should not confuse the public. 'Confusing the public' – that is a frightening phrase, that is a phrase which has echoes and overtones of fascism and echoes and overtones of the communism which we on this side of the House are supposed to believe in. Of course, the simplest way not to confuse the public is to brainwash them, to tell them nothing, to feed them with opiates or, best of all, to feed them only one point of view.

Let me make one last observation on my article. I wrote then with what has turned out to be horrible prescience:

> Politics is a game which only one contender can win at any particular time. The politician, therefore, logically views the communication medium as the cockpit of contention. He is constantly only totally satisfied when he is able to use it to gain advantage of his adversary. A good station is a subservient one.

Have we reached a point where this is what the government are setting out to do? Are the lights, as some of us feared, beginning to go out for freedom of television because, I warn the House, if they are, that is only step one. They will be going out for the newspapers next. We are a small country. We are lucky – a point which has been made in the press – that the newspapers at least are in competition, but one of the results of being a small country is that we tend very often to have only one of something – only one set of economists very often, for example – I exempt Deputy FitzGerald – only one set of economists and Deputy

FitzGerald supplying the government with information and, in this instance, just one television service – a terribly easy thing to tamper with.

I would ask the government, therefore, to treat the Labour Party amendments seriously, to draw back from a path which they can embark upon if they want to. Their majority entitles them to do so. Their majority entitles them legally to turn back the clock to the days of the whips' agreement of 1966, to wipe out the years of progress that have been made in independent broadcasting, to wipe out the memory of the integrity with which the present Tánaiste and Minister for Health once supervised the development of radio in the country. The government's majority entitles them, if they so wish, to wipe out that history and to launch an onslaught upon independent television. Is this motion the first step in that onslaught? I would like to think highly enough of the Taoiseach and some of his colleagues to believe that they would not stoop to that but, set in context, I cannot help feeling that the whole thing has a sinister contagion about it and the sequence of events by which one of the most aggressive, persistently intemperate, members of the government has set off a process from which nobody can emerge the winner, only truth can emerge the loser, is one which frightens me, frightens me because of my memories as a part-time journalist and frightens me on behalf of freedom of speech everywhere.

If this House is to turn the full weight of a judicial inquiry initiated by the parliament of the nation upon something, let it be upon the social evil of unlicensed moneylending. Let it not so lower and demean its own dignity as to show and enforce its authority as the first step in an onslaught to extinguish freedom of current affairs broadcasting in this country.

21

DEBATE ON CONTROL OF IMPORTATION, SALE AND
MANUFACTURE OF CONTRACEPTIVES BILL, 11 JULY 1974

MR SÉAN MOORE (FF):

One of the arguments put forward for the implementation of the bill is the fact that we have so many ills in our society that it would be a panacea for all these ills. We have at present a rash of people who go into various parts of the city, and particularly where the lower-paid workers live, and come back with horrifying tales of what they saw there. They then use this as an argument for supporting this measure. I want to point out that in the areas where lower-paid workers live, you may certainly have more children, but you have much less emotional disturbance, a much happier community and therefore the argument used by these people who have appointed themselves to work for this legislation does not hold water. Having said that and being aware of all the injustices in our society and the handicaps of young married people, I do not want to suggest that they are not suffering in lots of ways, but it is our duty to try to remove these injustices by a proper code of development to ensure that every young couple will be properly housed and have such means as will ensure a good standard of living.

On the other hand, it is always hinted that the manufacturers of these articles are some benevolent society whose only aim in life is to ensure that these are made available freely and cheaply. We have to face the fact that the name of the manufacturers game is profit. The people peddling these things at the moment, the vast majority of them, are doing it for profit and the advertising in some of the glossy magazines, which is contrary to the law and about which the government have done nothing, is also being done for profit. Let us get away from the idea that there is any benign design behind the campaign to have these made freely available, from the manufacturers' point of view. I emphasise that I am referring to manufacturers with their outlook of the profit motive.

We have to recognise this fact and the fact that in our society there are many injustices. We have also to recognise that it is being suggested that young married couples and unmarried people also in the use of these devices will find a kind of panacea or solace for all their troubles. The atmosphere has been created in the past three or four years. The decision of the Supreme Court brought the matter to a head. In fairness to the government, they did have to make some move, the Supreme Court having ruled in the McGee case, towards making certain changes and they introduced this bill. The people who examined it, even its technicalities, tell us that it is imperfect and will not serve any useful purpose whatever, but what we have to examine is what legislation would bring about such a situation as would go towards making a different society. In my view, this bill will make no contribution whatever towards achieving the common good. Therefore, it must be rejected by us because it is the job of legislators everywhere in the world to ensure the happiness of their people. They must ensure that every act must lead towards a better society.

If we look at other countries we will see that though they may have progressed as regards transport, housing and general wealth, the sum of their happiness has not been increased. Therefore, we must look further afield if we are to find a solution to the problems which this bill is supposed to remedy. It has been suggested that unless this bill is enacted and there is general availability of contraceptives here, our population problem will become frightful and that there will not be sufficient space to live in. This was said many years ago by Malthus. Few people listened to him. Of course, the population has increased since then to a great degree but there are still many uninhabited parts of the world. As well, the techniques of producing more food are being perfected all the time. So the Malthusian argument will not stand examination.

It has also been claimed that this bill is affording civil rights, but even humanists would question this because nobody has the right to do something or to propagate a cause which might eventually bring unhappiness. I know it is held sincerely by many people in this country that they have a right to use contraceptives. I recognise their right to think in that way but how often do we hear things which are not right, and is it not just as well at times that we are restrained by the laws of the country? I have often had beliefs on different subjects which I felt were for the good of society but as one becomes a little more experienced one sees that these beliefs do not stand up to examination.

It has been suggested that a referendum should be held on this question. One has noticed the great number of opinion polls that have been held, some of which, to my mind, were suspect. I have not sought to hold an opinion poll but I have kept every letter and message I got for and against this legislation. I represent a sophisticated, cosmopolitan area, Dublin South-East, which has a large section of the affluent society and a large section of not so affluent people. Of the letters and messages I got, 160 were against and 5 were for this legislation. I have the file upstairs and if I can be guaranteed anonymity anybody can see that file.

I am highly suspicious of the manufacturers outside this country who are propagating the need for contraception and of any advertisements I see. Believing as I do that this bill will not contribute to the common good, and because it is, as members on the government side have said, a faulty bill which is not workable, I must give due notice that I will vote against it.

DR THORNLEY:

I will only say of Deputy Moore's speech that I share his admirable desire to extend the sum of human happiness. I only regret that his party having spent almost forty-two years unbroken in power did not succeed in doing so. Unlike Deputy [Oliver J.] Flanagan (FG), I have not been thirty-two years in this House – I have only been five years here – but I agree this is a vital debate, so vital that I returned from Strasbourg for the special purpose of speaking in it. I can only say of the two speakers who preceded Deputy Moore – the short and explosive speech of Deputy [Michael] Kitt (FF) and the long and explosive speech of Deputy Flanagan – that they filled me with a mounting sadness about the manner in which this debate was being conducted. I felt somehow that time had stood still in Ireland.

I will make only one point on Deputy Kitt's speech. I, too, was brought up on the speech he referred to when he invoked the former President as a reason for voting against this bill – a form of logic which rather escaped me. I can almost recite that speech by heart about strapping youths and comely maidens living in frugality. Once upon a time I actually believed this until I found that under the regime of Fianna Fáil the strapping youths wound up digging the roads for the English and drowning their sorrows in Finchley Road.

As to the speech of Deputy Flanagan, I should like to make two points, one very simple and the other more complex. The simple one is that he made reference to the intake in mental hospitals in this country being very high. Anyone who knows anything about socio-medical practice knows that the statistics for intake in mental hospitals in this country are distorted by the fact that we do not have adequate home geriatric treatment and we have to put our old people into mental homes.

The other point is more complex. I do not want to criticise Deputy Flanagan who I assume spoke sincerely, but the constant linking of abortion and contraception by him is something which I found rather revolting. Speaking as a Catholic, no matter what the bishops may have said, I see no connection between the two concepts. There are absolutely no circumstances in which I would vote for abortion. I regard it as murder and I consider it completely unrelated to this bill. Indeed, a section of this bill prohibits the importation of abortifacients which gives some indication of the minister's intentions in this respect. They are the same as mine.

I should like to say with reference to Deputy Flanagan's speech that since I totally disagree with everything he said, I hope that if I can assume his sincerity he will do the same for me as a Catholic with two children. By way of preliminary, I shall make a couple of other brief points. If at times I appear to be flippant in this debate I hope, sir, you will not take exception to it – my flippancy does not derive from the position that I do not regard this subject as serious but rather from a feeling, as I listened to some of the speeches in this debate, which is best reflected in a line from one of Byron's more famous poems:

> And if I laugh at any mortal thing
> 'Tis that I may not weep.

Also I apologise to you if I introduce an element of realism into this debate by occasionally referring to rather unpleasant specific and anatomical details, although Deputy Flanagan was not exactly reticent in doing precisely the same thing.

I think this debate and all debates on this subject are surrounded by an element of hypocrisy, which I find distasteful. Everybody knows, of course, that contraceptives have been available for years in this country particularly to the affluent middle classes. Anybody who could afford the price of a return ticket to London, or who had a friend in England, was easily able to import these things. We are putting our collective national fingers in our collective national eyes when we pretend anything else.

Sometimes, listening with sadness to Deputy Flanagan, I felt there was no point in speaking in this debate at all, that everything that needs to be said about it has been said. It has been said in particular by two people, one a gentleman with whom I do not normally get on very well, 'Back-bencher' in *The Irish Times* who, in his articles, swiftly and brilliantly destroys the framework of hypocrisy which surrounds this controversy and the other, my good friend, Dr Patrick Leahy of Ballyfermot in a letter to *The Irish Times* for which he was disgracefully criticised, in my view, by Deputy [Noel] Lemass (FF). I should like to add in this slightly cynical vein that as a European parliamentarian and also as someone who is something of a linguist, I can tell the House to rest assured that the protraction of this discussion over the last few years in Ireland has rendered us the laughing-stock of western Europe.

Deputy Moore and others referred to receiving letters from large numbers of people telling us not to vote for this bill. I received those letters also; they were quite blatantly and patently part of an organised campaign, all verbally almost identical. In some cases they were even photocopies. Some of the admirable gentlemen or ladies who sent these letters descended to what I regard as the slightly un-Christian omission of not stamping them so that in order to find out about them not wanting us to vote for the bill, one has to pay a surcharge to the Minister for Posts and Telegraphs [Conor Cruise O'Brien (Labour)]. This is slightly unfair. All these letters began with the proposition that they had voted for me in the last election, a proposition which I found implausible in my case since my views on contraception are pretty well notorious, and went on to say: 'You have no mandate to vote for this bill, so do not vote for it.' I am happy to tell the authors of these millions of letters that at the next general election they can have the pleasure of not voting for me because I intend to vote for this bill.

With due respect to Deputy Flanagan who said that no matter what damage was done to his electoral chances by his voting against this bill he intended to do so, let me suggest that, particularly in the case of rural deputies, they are far more likely to do themselves electoral damage by voting for the bill than by voting against it.

Since I take such a depressed and slightly cynical view of this bill and this controversy or non-controversy, it may well be asked: why do I bother to speak on it at all. The answer is a slightly conceited one: I shall not allow myself to go into the record as having voted for what I regard as an insufficiently liberal bill without having explained the reasons why I shall take an apparently logically contradictory attitude. I confess that the Fianna Fáil speakers who have called this a badly drafted bill have a point. I can see Deputy [David] Andrews (FF), a lawyer, waiting to get in and I am sure he will say that this is a badly drafted bill. I am inclined to agree with this. I confess a little disappointment with my colleague the Minister for Justice in his drafting of this bill, particularly since I played a humble role in elevating him to the office he now holds by, as Labour's director of elections, transferring the Labour second preferences in Longford-Westmeath ruthlessly to him in the 1970 by-election, a process for which I was duly censured by my own Labour organisation. That was, of course, in the halcyon days of 'going-it-alone', before the Labour Party leaders put wet towels around their heads and by the application of simple logic and mathematics arrived at the startling conclusion, only equalled by that vouchsafed to St Paul on the road to Damascus, that under PR you could not turn eighteen seats into seventy-two in one election.

May I now make a few criticisms of the bill for which I intend to vote? The bill defines a contraceptive as 'any appliance, instrument, drug, preparation or thing designed, prepared or intended to prevent pregnancy . . .' As Dr [Paddy] Leahy pointed out – what is a 'thing'? Could I draw the attention of the House at the risk of embarrassing it mortally to some of the facts of life? Suppose, as Dr Leahy pointed out, a young lady having failed to menstruate decided to terminate a suspected pregnancy by the time-honoured method immortalised in literature by Alan Sillitoe in the novel *Saturday Night and Sunday Morning*, to wit, taking a steaming hot bath and consuming a bottle of gin. Does that constitute a bottle of gin a 'thing'? If an unmarried girl goes to a supermarket and seeks to purchase a bottle of gin, is she to be eyed suspiciously by her neighbours who may wonder whether she is buying the bottle of gin for the laudable and time-honoured purpose of becoming inebriated or whether she intends to use it as a 'thing' to procure the termination of pregnancy?

May I also draw some further facts of life to the attention of the House and particularly to Deputy Flanagan who appears to think that in this island, which Karl Marx once called this *sacra insula*, sin, fornication, abortion, contraception and things like that never happened until recently? As Dr Leahy also pointed out, many an Irish unwanted pregnancy, and the life of many an Irish mother, has been terminated by the use of a knitting needle. Does that constitute a knitting needle 'a thing'? If an unmarried mother goes into Woolworths to buy a pair of knitting needles, is she to be asked whether she intends to knit with them or to use them in a manner defined as illegal under this bill?

There are sections of the bill that I must in all conscience criticise even though I shall vote for it. Section 1 (2) for example says:

> For the purposes of this Act a person who has no living spouse shall be taken to be unmarried.

So, the young woman married at twenty and widowed at twenty-five, who purchases things between the age of twenty and twenty-five is acting perfectly legally but, at the age of twenty-five, such purchases ceases to be legal and become illegal. This is a concept which I find rather difficult to comprehend in terms of abstract logic. I also have a criticism of this bill which is at the same time a criticism of the Fianna Fáil Party for their persistence in opposition to it. If the minister feels I am criticising him, it is because this controversy has placed him in an utterly impossible position and the compromise he has endeavoured to produce is probably as good as he could produce in the circumstances. I hope he will accept my criticism in that spirit and that it can be seen in that light.

In a sense, this bill can be seen as a class bill – that is one of my objections to it. Because of its very complexity the people most likely to avail of it, if enacted, are precisely the people who are least in need of it because they are already provided for.

Let us again cut through some of the hypocrisy which has surrounded this discussion – and I do not mean that to apply only today but to the discussion over the past ten years. Everybody knows that anyone who belongs to the class of myself or anybody else in the House can contact a sympathetic Dominican who will tell him or her that *Humanae Vitae* can be liberally interpreted – *pace*, Deputy Flanagan, I have read *Humanae Vitae* – and that, therefore, the use of the pill is all right. Anybody who belongs to the affluent middle classes can find a sympathetic doctor who will indulge in the fiction that the pill is a menstrual regulator and not a contraceptive with the result that the middle classes can live happily ever after.

Deputy Moore spoke as if he was oblivious of the fact of a housing shortage in Dublin. I want to make a couple of points which are directly related to the class nature of our present contraceptive system which would not be ended in my view adequately by the passage of this bill. As I said, I have not been thirty-two years in this House but in the five I have been here I have experienced a pattern which is very common in a working class area which principally concerns me. The young pair get married: everything is blissful. They move into the front room of a small house in the working class area. They have a child. They go to the corporation requesting that they be given a house but they are told that this is not possible since they have only one child. The principle of the corporation in this context seems to be the ancient injuction to increase and multiply. So the couple go back and have a second child. Then, they go again to the corporation or they come to me or to Deputy [Seán] Moore or to some other deputy and, consequently, we write letters to the housing manager of the corporation but we are informed that Mrs X has only two children and so her name is down on the waiting list but that she will be notified when her turn is reached and that there are many cases worse than hers. The family return to living in their in-laws front room.

The in-laws are sick at the sight of them. The husband is sick at the sight of the wife and she is sick at the sight of the husband. The husband is on the booze while the wife is on librium and valium in vast quantities and the ultimate conclusion of this cycle, which is far more common than most deputies will have the honesty to admit, is that the husband perpetrates what Dr Noël Browne has described as the Irish form of divorce. There is no legal divorce here but there is a form of divorce in that a husband simply buys a one-way ticket to London or some other place where he disappears into a limbo from which he is not rescued. Luckily, progressive legislation in respect of deserted wives has brought this hideous problem to light in recent years. If I may, I shall borrow an expression used by Deputy [Dr John] O'Connell (Labour) at the last Labour Party conference when he said that in the case of housing applicants he never knows whether it is best to prescribe the contraceptive pill so that the couple might be happier or to prescribe the fertility pill so that they might qualify for a house. Any Dublin deputy who is not aware of that situation is talking through his hat.

The bill makes reference in Section 1 to authorised persons. I should like to refer here to statements made by Deputies [Michael] O'Kennedy (FF) and Flanagan which I found profoundly distasteful. If this bill is passed, which I hope it will be, will the millions of people who have been writing to Deputy Moore or to myself or to any other deputy on this subject desist from their efforts? I do not think so. This bill places chemists in a most unpleasant position. Deputy O'Kennedy suggested that the issue should be left to medical prescriptions but that would place doctors in an equally embarrassing position.

Deputy O'Kennedy referred to good, sound commercial practice per-haps dictating that a chemist would not apply to become a legitimate con-veyor of 'things'. That reminds me of the nice ladies in the League of Decency and in the Family Protection Association going along to the chemist in, let us say, Ballygobackwards, that village immortalised by the late Jimmy O'Dea and saying: 'I trust we can rely on you not to buy "things" because if you import things we will take our business in cos-metics and toothpaste ten miles down the road to somebody else because, great though that sacrifice will be, no sacrifice is too great to keep Ireland in a chaste and holy situation' – that situation in which Deputy Kitt thinks it continues to be.

Furthermore, I can envisage the local chemist playing eighteen holes of golf on a Sunday afternoon and the local parish priest saying to him: 'I know you are a good Catholic. I trust we can rely on you not to pollute our community with "things".' I can see the chemist succumbing to these pressures. This takes me back to my class point. If one lives as I live – in relative affluence in Ballsbridge or Sandymount – one can get hold of 'things' just as at the moment one can get hold of pills, but what about the people who really need these things, those people who are living in overcrowded circumstances? What about the people who are not depend-ent on my intellectual confessor who tells me that I am so valuable to the community that I can do almost anything that remains within the purview of the Catholic Church? What about the people who are dependent total-ly on the tender mercies of less liberal and older doctors and priests?

One of the weaknesses of the bill is in section 5, which provides for the restriction of sale of contraceptives to married people. That is not necessarily wrong but I would like to ask how it is to be enforced. My crit-icisms need not be taken as too stringent but if Fianna Fáil had the courage and honesty to allow the measure go to committee, there are details of the kind I have been discussing which could at that stage be tidied up by the introduction of amendments. I am sure that I speak for all of us over here when I say that we would be delighted to give every co-operation to the people opposite if they were prepared to do as I suggest.

Let me get back to the question as to how the restriction on the sale of contraceptives to married people would be enforced. If, say, I had a young brother who was not married and this young brother was fornicat-ing – to use a term employed by Deputy [Desmond] O'Malley (FF) with that wonderful Old Testament ring which he gave to the debate – I can assure Deputy Flanagan and also the hierarchy and the plain people of Ireland that the first thing I would do would be to try to dissuade my younger brother from fornicating with his girlfriend but, if he had lost his religion or had become converted to, say, Judaism or Protestantism, I would say to him to take precautions because it would be highly unfair to impregnate a single girl and consequently, to expose her to the consequences either of the production of an illegitimate child or to the horrific consequences, which are mentally unending, of an abortion.

So, I go to the chemist and I buy my things – in fact, I do not buy things, but that is my business and nobody else's – and my mythical young brother buys his things. We are known to everybody in Sandymount so when we emerge from the chemist's shop the people say of me: 'He is a public sinner, you know.' They look at me with scorn and the worst thing they could do to me would be to write to the administrator at St Andrew's Church, Westland Row, and propose that no longer should I be allowed sing in the choir. However, they take me away from my younger brother and they rush him down to the corner where there is standing the local garda, with thumbs in his pockets, like Jack Cruise in pantomime, wondering quietly whether he should move in and enforce 'holy hour' in the local pub. The people say to the garda: 'Arrest that young man: he is carrying "things" which he has purchased and to which he is not entitled.'

As a second proposition, suppose, because I feel so strongly about the horrors of impregnating unmarried women, that I swallow my principles and buy things and give them to my young brother, what would be the position? My young brother might say: 'I appreciate, David, what you are doing but you are putting yourself to untold expense and, therefore, I must pay you for these "things".' At this point I become an unlawful purveyor of things and, either I am fined £100 or am sent to jail for six months for my crime while my young brother is also fined £100.

MR [JOHN] KELLY:
I think it would only be the young brother who would be fined.

DR THORNLEY:
I am sorry if I appear to be funny in dealing with this matter. But I am not being funny because the subject is a very serious one. All I can say is that this bill will provide the gardaí with a very interesting time. Already they are busy dealing with the problems of arson, theft, vandalism and wandering horses. The bill, too, would provide the legal profession with a varied and interesting addition to their already substantial income.

Having said all that let me say now why I defend the bill. I shall attempt to do this as tactfully and as politely as I can but I must say that the Fianna Fáil legalistic arguments against this bill, strong as they may seem, are not put forward sincerely. The spectacle of a man of Deputy O'Malley's age thundering about fornication, like an Old Testament prophet, from the benches of this House, reduces me to a state where I do not know whether to laugh or cry. It reminds me of the equally nauseous spectacle which I had to endure about three years ago in this House when ex-Deputy [Brian] Lenihan threw out the Browne–O'Connell Bill on contraception thereby earning himself the prestigious reward of a handshake from Deputy Flanagan.

What is wrong with this proposal? No one is being forced to use 'things'. These things are simply being made available for those whose consciences entitle them to use them. Am I to say I am my brother's keeper as Deputy Flanagan says to the extent that even if my brother is a Protestant or a Jew, does not share my religious belief, I have got the right to say to him he cannot have these things?

The Minister for Posts and Telegraphs has been derided for bringing the issue of Northern Ireland into this debate. Nobody suggests that the importation of contraceptives is ultimately and determinately fundamental to the partition issue. Nobody suggests that the ordinary Northern Protestant is some sort of raving sex maniac who will join up with the Republic of Ireland if he can have contraceptives available but not otherwise. Nobody suggests anything of the kind. But, there is a principle involved here. Articles 2 and 3 of the constitution speak of this as one nation. If it is one nation it contains at least 25 percent of the population – at least 25 percent – whose consciences, unlike Deputy Flanagan's – I suppose he would regard them as uninformed consciences as they are Protestant consciences and not Catholic consciences – enable them to have contraceptives. Am I to say to that 25 percent that they cannot have contraceptives? I admit as some speakers say, that it is not fundamental but there is a principle at stake here. Are the proponents, like Deputy Flanagan, on the retaining of Ireland as Catholic and subject to the teachings of the pope, using a sort of paraphrase of Pádraig Pearse's famous remark, and I yield to no one in my admiration of Pádraig Pearse? What was it he said? – Ireland not free merely but Gaelic also. Are the Fianna Fáil Party saying, Ireland not free merely but Catholic also? Is this the message of peace we are taking to our friends in the North? It is absolutely farcical.

I once had the experience of being very close to and friendly with a distinguished Protestant rector who went on to become very high in his church who believed that his young parishioners were entitled to instruction in the use of contraceptives and used regularly to have to go to England and, like a thief in the night, smuggle them in. Is this the way to treat the 5 percent of our minority in the South and the potential 25 percent of our minority when we have reunited the country as the Fianna Fáil Party are so adamantly determined to do?

Deputy Flanagan made a reference to the fact that the Minister for Posts and Telegraphs – he said something patronisingly like 'an admirable and gifted man in every other respect' – had not enjoyed the benefits of a Catholic primary education. This is the kind of remark which induces nausea in me and it compels me to indulge in a little sort of breast beating because while it may be true of the Minister for Post and Telegraphs that he did not have a Catholic upbringing, in my case, while I did not have a primary Catholic upbringing, later in life I did become probably the only convert in the House. I am not giving that lecture so as to beat my breast because I dislike breast beating but I think my Catholicity is pretty well known. In fact, it caused me to be insulted at a Labour Party conference on one occasion.

Deputy Flanagan invoked the name of the pope a great deal. May I say that I had the privilege of an audience with the pope the other day? I did not bring this issue up at the time. Also, I have read my encyclicals. I have read my *Humanae Vitae, Populorum Progressio, Mater et Magistra, Rerum Novarum, Quadragessimo Anno* and *Mit brennender Sorge*, one of the less attractive encyclicals. I have also read the *Bull of Hadrian* which brought the English in here in 1169. I cannot quite see how this is particularly relevant to the way in which we should treat those whose religious beliefs are different from our own.

If Deputy Flanagan wishes further instruction in encyclicals I can come to his help because I have copies of every encyclical of Pope Paul, Pope John, Pius IX, Leo XIII, Pius XII, Pius XI and I have selected editions of every previous encyclical from the beginning of the time when encyclicals were issued. I can give these to Deputy Flanagan if he wants to improve his Catholicity still further.

As I have said, the North is not the issue really, although it is terribly relevant. To me as a Catholic, the point of view is whether the Catholic Church is a voluntary organisation of which one may or may not be a member and the state is something different or whether the two are coterminous.

ACTING CHAIRMAN (MR MOORE):
Would the Deputy return to the bill? We are not discussing Catholicity.

DR THORNLEY:
We are discussing a very important principle which affects our relations with the North. I think I am entitled to develop it very briefly. Deputy Flanagan was permitted to speak for three hours on almost nothing else but Catholic teaching. It may interest Deputy Flanagan and others to know that the church has abandoned the thesis antithesis concept, as it used to be called, and has moved over, under the influence of great theologians like the late Courtney Murray and our own Enda McDonagh, to the belief that the two are separate entities. While I accept the right of the pope to tell me what to do as a Catholic, I do not accept the right of the pope to tell somebody who does not believe in the pope what he should do. This is very good straightforward Catholic teaching to be found in Courtney Murray. I found all this out, by the way, it might interest Deputy Flanagan to know, in a period when I was lecturing in Catholic social teaching in St. Patrick's College, Maynooth as a substitute for the then Monsignor Jeremiah Newman, then President of the college, who has since been elevated to the hierarchy. So my credentials here are impeccable.

I would appeal to the Fianna Fáil Party not to treat this matter as one of purely politics. I would appeal to them to recognise – and I know this is a high-sounding cliché – that the eyes of (a) the North and (b) the world are on us when we consider this issue today. If the Fianna Fáil Party had come up with a single constructive amendment to this bill or were prepared to permit it to go to committee stage as it stands and bring up amendments to it then, I could understand their attitude but as far as I am concerned they are treating one of the most fundamental areas of private human conscience that it is possible to consider simply as a political football in the hope of embarrassing this side of the House. This is behaviour which is not worthy of them, particularly the younger members of their party. I respect the feelings of older people, just as I would allow a free vote on this bill. I respect the feelings of those who disagree with me on this though I know and we all know that there are men on the Fianna Fáil side of the House, particularly, as I say, the younger men, who in their heart of hearts believe that the importation of contraceptives is a perfectly legitimate natural right for those who do not share the acceptance of the teaching of *Humanae Vitae*. As I say, the eyes of the world and the eyes of the North are upon us in this.

I want to conclude by saying this: I very seldom agree with the Minister for Posts and Telegraphs on anything. I am, therefore, in a very particularly strong position to say what I am now going to say, a very strong position because my respectability as a Catholic has never been called in question, and a very strong position because my arguments with the Minister for Posts and Telegraphs over the issue of republicanism are also notorious, and it is notorious that we disagree profoundly on that issue. In many ways I am closer to the people on the Fianna Fáil side of the House than I am to the Minister for Posts and Telegraphs on the issue of republicanism. So I say, with all the force at my disposal: if this House renders itself ludicrous by throwing out this bill I will not be able to find an argument which will enable me to differ from the view of the Minister for Posts and Telegraphs that Articles 2 and 3 of the constitution should be repealed and the reality of the position accepted.

22

Adjournment Debate on Northern Ireland,

16 December 1971

Dr Thornley:

My apologies. I am not trying to rake over old historical ashes here. All I am trying to do is to grasp some unpalatable truth which is that this country was born and bred in violence and has been taught to love violence for fifty years; that the children have been brought to worship and make heroes of people who exercised violence. Perhaps we are wrong and that Deputy Dr Cruise-O'Brien is right. At least Dr Cruise-O'Brien's stand is consistent. He thinks 1916 was wrong. He thinks the whole thing was wrong. I do not. Perhaps he is right, but certainly he is consistent. He does not say: 'Violence was all right until I got into those benches in 1932 and then it ceased to be all right.' I can understand his position. I cannot understand the dismissal of violence by the pacifist federal Republicans of that side of the House who were born from this tradition. They attack bank robberies, so do I, but the greatest architect of bank robbery after Lenin, who invented the policy of appropriation, which was a polite word for bank robbery, was of course Collins himself.

We were taught to believe all these traditions were right. I was taught to believe they were right. In 1944 on my ninth birthday, my birthday presents were: Dan Breen's *My Fight for Irish Freedom,* Desmond Ryan's *Seán Treacy and the Third Tipperary Brigade.* I was brought up on this. Now I am to be told it is wrong. All right. I can make the transition. I am old enough, but what about the younger people who are bred on this, bred on the barrack attacks, bred on Seán South and the rest? I challenge any Deputy on that side of the House, even now, to deprecate violence. I challenge the Minister for Justice, Deputy [Desmond] O'Malley, to go down to Limerick and say that Seán South was wrong in 1957, or whenever it was, and that the song 'Seán South of Garryowen' should never be sung again. I wonder would he do it at the Fianna Fáil cumann. I somehow doubt it. Yet these are the people who, sitting upon an historical tradition of violence which they fostered themselves, tell us that we must eschew these people and possibly even intern them, as was suggested in this House.

Always we seek to sweep this problem under the carpet to make it go away. The Minister for Posts and Telegraphs went so far as to issue a ministerial directive not so long ago to Radio Telefís Éireann that they were not to show interviews with these people, the Provisionals and the Officials, a decision which placed him on all fours with his distinguished counterpart in Great Britain, Mr. Christopher Chataway, a fact of which I hope he is proud. Does the refusal to admit that these things exist, that these people are recruiting, that they have a glamour which appeals to the young, amount to statemanship? Does it make the problem go away? It is a fact of life which we have to accept. What directive will come next? Will a directive be made that public pronouncements from the Labour Party should cease? If I may introduce a note of flippancy to lighten the somewhat historical tone I am taking, if the Minister for Posts and Telegraphs were to make such a directive in our respect it might be the greatest electoral favour he could do us.

The Minister for Finance, Deputy [George] Colley (FF, Minister for Finance), has asked the IRA to step out of the way and stop hindering the processes in which that party is engaged to end partition. What steps have they taken to end partition? As far as I can see, there have been only two steps to end partition since the retirement of Mr de Valera and perhaps even further back than that: under both Deputy [Frank] Aiken and Deputy [Liam] Cosgrave, the ritual of getting up at the United Nations and saying that partition is a bad thing, provoking yawns of boredom from everybody, saying: 'Those Irish are at it again'; junketings of bodies like the Anti-Partition League, speeches to the Irish Club and the NUI Club in London. Are these serious attempts to end partition?

DR [JOHN] O'DONOVAN (LABOUR):
The late Michael Collins and the late Sir James Craig made an effort to end partition.

DR THORNLEY:
I am talking of more recent years.

MR [BRIAN] LENIHAN (FF, MINISTER FOR TRANSPORT AND POWER):
The deputies had better discuss that at the Labour Party conference. This
is Dáil Éireann.

DR O'DONOVAN:
I believe in historical accuracy. Fianna Fáil do not believe in the truth at
all. They believe in myths.

DR THORNLEY:
I am endeavouring to draw my remarks to a conclusion. To me, until the
civil rights movement came to attention in 1969, the desire and intention
of this government to end partition was a ritual lip service to the principles, expressed about as meaningfully as the comparable hypocrisy of
deputies who get up here in this House and speak about two sentences in
Irish which they repeat when they revert to the spoken vernacular of
everybody in this country, barring about 3 percent of the population.
What has changed since 1969? The civil rights movement changed it first
and when the British army went on the aggressive and the unionists went
on the aggressive at Burntollet, these changes began.

Does anyone think that Mr Harold Wilson would have come over
here to talk to the leaders of the three Irish parties and others two years
ago when he had the power to do so? Of course he would not. When the
Minister for Finance is finished saying that the IRA should get out of the
way let us grasp another unpalatable truth. It is unpalatable to me. If the
settlement of partition is in any way in the offing and if the Taoiseach has
his seat at the high table which settles it he will have been shot into that
seat by the events in the North not by any efforts of his own. He may not
like these truths but truths they are.

What have we in turn done down here to prepare ourselves for the
ending of partition? Nothing. Dr Paisley, Mr Boal and others have drawn
attention to the defects in our social services, in our legal code and in our
constitution. The most the Taoiseach has been able to reply to this is to
suggest that he would convene a meeting of the churches which might
throw up suggestions to change the constitution. He will not grasp the
nettle himself and make these changes. He will not accept the bill which
Dr Browne and Dr [John] O'Connell are putting forward in this House
on contraception, a bill with which I want to associate myself, whatever
cost that may be to me. He will not grasp that nettle. No, he prefers us to
make the running on that so that when the Taoiseach stands in that

corner there and says he is prepared to make constitutional changes, if he calls an election Deputy Paddy Power, Deputy Meaney, Deputy Flor Crowley and many others will be sent around the country to say that we in this party are alien, materialistic, communist, reds, pinks, queers and every other kind of thing.

What kind of hypocrisy is that, that one type of intellectual stance is maintained on the front benches thanks to the guaranteed loyalty of the sixty or so deputies who sit behind them and who can be guaranteed to go around the country and traduce our characters for putting into the cold light of print what the Taoiseach pretends he wants to do. What kind of honesty or sincerity is that? It is the most blatant, utter hypocrisy.

Let us face one or two final truths. If we are going to ask the North to join us in any other circumstances other than bombing and geligniting them into this part of the country, and I agree with Deputy [Patrick] Cooney (FG) that this is a horrible prospect to have to face, then we will have to grasp these nettles.

What is the record of Fine Gael on this? They have a similar ambivalence. Deputy Cosgrave boasts that the 1922 constitution was non-sectarian and he spoke today about equality before the law. Last Friday Deputy Oliver Flanagan got up and said that the constitution is sacrosanct as it stands at present and under no circumstances must it be altered. This is the same trick all over again. Who is sincere around here or who is not? I see Deputy Cooney grinning with embarrassment and I do not blame him.

I do not often speak in this House as frankly as I am speaking tonight but I intend to say what I have to say and nobody will stop me. If we mean anything here we have to show that this twenty-six county portion of this country is worthy to invite the North to join us. This means a revision of our laws. I see no moral worth in Catholic virtues which are retained in this state by the legal imposition of sectarian chastity belts. I do not think the Lord would welcome me into heaven on the grounds that I did not divorce my wife when the state made very sure that I could not divorce her in the first place. What sort of morality is that?

We will need true community schools. Question Time today showed how ready we are to embrace the concept of true community schools. I wondered, listening to the discussion on the community schools and other subjects today, how sincere the people on the government benches are about the ending of partition. I would love to see the ending of partition. I would love to see thirty or so Ulstermen come into this House with the Reverend Ian Paisley, the most vocal and pronounced of them all. I wonder how Deputy [Padraig] Faulkner, the Minister for Education, would like to have to handle the draft of questions he got today on community schools if he had Dr Ian Paisley sitting over here speaking on behalf not of 5 percent but 25 percent of the population? His face would be even redder than it was today and God knows it was pretty red then.

I see the necessity for a socialist solution to this problem in both parts of the country. My tradition is the tradition of O'Donnell and Gilmore. I am sorry to see some of my own colleagues are repeating the historical mistakes made in the past and apparently turning the path of Labour away from the Republican tradition. They shall not succeed in doing this and if they do this party will no longer contain me.

There is a socialist solution and it is the achievement of a pluralist society, a non-sectarian society on both sides of the border, and a just society on both sides of the border, a society of equal opportunity. In Derry, nothing was more tragic to me than to see the exchanges between soldiers and unemployed Derry youths on a Saturday afternoon. One set of unemployed workers fired rubber bullets at another set of unemployed workers which threw stones back at them. There were unfortunate English soldiers for whose trigger happiness and neurosis at the moment I do not greatly blame them. They are people transported from Lancashire towns, where they could not gain employment, and find themselves in this strange place where they need maps to find the border. Usually they cannot even find the border when they have the maps. They fire at people they do not know, unemployed Catholic youths who throw stones at them. I never in my life saw a more tragic situation.

One of the saddest sights I saw in Derry was a bewildered Negro soldier sitting at the wheel of an armoured car with an expression of stoic perplexity on his face, wondering what on earth was going on around him while the stones and rubber bullets flew. Of course, you have got to condemn those who indiscriminately plant gelignite in public places but you have also to accept the horror of institutionalised violence. To me institutionalised violence is only quantitatively and not qualitatively different from the violence of killing. If I was an unemployed Derry worker whose wife was a shift worker in a shirt factory, and I had a son and I saw the full lifetime before him contained only unemployment like my own unless he left this country, I would feel if someone handed me a gun or a rock that it was the proper thing to use it.

It is we, not them, who are to blame. It is not the violence that is to blame. It is the stagnation of this state that is to blame, the failure of this House that is to blame, the bankruptcy of these two statelets that is to blame. Sometimes, looking around at the irrelevancy of politics, looking around in a situation in which more time is spent on exchanges of personal abuse at Question Time here than has been spent in the last two years on unemployment, housing, redundancy, health, I sometimes feel even as Pearse felt that the generation of which I am a member, a relatively junior member, thank God has deserved the catastrophe it has brought upon itself.

Nothing the Taoiseach said today suggested that his mind was in any way open to a structural change in our society which would speed the ending of the division of our country. Nothing the Minister for Education said in his discussion on community schools would suggest that his mind is in any way open to structural change. I ask every member of this House, those few who have listened to me, those who have interrupted me and those who were not here to examine their own and our − I include my own − collective consciences as to whether we have not brought this disaster upon ourselves. I ask them to consider that, if we are washed away in a tide of violence, it may be precisely because we have ceased to justify ourselves as a parliamentary assembly. Certainly, if the suggestions, the ways of friendship, of amity, of pluralism, of social justice which go forth from this House towards the North and towards our underprivileged people, if they continue to be on the level of the contemptuous indifference of the Taoiseach's speech this morning, then we shall have no right to complain if the public turns its back upon this assembly.

Many years ago I wrote − I quote my own words −

> The day of the movement, of the charismatic leader, is for better or worse dead. The future is with the type of politician exemplified by Wilson, Maudling, Erhardt, Brandt. Whatever palms are going will be the prize of the party which finds such leaders and convinces an apathetic electorate of their novelty and their genuineness.

Perhaps the greatest danger is that no party should succeed completely in the immediate future in performing this operation. If this is so, young talent will be siphoned off from the political parties into non-partisan political activity.

AN LEAS-CHEANN COMHAIRLE:
Would the Deputy give the reference?

DR THORNLEY:
Studies in the spring of 1964. What a horror of a personal judgment that
was! What a judgment we are inviting upon ourselves in this House in
these days! No single man can take more blame for that than the
Taoiseach, the Taoiseach who has put his continuance in office before
every other consideration, put it to the point of humiliating his closest
colleagues and the traditional familial architects of his party's longstand-
ing success. I quote from Verdi's setting of Shakespeare's Falstaff:
'h'onore oladri,' 'Honour, you thieves'. Honour is dead in this House.

SELECTED WRITINGS OF DAVID THORNLEY

BOOKS

Isaac Butt and Home Rule. London: MacGibbon and Kee Ltd, 1964.

Introduction. *The Government and Politics of Ireland.* By Basil Chubb. London: Stanford University Press, 1970.

ESSAYS AND PAMPHLETS

Irish University History Students' Congress Bulletin. 'Isaac Butt and the Union, 1843-1870'. Dublin: n.p., 1956.

'The Irish conservatives and home rule, 1869–1873'. *Irish Historical Studies* Vol. XI. No.43 (March 1959). Dublin: Dublin University Press.

'The Irish home rule party and parliamentary obstruction, 1874—1887'. *Irish Historical Studies* Vol. XII. No. 45 (1960). Dublin: Dublin University Press.

'Political Prospects'. *The European challenge: its social, legal and political prospects.* Ed. D. Thornley and P. Jackson. Tuairim pamphlet no. 11: Dublin Branch, 1963.

'Wages, politics and planning'. *Chamber of Commerce Journal.* Dublin: n.p., April 1963.

'The Reunion of all Christians'. *Praying for Unity, A Handbook of Studies, meditations and prayers.* Ed. Michael Hurley, S.J. Dublin. The Furrow Trust and Gill and Son, 1963.

'The development of the Irish Labour movement'. *Christus Rex* (an Irish quarterly journal of sociology) Vol. XVIII. No. 1 (January 1964).

With Basil Chubb. *Irish Government Observed.* Dublin: Irish Times Ltd., 1964.

'Ireland: The End of an Era?'. *Studies* (An Irish Quarterly Review of Letters, Philosophy and Science) Vol. LIII (Spring 1964). Dublin: The Talbot Press.

(Note: Later published as Tuairim pamphlet no. 12, Dublin Branch of Tuairim, 1965)

'Patrick Pearse – The Evolution of a Republican'. Thomas Davis Lecture Series.

RTÉ Radio, Dublin. 20 March 1966. (Note: The Thomas Davis Lecture Series, transmitted on RTÉ Radio in 1966, was organized to commemorate the fiftieth anniversary of the Easter Rising.) This lecture can be found in the following print publications:

— 'Patrick Pearse – The Evolution of a Republican'. *Studies* Vol. LV. (Spring 1966). Dublin: The Talbot Press.

— *Leaders and Men of the Easter Rising: Dublin 1916*. Ed. F.X. Martin, O.S.A. London: Methuen and Cornell University Press, 1967.

Irish Identity'. *Doctrine and Life* Vol. 16. No. 4 (April 1966). Dublin: Dominican Publications.

'Eamon de Valera'. *New Knowledge* Vol. 6. No.1 (1966). London: Purnell & Sons Ltd.

'The Blueshirts'. Thomas Davis Lecture Series. RTÉ Radio, Dublin. 1 November 1964.
This lecture can be found in the following print publication:
— 'The Blueshirts'. *The Years of the Great Test: 1926-39*. Ed. Francis Macmanus. Cork: Mercier Press, 1967.

'Television and Politics'. *Administration* (journal of the Institute of Public Administration of Ireland) *Special Edition on Radio Telefís Éireann* Vol. 15. No. 3 (Autumn 1967). Dublin: Institute of Public Administration.

'De Valera Between the Wars'. *History of the Twentieth Century* Vol. 2. No. 46. Ed. A.J.P. Taylor. London: Purnell, 1968.

'Patrick Pearse and the Pearse Family'. *Studies* Vol. LX. Nos. 239–240 (Autumn-Winder 1971). Dublin: Talbot Press Ltd.

'Irish Politics and the Left'. *Hibernia* Vol 27. No. 6 (June 1963).

'Growth of a Power-Elite'. *Hibernia* Vol 31. No. 7 (July 1967).

NEWSPAPER ARTICLES

'The Common Market and You . . . ?'. Interview. *The Irish Times* 12 Jan 1963. (As part of a series of articles on the Common Market)

'What's wrong with the Dáil?' series of four articles. *The Irish Times* 19–22 Aug 1963.

Series of three articles for *The Irish Times* assessing the Labour Party, Fine Gael and Fianna Fáil, in that order, 30 and 31 March, 1 April, 1965

With Basil Chubb. 'In Pursuit of a Majority – Some possible results of changing the election system'. *The Irish Times* 15 Jan 1968.